ageproof

ageproof

Living Longer Without Running Out of
Money or Breaking a Hip

JEAN CHATZKY

MICHAEL F. ROIZEN, MD

with Ted Spiker

Foreword by Mehmet C. Oz, MD

GRAND CENTRAL
PUBLISHING

NEW YORK   BOSTON

Grand Central Publishing
Hachette Book Group
1290 Avenue of the Americas, New York, NY 10104
grandcentralpublishing.com
twitter.com/grandcentralpub

First Trade Paperback Edition: August 2019

Grand Central Publishing is a division of Hachette Book Group, Inc. The Grand Central Publishing name and logo is a trademark of Hachette Book Group, Inc.

The publisher is not responsible for websites (or their content) that are not owned by the publisher.

The Hachette Speakers Bureau provides a wide range of authors for speaking events. To find out more, go to www.hachettespeakersbureau.com or call (866) 376-6591.

Dr. Sheldon Cohen and Carnegie Mellon for Perceived Stress Scale, page 16.

Print book interior design by Fearn Cutler de Vicq.

Library of Congress Cataloging-in-Publication Data has been applied for.

ISBN: 978-1-4555-6730-0 (hardcover),
978-1-4555-6732-4 (trade paperback),
978-1-4555-6731-7 (ebook)

Printed in the United States of America

LSC-C

10 9 8 7 6 5 4 3 2 1

To all who want to
live AgeProof:
Longer and Stronger

contents

«←————————→»

foreword

《←————————→》

How do you define a winning life? I would define it as living strong, living healthy, living with low stress and high passion, living with security, and living with the people you love. If you agree, then the next question becomes:

How do you achieve those things?

In my mind, it's about knowing how to navigate the daily collisions.

What do you do when your eyeballs collide with a bakery window? What do you do when your toddler's pranks collide with your patience? What do you do when your viewpoint collides with your partner's? How you manage those daily conflicts—big and small— will go a long way to determining how well and how happy you live. That's one of the reasons why I spend a lot of time thinking about life's intersections—the places where seemingly opposite forces come together to influence the way you live.

I'm happy to see that one of the most crucial intersections in life— that between health and wealth—is being tackled by two of the foremost thinkers of medicine and money. In *AgeProof*, Dr. Mike Roizen and Jean Chatzky examine one of life's most important collisions. My friend, Mike Roizen, the longtime wellness expert of the Cleveland

Clinic, and Jean Chatzky, the financial guru of NBC's *Today* show, have come together for a one-of-a-kind look at two seemingly different but absolutely related areas.

Not only are these two areas the most important issues when it comes to life satisfaction—that is, you want to live healthy and with as many resources as you can. But they're also cyclically connected—that is, how healthy you are has an effect on your bottom line, and your handling of money issues has an effect on how healthy you are. That's because getting sick can be extremely costly (in direct ways, like the actual expenses of insurance and medical procedures, and in indirect ways, like being out of work because of health problems). It's also because money problems are the biggest source of stress for Americans. Stress has been linked directly to a whole bevy of medical issues, including heart disease, sleep problems, weight issues, and depression.

What I like most about their approach is that it's not all about tips and tactics (though you'll find plenty of them), but that they have found the common principles and themes for how to approach improving both your health and wealth. When you see the links, you'll gain inside insight into how you can use the same principles in both areas. For example, you may think of budgeting as something you do with money, but you can take the same approach to how you eat as well. You also will learn how to develop teams of comrades—professional and personal—who can help you face obstacles, make smart decisions, and fend off temptations.

This book has a safety deposit box full of information, and Mike and Jean are giving you the key. Their prescriptions are doable, are helpful, and make sense.

In the end—if you understand their principles and take their advice—you will be well on your way to achieving what you want out of life.

The chance to live long and strong, with health and wealth.

—Mehmet C. Oz, Professor of Surgery at New York
Presbyterian/Columbia University and multiple
Emmy-winning host of *The Dr. Oz Show*

introduction

«‹———————›»

AgeProof Your Life

We can't know *exactly* what's on your mile-long to-do list. It probably contains some combination of work tasks (tomorrow's deadline), home tasks (stack of bills), things you dread doing (22 miles of errands), and maybe a couple of things you can't wait to do (cappuccino with friends on Friday!). As you accelerate through life, the day-to-day drudgery often means you put off taking care of or ignore the two most important things you need to pay attention to for a long and vibrant life—your body and your bank account.

In the end, aren't these two things—your health and wealth—the two things you want most?

You want to live long, with enough money to do the things you want to do (and to still be able to remember where you put it). You want your body to be strong and your family to be secure. You want to age so that you are in control of your destiny. You want power over your life, and the freedom and energy to enjoy your passions.

You want to be AgeProof.

That's what this book is about. And the two of us—one an expert in medicine as the chief wellness officer of the Cleveland Clinic, and one an expert in money as the financial editor of NBC's *Today*—have joined together for a one-of-a-kind look at how you can make your health and wealth work together to help you do just that.

We have found that there are eight important ways to stay well and eight just as important ways to stay flush, and they intersect—and your future happiness depends on them. By diving into those areas—and, more important, the science behind them—we've developed a new approach to help you manage your life. What we're giving you is a new lens through which to view the choices you face, the decisions you make, the behaviors you adopt, and the goals you reach for. All drive toward the ultimate goal: AgeProofing your life by keeping your body young and your finances secure enough to go the distance.

We know, we know. You still may be a little skeptical: What does a 401(k) have to do with trans fats? What does homeowner's insurance have to do with a beautiful EKG? And, for the love of your preferred deity, what does credit-card debt have to do with a herniated disk?

Good questions.

On the surface you can see some quick similarities between health and wealth. We count our pennies and our calories. We're tempted by things we want but don't need (red pumps, red velvet cupcakes). We often try quick fixes (condo-in-Florida investments, liquid-only diets). We sometimes avoid what we know is the right thing to do (by splurging instead of saving, by eating fries instead of fruit). And we know that piles and piles of green things (broccoli or hundred-dollar bills) are a very good thing.

But this book isn't about surface-level comparisons between money problems and health issues. This book is about the fact that if you want to have a solid handle on your future, you need a true grip on both of these things.

Wealth without health? It's not going to last; your physical problems will wreak havoc on your bank account. Health without wealth? Maybe while you're young. But as you age, you need more resources to keep you that way.

Being AgeProof is about longevity—living strong and secure for your *whole* life.

Now, don't think that mastering two disciplines means adding more and more items to your to-do list. That's the thing. It doesn't. As this book will show, becoming AgeProof—philosophically and strategically—is a matter of taking the same approach to both.

Take, for instance, the idea of budgeting. A budget, we all know, is what allows us to manage our inflow of income and our outflow of expenses. Managing your health is all about budgeting, too, though very few people think about it like this; you have to manage the inflow of nutrients and the expenditure of that energy to maintain a balanced caloric budget. Another example: You could argue that one of the greatest threats to your longevity is temptation. When it comes to food, giving in to deep-fried cheese leads to weight problems, which lead to inflammation problems, which lead to sugar problems, which lead to heart problems, which lead to extended "vacations" at the county hospital. When it comes to money, giving in to the latest and greatest and loveliest gadget/diamond/vehicle leads to credit-card problems, which lead to bill-paying problems, which lead to extended "vacations" with the in-laws. So learning the science behind overriding the natural urge to give in to temptations is something that will help you manage both areas of your life.

And not only are health and wealth similar in principles and tactics—and this is the bigger point here—they're interconnected like strands of DNA. Our goal is to help teach you about that intersection so you get comfortable with the science and adopt the strategies—both of which will help you AgeProof your entire life.

• • •

At no other time in our history has AgeProofing been as important as it is now; that's because we're living longer and longer—and need more money and better health to last those extra decades (yes, decades). The problem that many of us face is twofold. For one, we think of money and health the way we think of large-toothed forest-roaming beasts—they scare the heck out of us. Much of that fear is caused because we close our eyes, hope for the best, and are timid about confronting issues that feel as comfortable as a pair of not-quite-dry-from-the-dryer underwear. And that's something we have to change (our attitude, we're talking about). We have to be open and honest, and have frank conversations about subjects that can make us squirm.

Second, we're a society known for making collectively bad decisions about money and health. For example, you might buy an industrial espresso machine, then end up using it once a year. While the java (if filtered through paper) may be good for your health, it may not have been the wisest investment. On the flip side, sometimes you make good decisions about eating and exercise. Other times you rapid-fire cheap bacon burgers down your throat. And while that two-buck burger may be good for your financial bottom line, it's probably not so good for your anatomical one.

While we all worry about running out of money (and running out of steam to walk from the bed to the bathroom), the biggest angst in the health and wealth arenas comes about because we often pit instant gratification against long-term security—what can we have now against what we should do to save for later. Sometimes it's presented as a binary approach, in that there's good and bad and only one proper way to invest—by saving for later. But we want to teach you how to satisfy both ends of the spectrum—how to gain financial security and health for the long haul without giving up the comforts of everyday life. We want you to get these two things:

- a healthy portfolio of assets that will last you for your entire life—and then some
- a wealthy body that is years younger than the calendar says it is

The reason this is so important—right now—is that the world is in the middle of a pretty large shift when it comes to aging. Because of this, we want to ask you a question. How old do you think you'll get to be? Sixty-eight? Seventy-seven? Eighty-four? Whatever number popped into your head, chances are that you're about as wrong as a steady diet of Big Macs. You're going to live longer than whatever number you picked (as well as longer than a Big Mac, which can last in your refrigerator for years, by the way Q). Just consider this: in the past three decades, life expectancy in the United States has jumped for men from 70 to 79 and for women from 77 to 83.

> **Q JEAN SAYS:** Mike, I didn't need to know that.

That statistical observation may not surprise you. But how about this one? The longer you live, the longer you're going to live. While that last line might sound like some spiritual platitude you'd find in your Twitter feed, it's rooted in #scientifictruth. Let's say you make it to 65; that means you're more likely than not to Energizer Bunny your way through a long life. Today the average 65-year-old will live until age 85. But that means *half* of all 65-year-olds will surpass that. One in three will pass age 90. And one in 10 will pass 96. As for the number of Americans who are age 100 or older? It has gone up 2,200 percent since 1950. And in February 2015, *Time* magazine declared it likely that the first person to live to 160 has already been born.

And while you're processing all of that, we've got another question for you: What do you want aging to feel like? Do you want to be taking walks, playing tennis or golf, swimming, jumping rope like a six-year-old with your six-year-old granddaughter (jumping rope is good for your bones), traveling with your family, walking through the woods, launching a business and/or starting a new career? Or do you want to be couch-ridden watching *Simpsons* reruns because you have too many ailments and not enough resources to get up and go? We're hoping you didn't choose the latter (though please enjoy *The Simpsons* at any time).

Far too few people are planning for the inevitable reality that we're living longer—and taking steps to get themselves the assets and body to do so. In fact, 90 percent of people don't spend time thinking or talking about financial longevity. That's frightening. Because when you either run out of money or lose your anatomical and biological juice, you're simply up a river without a paddle (and you wouldn't have the money to buy a paddle or the body to use it even if you did).

So envision what you want your life to become after the age of 50. Trips to Europe, fun with friends, hiking and biking in the countryside, opening your own little taqueria on Main Street? It doesn't matter what your passions and dreams are. What matters is that without *both* wealth and health, you *will* live on a dead-end street.

Over the past 100 or so years, one innovation after another has prolonged life: the tuberculosis vaccine (1921), penicillin (1929), high-blood-pressure meds (1947), the surgeon general's warning on cigarettes (1969), seat belt laws (1984), tests for inflammation becoming routine (1986), vaccines for preventing cervical and throat cancer (2004) and for treating a specific cancer (2006). With so many life-threatening problems not needing as much attention, medicine can focus on managing chronic conditions: arthritis, asthma, diabetes, osteoporosis. Even some types of cancer and HIV/AIDS are now considered manageable. The result? Life goes on—with you being able to live younger no matter what your age—longer than ever before. It's like cars now lasting 200,000 miles, compared to 60,000 miles decades ago. This book is about giving you the power to change your own oil, fill yourself up with fuel 🗨, and take the ride of your life—all without crashing, without breaking down on the side of the road, without limping through life with duct tape over your rear bumper. And by taking good care of your health, you will live a long and energetic life.

While this change in longevity should be exciting, the truth is that longevity comes with a price. One, because we're living longer, it's more expensive to fund retirement. That's true even if you're in good shape (traditionally, maybe we lived only a decade or so past retirement, but what happens when we live for 30 or more years after we stop earning?). Surveys from financial institutions note that running out of money before running out of time is by far our biggest financial fear. One even found that running short of funds is a bigger fear even than death. Going the distance means we need a new set of skills, new strategies, and a new way of thinking.

We will teach you how to make your money and good health last decades longer, and then use both to build a legacy by supporting your favorite people and/or institutions, or helping that six-year-old granddaughter of yours learn enough and have enough to attend college. No longer will you be afraid of your money running out or your

🗨 **DR. MIKE SAYS:**
Or battery fully charged with electricity.

hips not holding up—and forced to deal with the stress that accompanies those worries.

Living longer also means that we as a nation are spending more on medical expenses—even without a significant health event. Care for people with chronic diseases now accounts for 84 percent of all healthcare spending. And that doesn't happen just in the last year of life. We're spending much more along the way to manage chronic disease. Medical and health issues are not top of mind only when you have an illness or a credit-card issue. They are everyday issues that together affect your happiness. But if you can take the steps we outline here, you'll reduce your risk of developing chronic conditions, save more of those out-of-pocket and horrendous hospitalization costs, and live longer with fewer disabilities. So you'll be able to feel, act, and actually *be* younger and happier.

For example, you will learn how to:

Assess. Use diagnostics to figure out where you stand financially and medically, so you know where to go.

Easily Change Behaviors. The key to success in both arenas is to eliminate the idea that you have to work hard and try hard. When you use automatic systems and create automatic habits, you win.

Slash Stress. As the number one driver of poor health and poor wealth, managing stress—the intersection point between the central nervous system and the emotional faculties—has to be a top priority. We'll take you through the science of stress management.

Build Strong Teams. One of the biggest mistakes people make in both areas is keeping everything private. Doctor's offices and bank accounts should be private, but that doesn't mean you should go it alone; in fact, having the proper team around you (including family and professionals) is key to helping you achieve optimum levels in health and wealth. Socializing your progress allows you to help others as well as yourself.

Budget. Your finances *and* your calories.

Erase Mistakes. Even if you're in bad shape, you can dig yourself out. We'll teach you how to reverse financial and health patterns to catch up. You will learn to adopt small continuous changes that will help you see results.

Create Strong Environments to Make These Dual Goals Easier. Both at work and at home.

We structured the book to help you best navigate these two worlds. Each section begins with the science and overarching theme that links health and wealth. That provides the prism through which you should read each of the following chapters—one each on the health arena and the financial one. (From time to time you'll also see some individual perspectives from us dropped into the margins.) At the end of each section, you'll also get the quick-hit list of **AgeProof Essentials**—the three quick you-can-do-it takeaway steps that you can put into action right away.

We hope that you come away with three things that can change your life for the better: one, specific strategies for how to improve your money situation and your body, two, an understanding of the unique relationship between health and wealth, and three, a way to measure, monitor, and be aware of your progress.

After all, AgeProof doesn't mean immortal. But it does mean that you live as long as you can and as strong as you can.

Strong in your body.

Secure with your money.

Set for life.

Part I
System Checks

The Science of Diagnostics

*Why we all need a thorough once-over
before we make any significant changes*

Your morning is a whirlwind. You wash your face, fix your hair, brush your teeth for two minutes after flossing, which you do after a 20-second brushing of your teeth (at least that's how you should be doing it, while you practice balancing on one foot Q), make the breakfast smoothies, get the kids going, brew the beverage, peek at your phone to see the status of Barbara's sick pup, on and on. And then you do this (maybe five or 500 times): you check yourself in the mirror.

Q JEAN SAYS: That's a Dr. Mike Rx, he's not kidding.

How does your hair look? Your makeup? Your clothes? Your butt (no VPLs, please)? Your skin? Your hair again? Everything? You assess, you make changes, you assess again, and you go on about your day. You perform this very basic test throughout the day because (1) you care about your appearance and how you project yourself to the outside world, and (2) nobody likes buzzing about the day with a peppercorn-decorated incisor.

What's the point?

Every day of your life, you perform this quickie diagnostic test on yourself to evaluate your current state of affairs, because you inherently know there's a value to the process of self-evaluation. You assess, you evaluate, you adjust. And then you repeat as necessary.

Yet when it comes to perhaps the two biggest issues in your life—your health and your financial status—you're scared to look in the mirror. Maybe you're afraid of what you'll see. Maybe you just don't like what you'll see. Maybe you don't want your bank account or your blood pressure barking back at you. Maybe the truth hurts so much that you can't stand to see—and address—this kind of reflection. Or maybe you're afraid you'll pale in comparison to the others in your world.

But avoiding the metaphorical mirror means that you'll never notice when you have lipstick smudged across your face. That is, you'll never know if something is off—or how badly it's off—if you haven't taken the time to look. And hiding from the truth doesn't mean the truth doesn't exist.

The reality is that before we start any meaningful discussion of health and wealth (and changing both for the better), there's one thing you have to do: embrace your *current* reality. That means embrace the data. Embrace the diagnostics. Embrace the fact that you need to measure exactly where you are so you can determine where you want to be—and chart a course for how to get there.

In the next two chapters, we're going to walk you through the diagnostic tests you need to take (some by yourself, some with the help of others) before you get started. No matter what your financial or bodily goals are—whether they involve earning a million bucks or weighing a buck twenty-five—you have to know where you're starting.

An easy way to think of your journey is like this: Picture your dream goal as a destination on a map (a Malibu beach, an urban loft, a country farmhouse). You can see where it is, you've heard all about it, and you know what pleasure awaits when you get there. But what if you had no idea where the heck you were at this exact moment? You wouldn't know where to go, when to make turns, when to go straight, when to turn around, and so forth. You need to know where you're starting before you can chart your course.

The tests we'll outline in the next two chapters will give you your coordinates and show you where to go. The reasons:

Data Matters. One of the buzzwords you'll see all throughout the media today is *data*. We use data to find stories, to make decisions, to support theories. Yes, data can feel like an intimidating concept—spreadsheet upon spreadsheet, numbers upon numbers, formula upon formula. But there's a reason the word *data* and the practice of analyzing data are so prevalent today. Making sense of data matters, and we'll make it easy for you.

Data gives us clues about our worlds by enabling us to see patterns and changes, as well as absolute numbers. This is also true in the worlds of health and finance. Data serves up *big* pieces of the puzzle in terms of figuring out what you need to know and where you're striving to go. For instance, in health, we know the exact blood-pressure reading that serves as the line between healthy and unhealthy. In finance, we know the exact debt-to-income ratio that's deemed safe for lending.

So through the next two chapters we're going to present many of those benchmarks, not only because that data provides clues as to how well (or not) you're doing, but also because those absolute numbers really serve as gateways into a better life. When you reach those absolute data points, you know that you've reached a safe zone. That's why knowing your numbers is so vital to beginning this whole process (and it can actually serve as a great motivator, as well as be fun if you make a game or challenge out of trying to reach your goals).

Fear Can't Be the Long-Term Motivator. Chances are you've heard plenty of "scared straight" stories. Your overweight friend who had a heart attack now eats salmon and broccoli and walks five miles a day. You know a couple who were *this close* to a divorce because they couldn't come to an agreement about how they should spend their money. All of these uh-oh scenarios are based in the same emotion: fear. Fear of losing life. Fear of losing relationships. Fear of losing property. You get so scared that it's like a life-changing splash of cold water on your face. You change because you got dangerously close to something ugly, and you don't dare get that close again.

Here's the thing. Fear can work very well in the short term. If you

DR. MIKE SAYS:
The ideal is 115/75. Anything less than 125/85 seems OK, but blood pressure is one of the numbers you really do need to pay attention to. The simple and accurate BP machine I have at home (and use monthly even though I am at 115/75) costs less than $40 at the neighborhood drugstore.

JEAN SAYS:
36 percent, tops. More on that coming up.

take an ambulance ride thinking that's the last thing you're ever going to do again, darn right you're going to swap your French fries for snap peas. But what happens when you're two weeks or two months or two years removed from your ER visit? You forget. You forget what fear feels like. And you go back to the bottomless bucket of *queso*. Fear is a hard punch, but it's not the basis for lasting motivation. (We'll discuss motivation throughout this book; it's a core subject when it comes to prioritizing your behaviors and habits.)

Lasting motivation comes from many sources. There's the intrinsic motivator of wanting to do better because it improves your life and makes you feel better; in this way healthier living and more prudent spending in themselves provide rewards. But we would also argue that one of the best long-term motivators comes from the thrill of the chase—and the joy of seeing and feeling improvement. These are often what inspire people to keep going, to live better. They're positive reinforcement that drives positive action, which ignites even more positive energy. The thrill of the chase is a big motivator—visualizing yourself in a better reality, seeing yourself approach this reality. So part of the reason diagnostics are so important is that they allow you to set attainable benchmarks—long-term ones and short-term ones—that can serve as a steady rhythm of motivation throughout your life. Granted, seeing numbers that are bad (skyrocketing debt totals, soaring LDL cholesterol levels) may be jarring at first, and fear of what those numbers mean to your life may drive your initial actions. But at some point that fear has to switch over to something more positive—and more inspiring. Quantifying your success will then motivate you to continue your program. And that, we believe, is what ultimately will help you sustain long-term change.

You Must Compare Only to Yourself. In this journey to better health and wealth, you will face many hurdles. Perhaps one of the biggest: keeping up with the Joneses/Kardashians. That is, you feel the need to have what others have, to be as others are. You can't stop comparing the size of your house or the size of your waist with those of the people around you. Sometimes that can be motivating; other times it can be more frustrating than a wine cork that just won't budge. But we do know this: for most of you, comparing yourself to others won't do you a lick of good—and most likely will hold you back.

Consider this famous survey by economists Sara J. Solnick and David Hemenway. A question was sent out to more than 250 people at the Harvard School of Public Health, asking them to imagine two worlds. In the first they earned $50,000 a year while everyone else earned $25,000. In the second they earned $100,000 a year while everyone else earned $200,000. Then it asked which world they'd rather live in. What would you choose? Seems like a no-brainer. Of course, you'd want to earn twice as much, even if others would make more than you. But a whopping half went for world number one—they'd rather take a huge pay cut and be on top of the heap.

It drives us crazy when we think others have what we want. That's natural. But it's also destructive. Why? Because it takes you away from your own goals—and likely drives bad habits, such as spending money on things you can't afford.

So here's what we want you to do: Look at yourself in the mirror. But stop gawking at others. Gather your data, and think about your data. There will always be people in better conditions and worse conditions than you, so if you can remind yourself that you likely fall somewhere in the middle of a bell curve, you don't need to beat yourself up because the McDonoughs have a hot tub and Shannon wears a size two. Admittedly, this is a difficult habit to break, but we think that using your personal diagnostics as both a barometer and a motivator is the way to do it. Seeing your own data allow you to focus on minigoals (sometimes called benchmarks)—and concrete ones, rather than emotionally charged ones wrapped up in other people's lives.

Data Should Help, Not Overwhelm. Throughout the book we're going to be sending a lot of numbers your way. Sometimes it may feel as if we're rapid-firing a round of Ping-Pong balls. Interest rates, blood sugar levels, asset allocation, blood pressure—zing, zing, zing, zing. These are not meant to scare you or intimidate you. (Truth is, many people associate numbers with math. And with math comes fear. Math anxiety is a real disorder defined by the American Psychological Association. And it's often rooted in one bad childhood experience. For a lot of people, fear of math translates directly to fear of money, but it can also extend to other numbers-oriented subjects.) Rest assured, the numbers we'll discuss in this book are not all that difficult. We'll walk you through them, show you the calculations, and teach you what they mean—and, most important, how to use them.

The numbers we'll show you will help you budget—financially and health-wise. You'll see what you're earning and spending, but also what you're taking in and burning off. The baseline budget you create gives you your starting point for meaningful change.

And, perhaps above all, the real gritty truth about diagnostics is that they're data-driven truth serum.

You can't hide from the numbers. They tell you where your flaws are and where you can improve, and force you to evaluate the behaviors needed to get and do better.

In the next two chapters, you will close the door and strip down.

The raw data will be revealed. Some of it you may like, and some of it you may not. But it's what you decide to do with this raw data that really matters.

CHAPTER 1

Body Checks

*These tests will give you a snapshot of your overall health
to tell you where you are and how far you need to go*

The most common question you hear is probably the one you
most ignore.

How are you doing?

Oh, sure. When a clerk asks you that question, you say, "Fine, you?"
When a coworker asks you that question, you say, "Hanging in there."
When your best friend asks you, you launch into a diatribe wondering
how in the world a kid can drop his phone in the toilet for the third
time in two weeks. Sure, it's easy to answer "How are you doing?" if
it's a surface-level conversation starter. But if you want to peek a little
deeper into the recesses of your brain, your heart, your joints, and your
everything else, the question is a little more difficult.

How are you doing?

In the realm of health and medicine, some people are overtesters—
they know every piece of data, from cholesterol numbers to bone density numbers. Anytime they feel a twinge, they want an MRI.

More people are health ostriches—nope, nothing to see here,
don't want to know my weight, what that mole means, or why my
knees creak like the floors of an 1893 farmhouse. While knowing too
much or thinking that something's always wrong can send you into

DR. MIKE SAYS:

In fact, one set of gut feelings is a kind of data. Answer this question: Compared with others your calendar age, how is your health? Very Bad, Poor, Good, Very Good, or Excellent? Those who answer "Very Bad" or "Poor" are much more likely to suffer a disabling illness in the next two years than those who answer "Good," "Very Good," or "Excellent." Most of the data we ask of you is numbers that you cannot fool yourself on, like your blood pressure. (Even stress can be quantified, as we'll show you on page 9, via the Sharecare App.)

a high-stress tailspin of anxiety that has far more destructive effects than positive ones, it's far more threatening to know nothing. Staying ignorant about your health status is essentially an express-lane pass to the ER (or an urn, to be blunt). What you're striving for here is something in the middle—testing yourself enough to give yourself an accurate and revealing picture of your health to help guide you to make smart decisions, which will help you improve the areas where you're weakest (and thus make you healthier).

Now, our hunch is that even if you've avoided physicals the way raccoons avoid the sun, you probably have a pretty good idea of where you fall on the spectrum between healthy and unhealthy. For instance, you *know* if you're carrying too much weight or are sapped of energy all the time or things just, well, hurt. But here's the thing. Your gut feeling—as powerful as you think it may be—can't replace data . Data not only gives you tangible benchmarks to track from one period to another (to assess change over time), it also gives you a standard set of markers so you know whether you've crossed the line from healthy to unhealthy (or vice versa). That's because for virtually every test we have, there's a clear line in the sand—that is, the mark that serves as the threshold between "you're in good shape" and "you qualify for frequent user status at your doctor's office." So don't be afraid of the data. The data are there to inform you—and perhaps inspire you.

The last thing we'll say before we get into the nuts and bolts of the tests you should take is this: Your health is always in a fluid state as your body changes for better or worse. And oftentimes these tests are like snapshots compared to videos—that is, the tests reflect one moment in time as opposed to a series of moments over a longer period. That said, these snapshots—whether they come in the form of blood tests or self-tests—are pretty darn accurate representations of your health picture. Translation: there's not too much variation in what your cholesterol numbers look like, whether you have your blood analyzed today or tomorrow or two weeks from now.

Here's the other thing about numbers—something that a lot of people discount, but that can still be very powerful. Numbers can be motivating. When you start seeing some of these numbers moving in the right direction, that can inspire you to take a little more time to eat well, exercise when you may not feel like it, and make smart choices all the way around. In the same way, numbers can work against you; if you do a lot of work and don't see progress, frustration can lead to stress, which can lead to unhealthy habits. So you do have to be smart and realistic and patient when tracking medically or physically oriented data.

For this reason we are not going to recommend that one of your tests be stepping on the scale. While it is smart to know your starting weight, we don't want you to use your weight as a major driver for motivation (as so many people do). That's because weight is like the stock market on a crazy day—it fluctuates a whole heck of a lot in a short time. Plus a lot of things can influence weight, including muscle gain and hormonal ups and downs. So take a baseline measurement and then revisit every few weeks, but don't obsess about it, and don't use your weight as your main data point Q.

JEAN SAYS:
I never get on the scale. I use my clothes—and whether they fit—as my barometer.

☞ What's Coming Next

It likely goes without saying that our smartphones and mobile devices have changed the way we live, think, and feel. It's no different in the area of health and diagnostics. Many wearable devices and apps make it much easier for you to track everything from calories consumed to calories burned to hours slept to steps climbed. This technology makes it easier to have a sense of what you're doing every day.

We—in conjunction with Sharecare.com—have developed the free Sharecare App, for "Living in the Green," which tracks when you stay in what we call the green zone of health. When you're Living in the Green (as shown in deep green on the app)—by getting enough exercise, eating smart, and keeping stress low (we track this with voice technology, believe it or not)—you're decreasing your risk factors for chronic disease, and thus making your RealAge, the actual age of your body, younger. The app works by objectively analyzing and scoring behaviors and emotional states against the user's RealAge score (to get yours, see page 19). But overall, trying to boost your number of Green Days is both a philosophy and a meta-algorithm for healthier and happier living. Best of all? It works in real time—correlating events and behaviors to give you insights about what's happening right now, so you can be aware and make adjustments as needed. After all, insights drive awareness, and awareness drives action, and action drives change.

While the type of device you choose to put the app on largely depends on your own personal preferences (do you want to wear it on your wrist or have it on your phone), we do recommend that you get connected to some kind of tool that makes tracking your data simple—and motivating in return.

One of the things we like best about the Sharecare App, which can go on your phone and work by itself or with other data-tracking devices, is the insight it gives you into your own stress levels. After all, awareness of your problem is the first thing you use to overcome it. Erik A. Feingold, chief innovation officer of Sharecare developed the app to use "fractal variation," changes in your voice, to let you know where your stress levels are. Just as muscles in your back may tighten up when you're tense, so do the muscles in your vocal cords (in fact, they're very sensitive to stress, making them perfect as indicators). The microphone in your smartphone picks up these variations anytime you're talking, to quantify your stress, much as a pedometer or accelerometer measures your steps taken. Once you're alerted that you're in an aging zone (red or orange), you can take steps to mitigate the stress (fix it) and get into the green, or healthy, level.

And, frankly, awareness is a big part of the issue. Sometimes we may feel stress but not know how bad it is. Awareness is what gives you power. The Sharecare App is so helpful because it can measure stress when it's not so horrible as to make you sick—making you aware and nudging you to take action before the issue becomes serious. In fact, 90 percent of the stress detected by the Sharecare App format is from common relationship situations and nagging events (many of them financial) that can have a huge impact over time. And like a low step count that can trigger a healthful response from you (more steps), you can use that nongreen info to develop new automatic responses that reduce or manage your stress and help you stay younger, healthier, and happier.

Ultimately, that may be the greatest benefit of the Sharecare App. It detects your stress even when you are not consciously aware of it. We have found from the people who use it that its integrated behavioral and emotional analyses work sort of like an "emotional selfie" in that they help give insights so you can make behavior changes and take different actions to get out of the danger zone and into the green one.

Bottom line: diagnostics work. For instance, in the Cleveland Clinic Executive Health Program—in which people get a full work-up and we gather all the data points—83 percent of those who start get a major change in care or a diagnosis in the first year that changes their health for the better. The extrapolated and simplified conclusion: when you know where you're starting, are getting the right advice, and have ample motivation (some of it through these numbers), you can and will change your health outcomes, and often can and will sustain the changes. Yes, tests make you aware of where you are in health (it works the same for finance) so you can be aware of the choices you have. Changing your behavior requires that you be aware of the situation you're in, as well as the choices you have. That's why automation is so important—so that your brain defaults to good choices, rather than giving in to the reptilian side of your brain that's more likely to give in to temptation.

In this chapter we'll outline the tests you can perform to get a picture of your real status; some you can do by yourself and for some you'll need help. Don't dismiss these points of data. Test them. Track them. Use them. Learn from them and be motivated by them. In essence, AgeProof yourself by using them to help you get stronger, more fit, and less stressed, as well as to sleep better.

After all, if a picture is worth a thousand words, this picture is the most important of all, because it's the story of your current state of life.

Self-Tests

✏ Self-Test 1: **The Fitness Test**

No, no, no. We're not going to send you back to middle-school gym class where you have to humiliate yourself in front of 22 classmates waiting to see if you can do a pull-up. Well, in a way, maybe we are—minus the classmates and the 1970s-style shorts. While it's true that we all have varying levels of strength and endurance, depending on genetics and how much and often we exercise, there's some truth to be learned from testing your physical fitness. The military, police, and fire agencies do this kind of testing all the time, but the rest of us rarely assess how well our bodies can handle any number of physical challenges. Yes, the chances of your using a sit-up in your day-to-day life are small, but these abilities are proxies for more important ones. The stronger your body, the longer you will live. The stronger your body, the less likely you'll sustain injuries. The stronger your body, the higher the chance that you'll live life with energy and vitality.

These tests aren't meant to measure whether you can compete in an Olympic trial; they're about giving you data points that tell you whether you're on the healthy side or the unhealthy side. (Think about what a push-up actually means—that you're strong enough to move your body weight through space. Does that mean we're testing whether you can lift a car off someone in an emergency? Of course not. But we're testing how you can handle your own body, which is what you do every day, even if you're not nose-close to carpet crumbs.)

So we recommend that after a short warm-up of 10 minutes—walking with some vigor and some dynamic moves like circling your arms and swinging your legs—you perform each of the following tests to give yourself an initial baseline set of data. For all the tests, the number listed is your goal; you want to be at that number or better. If you're not there, it gives you a goal that you can work toward.

Push-Ups. This test measures your muscular endurance. Men perform with toes on the floor; women perform with knees on the floor. Keep your spine straight and your head in line with your spine. Do not allow your back to sag or your butt to stick up in the air. Make sure to place your hands directly under your shoulders. Lower your chest toward the floor until it comes within three or four inches of the floor, and then push yourself back up. Inhale as you lower, and exhale as you push back up. Perform as many as you can in a minute.

Age	Number of push-ups (men)	Number of push-ups (women)
20s	35 or more	18 or more
30s	25–29	13–19
40s	20–24	11–14
50s	15–19	7–10
60s	10–14	5–10
70s	6–9	4–10
80s	3–5	2–6

Curl-Ups This test measures your muscular endurance in your abdominals. Core strength for both men and women is key for good posture, injury prevention, and day-to-day functioning. Lie on your back with your knees bent 90 degrees and your feet flat on the floor. Place your arms at your sides, palms down. Flatten your lower back and curl your head, shoulders, and shoulder blades four to six inches off the floor. Return to the starting position. Perform as many as you can in a minute.

Mile Walk Test. You can premeasure a course with your car, use a track (a standard track has four laps to a mile), or use a watch that has a GPS signal on it to measure a mile. Walk one mile as quickly as possible without causing yourself pain or discomfort. (Do not run

Age	Number of curl-ups (men)	Number of curl-ups (women)
20s	45 or more	35 or more
30s	30–34	25–29
40s	25–29	20–24
50s	20–24	15–19
60s	15–19	10–14
70s	10–14	7–9
80s	6–9	4–6

on this test, even if you can, because the test was developed to, and is calibrated to, measure walk speed.) Wear a heart rate monitor or take your pulse for 10 seconds immediately after completing the walk. Multiply the number you get by six to obtain your one-minute heart rate. Record your walk time and your one-minute heart rate. Keep track of your progress. You can be your own goal setter for changes in time and heart rate over time. Over the course of several weeks, if your time on the one-mile walk decreases without a rise in your heart rate, you have become more fit. If your time on the mile walk stays the same but your heart rate drops, you have also improved your fitness level.

Get-Up Test. This test has easy metrics, because there are only two possible answers. Can you get out of a chair without using your arms to lift or balance yourself? This test measures your overall lower-body

Age	Time to complete one mile (male or female)	Heart rate
20s	18 minutes or faster	130 or lower
30s	19 minutes or faster	133 or lower
40s	20 minutes or faster	135 or lower
50s	23 minutes or faster	140 or lower
60s	26 minutes or faster	140 or lower
70s	29 minutes or faster	140 or lower
80s	32 minutes or faster	140 or lower

and core strength, your balance, and your overall risk of injury. As if it weren't obvious, you're aiming to score a "Yes, yes I can."

⬡ Self-Test 2: **The Perceived Stress Test**

If you or someone close to you has ever had a heart problem, you likely know what a stress test is: The patient gets on a treadmill, hooked up to all kinds of machines and monitors, and the technician cranks the incline and intensity of the treadmill until the patient says he or she can't do any more. All the while your heart is being watched and monitored for any of the blips or problems that occur when you're straining yourself. The results can show what kind of shape your coronary arteries are in.

But that's not what we're talking about here—and not just because we don't expect you to keep cardio-evaluation equipment in your attic. What we're talking about is you asking yourself a series of questions (this requires no warm-up) and then giving an honest answer. If you're honest about your answers, you will actually gain tremendous insight into your health, because the number one driver of health-related problems isn't triple-decker grilled cheese sandwiches. It's your perceived level of stress. Awareness of when stress occurs—like awareness of any issue—is the first step in developing a strategy and tactics for dealing with it. For reasons we'll talk about starting on page 71, stressful situations can be destructive to your health, because of the way your body reacts to high levels of chronic stress—through elevated heart rates, raised blood pressure, and hormonal surges that throw your body completely out of whack.

Above all, you're aiming to live in a more peaceful zone—an idea that connotes tranquillity and optimum health. In fact, by keeping your stress levels deep green on the Sharecare App (page 9), you will dramatically decrease your risk of poor health. Deep green is optimum, while light green is good, and the danger zones are yellow, orange, and red.

Take a moment to take this test developed by Dr. Sheldon Cohen at Carnegie Mellon.

Perceived Stress Scale. Use this scale to measure how you felt during the last month. Mark an X next to your feelings and then add up your total points.

In the last month...	Never (0)	Almost Never (1)	Some-times (2)	Fairly Often (3)	Very Often (4)
1. How often have you been upset because of something that happened unexpectedly?					
2. How often have you felt that you were unable to control the important things in your life?					
3. How often have you felt nervous and "stressed"?					
4. How often have you felt confident about your ability to handle your personal problems?					
5. How often have you felt that things were going your way?					
6. How often have you found that you could not cope with all the things that you had to do?					
7. How often have you been able to control irritations in your life?					
8. How often have you felt that you were on top of things?					
9. How often have you been angered because of things that were outside your control?					
10. How often have you felt difficulties were piling up so high that you could not overcome them?					

With permission of Carnegie Mellon

Figure your score:

Give yourself points for items 1–3, 6, 9, and 10 (4 if you marked 4, 3 if you marked 3, etc.).

Reverse the score for items 4, 5, 9, and 10 (that is, 0 points for an answer of 4, 1 point for an answer of 3, etc.).

Add your total points.

Calculation = Add up all your points		Numeric Range
	Low	0–12
	Moderate	12–19
	High	19–40

✏ Self-Test 3: **The Tape Test**

In your mind, the most valuable thing in your closet may be your favorite black pumps or your worn college sweatshirt. But when it comes to your health, the most valuable thing you have is your tape measure. It's decidedly simple and almost always scary, but the measurements you take can serve as great indicators of your current health status.

Best of all, there's only one formula you need to know: your waist size should be less than half your height. So if your height is 64 inches, your waist should be no larger than 32 inches. Take the measurement level with your belly button (it's OK to suck your stomach in).

The reason waist size is so important? Abdominal fat. It's the most dangerous kind of fat, because it secretes chemicals that cause inflammation, and because it's so close to your vital organs. This proximity means that toxicity from fat is more likely to influence these organs' functions and create all kinds of health dilemmas.

This formula is the one we recommend paying attention to much more than your weight, because it takes into consideration your size, rather than an absolute number of pounds. You can do this test once a month, and because it takes some time to change body shape, we don't recommend gauging it much more often. The best part: if you keep your waist size below this level and do only five other things or get to 6+2® normal values (which we'll cover in the next section), you have only 10 to 20 percent of the risk of contracting *any* chronic disease, including cardiovascular disease and cancer, of the typical American of your age. That reduces your lifetime health-care costs by more than 50 percent, even though you'll live 33 percent longer and with 33 percent fewer years of disability. (Yes, you read those percentages right; and if you read the rest of this book and act on it, you'll live with enough money to really enjoy those extra disability-free years, too.)

The things that will move the tape measure in the right direction? They all stem from the behaviors that we'll cover in the next sections (pages 71 to 167). Be aware of the situation, then make the changes.

JEAN SAYS:

Is there any easier way to do this? I've been wondering for a while. I don't think I'd buy 25 pounds of rice for this purpose.

DR. MIKE SAYS:

You can keep using the rice over and over to strengthen your grip. But if that doesn't work for you, many gyms and doctors' offices have hand grip meters that you can use to test yourself.

✏️ Self-Test 4: **The Grip Test**

What does it matter if you can open the jar of pickles? On the surface, not much, unless you really want some pickles. But a deeper dive into the research shows that your grip strength is strongly associated with longevity and good health. Several studies indicate that your grip strength predicts your risk of disability and even death—it literally predicts your rate of aging. While we don't know exactly why, the research shows that grip strength is an even better predictor than your overall muscle mass, your blood pressure, your LDL cholesterol level, and many other markers. (The one thing we haven't done is determine whether changing your grip strength can actually slow your rate of aging. That said, it's still a good number to know.)

You can test it by filling a five-gallon bucket with rice (this is what many athletes like pole-vaulters, rock-climbers, and football players do to increase grip strength). First place a packet of walnuts at the bottom of a bucket, and then fill the bucket with rice (30 pounds for men, 25 pounds for women). Take off any jewelry. Now time yourself as with one hand you try to dig down to the bottom of the bucket. Get the pack of walnuts in faster than 15 seconds? That's associated with more longevity and better health . (You can order the entire set of products to do this, plus extra free walnut packs, at NuttyRiceBucket.org.)

✏️ Self-Test 5: **Blood Pressure**

Most times we hope you never end up in cuffs, but this is the exception. We want you to spend some time in one—to measure your blood pressure regularly. That's because blood pressure is a top-three predictor of your risk of developing chronic disease. High blood pressure—blood pressure being the force with which blood travels through arteries, indicating possible clogs along the way—is often associated with high stress, heart problems, and many other ailments. And blood pressure is also the easiest measurement to take—with a home blood-pressure cuff, or by going to a pharmacy or gym or any number of other places.

Note: you don't want to take your blood pressure after exercise or drinking caffeine, because those things will cause it to decrease or increase. But you can take it regularly—say once a month if it is under 120/80, or daily if it's over that (yes, it is that important). Your goal: to have a blood-pressure reading lower than 120/80 (the ideal for slowing aging is really 115/75). Engaging in the activities that we'll describe throughout the book will help you lower it in the long run. But in terms of tracking, this is one of the most motivational numbers, because you can see it move down with just some simple diet and activity changes after only a few weeks. (Plus this number doesn't come with the same emotional baggage that's attached to your weight. So if it hops up and moves down a bit over a two- to three-week period, you won't beat yourself up the way you would if the scale did the same thing.)

✏️ Self-Test 6: **The RealAge Test**

The RealAge Test (found at RealAge.com or on your Sharecare App) assesses your eating, exercise, and sleep habits, along with family health history, behaviors, and existing conditions. Developed by Dr. Mike, this test tells you how much older or younger your body is than it really is— that is, your biological age as opposed to your calendar age. Taking it is a way to get an awareness of your overall health picture. So if you have things going your way, you may be 50 by the calendar standards, but 39 biologically because of your healthy habits and history (the maximum changes are about 20 years younger or 32 years older at age 55). You can use your RealAge in conjunction with the Sharecare App, which allows you to track health, stress, and more (more on this on page 9).

Professional Tests

✏️ Pro Test 1: **Blood Test**

Your blood is the town crier of your body—because it tells you an awful lot about much of what you need to know. Every year, as part of your annual physical (see below), you'll get blood taken from your body and sent to a lab (or two, as some tests are specialized ones not done in your typical hospital or doc's office). And when the lab results come back, you'll get a series of numbers that look as if they belong more in a mathematician's notebook than in your mind-set. But don't get intimated by the 6.3 this or the 92.4 that. Lab results also come with a context column—telling you whether you're in the normal or abnormal range on whatever is being evaluated. For our purposes you want to look at some of the more major numbers, because they're the big indicators about how you're doing health-wise. These markers give you insight into what's going on in your body. They are not just numbers, but a revelation of processes that either are working or aren't. Here's where you want to be:

> Waist is number 1, BP is number 2
> 3. LDL (bad) cholesterol: Less than 100, and
>   Triglycerides: Less than 100
> 4. Fasting glucose: Less than 107, or Hemoglobin A1C:
>   Less than 6.3
> 5. No cotinine (a tobacco end product) in your urine
> Soon (in the future): Telomere length compared with the
>   average for your age
> 6. Perceived Stress Scale: Less than 14

Plus 1: hs-CRP (measures inflammation): Less than 1.0, and TMAO (a measure of inflammation from carnitine, lecithin, and choline, as in red meat and egg yolks): Less than 2

Plus 2: Immunizations Current

✏️ Pro Test 2: **Annual Physical**

There are three good reasons you need to schedule annual exams. One, you should get the green light from your doctor before doing any activity more vigorous than walking. Two, your doctor can be on the alert for changes in patterns from year to year (be they weight gain or changes in your skin or alterations in blood tests). And three, annual exams give you a chance to be proactive about your health.

See, you shouldn't just treat a physical as the time when the doc looks down your throat, knocks your knee with a little hammer, and asks you a few questions about your social drinking habits. You have to reframe what a physical should be, and we recommend that you go on the offensive. Go in with a list of questions  (we give you a list on pages 133 and 136).

Direct your doc's attention to something that's been bothering you (even if it doesn't seem all that major). Ask about the latest trends in medicine and health that might be pertinent to your family history and to you. Use the opportunity to explore how you can identify your greatest risk factors and what you can do to reduce them. Too often people approach a physical as a ho-hum, check-the-box activity—without taking advantage of the one-on-one time.

JEAN SAYS:

You should do this when you meet with a financial pro, too. More on this in the teamwork section, chapter 7.

☞ This Is Only a Test

While you don't need to test everything all the time, there are points in your life when you should be getting a little more time with the pokers and prodders. That's because of the increased risk of various ailments as you age. Here are the recommended tests (which, because you're doing annual exams, your doctor should alert you to):

Bone mineral density: Around menopause for women, and at age 60 for men, and every five years for both afterward if levels are normal. If they're abnormal, get regular screenings to see if your treatment plan is slowing bone loss.

PSA and free PSA test: Men at high risk (African Americans and those with a first-degree relative who had prostate cancer before age 55) at age 45, and yearly until life expectancy is less than eight years.

JEAN SAYS:

My doctor recommends this every year. Am I overdoing it?

DR. MIKE SAYS:

Maybe. The data says you will prevent as many dangerous breast cancers with a breast self-exam monthly and mammograms every other year as with yearly mammograms. So no need for this yearly usually uncomfortable squeeze and extra radiation unless a mammogram reveals "iffy" lesions that need to be followed yearly. Your doc will tell you if you are in that category.

All other men at age 50 and yearly until life expectancy is less than eight years. (Note: our recommendation is different from current official government guidelines, but aggressive prostate cancers increased 72 percent in the last decade, probably because of lack of screening.)

Mammogram: Every two years after age 40 for women .

Colonoscopy: At age 50 and every 10 years thereafter, with a yearly stool hemoccult test.

Pelvic and rectal exam (women): Yearly when sexually active, and/or at age 50 and every year thereafter.

Rectal exam (men): At age 50 and yearly thereafter.

Eye exam: Every two years by an ophthalmologist.

Hearing exam: At age 65 and yearly during physical.

Oral exam: At least yearly by a dentist. Couple this with a cleaning, please, as periodontal disease is a leading cause of inflammation.

Mental health exam: At age 20 and yearly by your primary care doc. An initial screening of questions can alert her to depression and any other issues.

Echocardiogram and cardiac calcium or stress test (if you have more than minimal coronary calcium, your docs may suggest you move to the stress test; no or minimal coronary calcium and they'll usually skip it): Once at age 50 as a baseline, and then every five years till age 65 or till symptoms develop. Every other year after age 65.

CHAPTER 2

Your Fiscal Physical

*A bank balance isn't the only financial figure you need
to keep your eye on. These tests will help you survey
your complete monetary landscape.*

In so many aspects of your life, you get checkups. You have your
annual physical, weigh-ins, and blood tests. At work your bosses
like to classify you as excellent, satisfactory, or "shape up or ship
out." Your car? You have mileage benchmarks for oil changes and service calls. Heck, you've put yourself through diagnostics your whole
life—from report cards to SATs to GPAs. Data points tell you where
you fall on various scales of success. You use these tools not only to
make judgments, but also to make adjustments—to tell you when
things are going well and to tell you how to make things better.

But when it comes to money, so many people shy away from diagnostic tools the way we shy away from a second "serving" of cod liver
oil. After all, there's no real formal or ingrained system for really
assessing your financial picture. Nobody is sending home a report
card if you don't earn as much as you'd like. There's no scale to step on
to tell you that—oops—you overdid it when you spent next month's
savings allocation on last month's vacation. Often people judge their
financial stability in subjective ways that don't have much context—
how big their car is compared to the neighbors', what floor their office
is on (or whether it's in the corner), and how big their ring/house/TV/

boat is. And while those things may be indicators of your financial performance and your security, that's certainly not the scientific way to give yourself a fiscal physical. In fact, it can often be misleading; just because your ring is the size of a volleyball doesn't mean that you have enough money saved for retirement.

So what does that all mean? It means you should treat your financial picture the way you treat your heart health and the treads on your tires. If you don't take stock of where you are, you never know when you're going to fall apart. And what you're trying to avoid is a financial flat tire that leaves you stranded and desperate, without a spare to let you limp along to the next paycheck. Not only that, but you also want more than just "avoiding disaster." You want wealth and comfort—to earn and increase your money so that you do more than just get by, but also enjoy things, experiences, and family because you have the means to do, explore, dream, and live.

The real question is: Are you analyzing and understanding all your data correctly in a way that doesn't just stress absolute numbers but also reveals information about trends and what you need to do to reverse bad ones and maximize good ones?

While we won't take your blood pressure in this chapter, it may spike a bit as you assess your overall financial picture. Just keep going. As uncomfortable as it may be, you need to see and be aware of where you are, so you can learn about the (often simple) steps you can take to deal with any shortcomings. Your health, your finances, and, yes, even your mental well-being can be measured in numbers—helping you be younger, happier, and financially stable. Best of all, for these assessments, you don't need an expert or high-tech equipment to get results. You just need to log on to your accounts or pull out your latest statements to see exactly where you stand.

✏️ Test 1: Income Level

Your Gross Income: _____ (Not just your salary, but all income your family earns in a year; include interest at banks, dividends, income from rental properties, second jobs and side gigs, and Social Security—essentially any money you bring in annually.)

Your Take-Home Income: _____ (Your net income, or gross *minus* federal income tax, Social Security and Medicare taxes, state and local income taxes, health insurance premiums, and contributions to 401(k)s or other work-based retirement plans, health savings accounts (HSAs), flexible-spending accounts, and anything else deducted from your take-home pay. In other words, your discretionary income.)

How Often to Assess: Annually

You know how the first thing doctors do for a checkup is take your weight? (Of course you do.) Well, this is one of the first things to look at when assessing your financial picture. The reason: all other monetary values flow from this number. It's one-half of the major money equation: what comes in versus what goes out. And oftentimes it's one of the hardest things to control, because you're essentially at the mercy of a salary (and a growth rate) that's controlled by someone else (we'll talk more about income-boosting strategies and side gigs in chapter 3)

While we all *want* higher incomes because we think that's the route to more beach vacations and bigger kitchen islands, the fact is that the absolute salary doesn't always matter. Oftentimes when income goes up, so does spending. That means the net gain in the household is nada. So what are you after? Well, research from Daniel Kahneman, winner of a Nobel Prize in Economics, suggests that the benchmark for income should be about $75,000 a year. That number, according to his 2010 study, is the dividing line between those people who are happy and people who are not. While that may be a good starting point, you also know that $75,000 in San Francisco looks a heck of a lot different from $75,000 in Small Town, Middle America, or even in Cleveland. Therefore, it's impossible to really give you the pot-of-gold magic number you should be hitting when it comes to salary, and to your ability to save for retirement and emergencies. Instead, the way you value income has to be in proportion to your expenses.

DR. MIKE SAYS: And for those of you contemplating (or in) retirement, there's an interest rate manipulated by Federal Reserve members who seem to want to abuse those who save and motivate people to live for the day.

That means you have to make another calculation: How much are you spending? This exercise, if you're not already doing it, will require some time. You need to manage and track your monthly expenses—folding in categories that may not always be paid monthly (say your property tax or life insurance bill). And then factor in that 15 percent of your income *should be* earmarked for savings (if you're making a 401(k) or other retirement plan deduction off the top, you can lower the 15 percent by that percentage plus the percentage of any matching dollars you receive). After expenses, if you have some left over in your income, then you're ahead of the game. So this is how your equation should look:

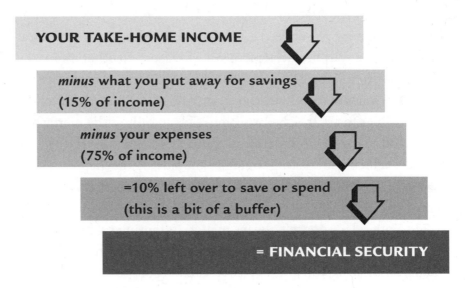

YOUR TAKE-HOME INCOME

minus what you put away for savings
(15% of income)

minus your expenses
(75% of income)

=10% left over to save or spend
(this is a bit of a buffer)

= FINANCIAL SECURITY

✏ Test 2: Your Expenses

Your Household Expenses: _____ (Everything you spend money on each month. This includes both the predictable—rent, gas, food, clothing, insurance—and the unpredictable—the dog goes to the vet, your brilliant child is invited to travel to the other end of the country to perform.)

Your Total Payments Involving Loans: _____
(Payments you're making on mortgages, car loans, student loans, credit-card bills, and personal loans.)

How Often to Assess: Annually

This is a simple—yet perhaps more depressing—equation: add up all the things you have to pay for every month. This total is what makes up your monthly budget, but also is the second piece of the financial puzzle that will determine your financial health. It includes regular expenses, as well as payments for anything you're borrowing money for. Debt, as you know, particularly high-interest-rate debt, is like the junk food of your financial picture. A little may harm you, may age you, but won't kill you; the more you have, the worse it gets. And for some people that junk-food addiction gets worse and worse, as you accumulate more and more debt and your expenses exceed your income. If you haven't already, you need to create a budget that allows you to see the inflow and outflow of money—taking into consideration all the payments you need to make regularly. While it may not be simple to actually reduce your expenses (we'll show you how throughout the book), it is fairly simple to create a diagnostic tool for determining whether your expenses are too far out of whack with your income. The three rules to follow:

⮑ Your total expenditures (including those dollars you put into your savings accounts) should not exceed your take-home income.

⮑ Your housing expenses (including mortgage payments, taxes and insurance) should not exceed 28 percent of your gross income (this is a measure lenders use to figure out if you qualify for a mortgage).

⮑ Your total debt payments (including those for housing, plus your credit cards, student loans, car payments, etc.) should not exceed 36 percent of your gross income.

(As you approach retirement, your total debt—not including the revolving credit-card bills you pay off in full every month and a car loan or lease if you have one—should be approaching zero.)

✏️ Test 3: Your Net Worth

Your Net Worth: _____ (Your net worth is the value of all your assets minus your liabilities. Calculating it means adding up the balances in your retirement, brokerage, savings, and checking accounts, then tacking on the value of the equity in your home (the price it would sell for minus the balance on your mortgage) and the value of the equity in your car (again, what it's worth minus what you owe on it). You can include other assets in your net-worth calculation—art, jewelry, etc.—if you wish, but only if you'd be willing to sell them to fund your future.

How Often to Assess: Annually

Taking a look at your net worth—that is, what you own versus what you owe—can give you a good look into how financially healthy you are. This is different from just your yearly salary, because basically it takes the pulse of your entire financial picture. What's important here is trend lines. Is your net worth going up or down from year to year? Sometimes your net worth can drop even if your salary goes up, because you take on more debt in the form of mortgages and loans. And sometimes your net worth may go up even if your salary doesn't, because you're paying down debt. There are some online tools that will make these calculations easier. They work just like medical apps or electronic medical records (EMRs) that track your performance on the same health tests over a number of years. Track your net worth now and make it one of those things you test every year. Here's what to calculate: assets minus debts equals net worth.

Once you've calculated your net worth, you should be asking yourself one question: What does it all mean? What if you're worth a hun-

Assets	Debts
Balance in all accounts (checking, savings, portfolio, retirement)	Credit-card balances
Equity in homes	Mortgage balances
Equity in cars	Other loans, such as car, student, 401(k), personal
Cash value in life insurance	

dred bucks or a hundred thousand or a million? Well, unlike some of the arenas of health, where a blood-pressure number is a blood-pressure number and you're either healthy or three bites of cheese away from a heart attack, net worth is a little more fluid. That is, your net worth can be very different from your neighbor's, even if the two of you have the exact same number. That's because net worth is all about context for retirement in comparison to income. Certainly we all want as high a number as possible, but more important, we want to keep it trending up, up, up. As long as you see yourself heading in that direction, steadily, you're on the right track.

✏ Test 4: Emergency Savings

Your Pot: _____

How Often to Assess: Once a Month

Life happens. Roofs leak. Cars break down. Medical mysteries happen. People lose jobs. Repairing any breakdowns can take a lot of money—money that is not included in your monthly budget. And finding a new job doesn't happen overnight. Oftentimes, when these emergencies arise, you rely on credit cards to pull through, which then turns into a dangerous game of dominoes as you come under financial strain attempting to climb out of debt (especially with cards that have huge interest rates). To avoid this burden—and keep your monthly budget in good shape and your net worth growing—you can and should earmark some of your budget for an emergency savings account.

This isn't where you save your money to grow. This is the old money-under-the-mattress trick, except you're not actually using a mattress. You're keeping a pot of easily accessible money to handle life's emergencies and put out financial fires. The danger, as you know (or have experienced), is that when money is easily accessible, it's, well, easily accessible—and that makes it awfully tempting to pull out that cash and use it to pay for a purebred Tibetan mastiff. But an emergency savings account counts only if you forget it's there—and tap it only if an unforeseen crisis would crush you financially. So here are the guidelines for your emergency account:

> This money needs to be liquid, meaning it should be in a savings or money market account that you can access immediately (not in a CD, where there may be a penalty for pulling it out, or in the market, where you could potentially lose principal). This account should be separate from the account you use usually for everyday expenses.

> Focus on creating a small pot first. Save $2,000 before turning your energy to building the bigger pot. About half of all Americans would find it hard to come up with this sum in a pinch, so having a fund this size at your disposal is a substantial achievement. This baseline can get you out of immediate jams, even if it can't do much if you lose a job.

> Once you're at the baseline, work on increasing the account until it could handle between three and six months' worth of expenses (six months for single folks, three months for two-income couples—if one loses a job, the other income can help fill the gaps). Retirees should have enough in an emergency account to cover one year of expenses and enough sheltered from the whims of the stock market to cover three years (we'll talk more about where to put

that money in chapter 10). Just don't let building this bigger cushion get in the way of saving for retirement and capturing matching dollars. Split the difference if need be, putting 3 percent toward this fund and 12 percent toward the long term, until your cushion is created.

✏️ Test 5: **Retirement Options**

In Your Retirement Accounts: _____ (total amount)
     Social Security Pot: _____

How Often to Assess: Annually

What does retirement look like to you? A beach? A hammock? Golf or tennis? Travel? Hanging with your spouse or the grandkids? (Men, it seems, are looking forward to hanging with their significant other, according to some new research. For women it's all about the little ones.) Any or all of those? Sounds lovely. If you're lucky, retirement will include whatever you want, even if that means working at a job you love or inventing a side career for yourself or pursuing a passion. No matter what retirement looks like to you, two truths apply to virtually everyone: your health costs are going to go up (even if you do follow all our advice, the body will betray you from time to time), and your income from working is going to go down (and, eventually, just stop).

All that's a different way of saying that one of your priorities has to be pocketing enough money to take care of yourself in retirement. While some expenses will certainly go down (the days of buying prom dresses and basketball shoes may be over), other expenses (greens fees and entertaining friends, for example) will not. And you want that retirement stash to be able to handle your living expenses, your medical expenses, your unforeseen expenses, and your spoil-the-grandbabies expenses—without ever having to worry about outliving your savings.

Now, there is some debate as to the optimal number in terms of how much you actually need to retire. So many factors play a role—how much you earn, how long you plan to work, how much you plan on spending, and how long you live. You can use an online calculator to calculate your optimal number (find ours at JeanChatzky.com/tools). But if you just want a ballpark number, use this chart to guide you:

By the time you're...	Your retirement stash should be...
30	About the size of your annual income
40	3x your annual income
50	6x your annual income
60	8x your annual income
At retirement	10x your annual income

Source: Fidelity Investments

What if you're not there yet? Don't panic. That's precisely what these benchmarks are for. Remember how on page 26 we said that you should be saving 15 percent of your income, including matching dollars from your employer? If you're not hitting these marks, that's a signal to you to adjust that 15 percent higher—try to ratchet your savings rate up by 2 percent a year, and/or plan on working a little longer and taking Social Security a little later. (We'll talk more about that in chapter 10; for now you can see what you stand to receive by going to SSA.gov and checking your current statement.)

Just note: These numbers were developed specifically with people who earn $50,000 to $300,000 a year in mind. The way they work, your savings (the multiple of your annual income in the above chart) are designed to replace 45 percent of your preretirement income while Social Security covers the rest. The amount Social Security will cover slides based on your income. See the chart below:

Where Retirement Income Comes From			
Preretirement Income	Income Replacement Rate		
	From Savings	From Social Security	Total
50K	45%	35%	80%
100K	45%	27%	72%
100K	45%	16%	61%
300K	44%	11%	55%

Source: Fidelity Investments

This analysis raises some important questions. Here are the answers.

Do you have to worry that, if you're earning $100,000 a year, the 27 percent of your nut that you'll replace with Social Security plus the 45 percent you save adds up to only 72 percent? No, because you're not consuming the full $100,000 that you're earning. You're paying taxes, living, and—most important—saving at least 15 percent a year. You're already living on less. For those reasons you don't have to replace the full amount.

What if you are one of the people with pension income that will replace a certain percentage of your retirement income, in addition to your 401(k) or other retirement nest egg? Lucky you! You can reduce the amount you have to save to replace the first 45 percent you need for your future retirement paycheck. For example, if you can see that your pension is going to replace 15 percent of what you believe will be your final income, you are responsible for replacing only the other 30 percent. Figuring out how much that is means doing a little math:

30% (or the amount you want to replace)/45% (or the full recommended replacement rate) = x (the new multiple of your final income you want to save by retirement)/10

In other words: 30/45 = x/10. Do the math and x = 6.67. You need to save 6.67 times your final income by retirement.

What about health care? These recommendations are based on actual consumption patterns of people in retirement, so health care is included. Although you can expect health expenses to start to rise as you age, other expenses taper off simultaneously. By age 80, health-care expenses have essentially replaced transportation expenses.

What if you earn more than $300,000 a year? In general, the more you earn, the less of those earnings you consume. We're in no way suggesting that someone who makes $5 million a year needs to save $50 million to retire comfortably. But one way to gauge how much you'll need is to pay attention to how much of your income you're actually consuming in the years before retirement. In many cases college expenses and, perhaps, the mortgage will be satisfied by then, so you can eliminate those from your list of outflows.

✏️ Test 6: **Your Credit Score**

Your Credit Score: _____

How Often to Assess: Every Six Months

A vital piece of financial data, your credit score usually determines what interest rate you'll pay on mortgages and other loans. It even factors into the price of your homeowner's and auto insurance premiums. So the better your score (and there's a proven way to raise it if you're not satisfied with where yours is right now—we'll talk about it in chapter 11), the more money it can save you in the long run. Monitor your credit score as regularly as you change your oil (unless you've got one of those cars that needs oil changes only every 15,000 miles; in that case check it twice as often), so you know where you stand with people who will be making financial decisions that affect you (and check your credit report regularly to make sure you haven't become a victim of identity theft). You can request a free copy of your credit report each year from each of the three major credit-reporting agencies at AnnualCreditReport.com. Your credit score is based on the information in these reports, so look for errors you can correct or bad habits you can turn around 💬. You can also review your credit score free each month at CreditKarma.com, Credit.com, or SavvyMoney.com.

Most credit scores operate within the range of 301 to 850. How the scores stack up:

> Excellent credit: 750 and up
>
> Good credit: 700–749
>
> Fair credit: 650–699
>
> Poor credit: 600–649
>
> Bad credit: Below 600

💬 DR. MIKE SAYS:

And I bet your bad health numbers go down as your credit score goes up—financial stress has that much of an impact on your health.

✏️ Test 7: The Mirror Test

How Often to Assess: Annually

All the above tests have one thing in common: they're all about the numbers. Tangible data, hard-line metrics, percentages, additions, subtractions, goals that you can tangibly see and achieve. But we don't want you to think that financial security is solely about digits. In fact, we'd be remiss if we didn't explain that much of what drives our financial decision-making isn't numbers, but emotions. Therefore it's not only smart, but advised, to make one of your financial assessments about something that doesn't include a single dollar sign. You'll think about you—your life, your goals, the changes you've experienced over the past year. Why? Because the changes in your life can change your decisions—and those can change budgets, outlooks, expenses, and all the things that influence the numbers in the rest of this chapter.

So with this assessment, your goal is simply to answer the following questions—not just to give yourself a tangible piece of data to work with, but also to help yourself think about how these things may affect your approach to money and wealth. Ask yourself:

⮕ How has your life changed? (In terms of marital status, a new job, relocation, or any other big life events.)

⮕ Have your financial goals changed? (Do you want to donate more to charity [before or after death—consider a "charitable annuity" that allows you to receive interest payments on donations till you and your spouse die], spend more time with family, travel more, start a business?)

⮕ Have your views on risk changed? (Has the market or your life status made you more or less averse to risk, more or less aggressive with your portfolio and investments?)

While you don't need to do anything specific with those answers, you should spend some time letting them percolate and thinking about how these changes may influence your money issues.

☞ Three Advanced Checkups

If you're in good shape with most of the above tests, you're probably ready to take a look at a few other key areas (all of which we'll discuss in detail later in the book, but all of which are worth mentioning here as you do annual diagnostics). We'll be covering all of these in more detail throughout the book, but you can use the total numbers for taking stock of where you are.

Other savings accounts: How much do you have earmarked for college education, health care (via a health savings account), or other specific uses? Are those numbers heading up as rapidly as you'd like?

Asset allocation: This will determine the percentage of your portfolio that goes into, say, stocks or bonds. If you have investment portfolios (including your retirement and other brokerage-based accounts but not your bank-based emergency ones), assess how your assets are divided every year. One rule of thumb: the percentage of your portfolio in stocks should be around 110 minus your age.

Insurance: Every year you should look at what you're spending on various forms of insurance and make sure that your coverage is sufficient for your needs and that you're not spending more than necessary. This may entail shopping around.

AgeProof ESSENTIALS

1. The "mirror test"—checking yourself out in terms of health and finances—is a mandatory part of improving both areas of your life. Combining do-it-yourself tests with some professional ones will tell you where you are and what you need to do.

2. The no-argument tests everyone needs to do: blood pressure and the line earmarked for savings in your budget. If those numbers aren't where they need to be, you need to change what you are doing and keep assessing until they are.

3. The first step is the hardest. That's OK. Take the leap now and you'll be more confident and empowered to change what you need to after that.

Part II
Breaking Bad Behavior

The Science of Habits

Changing your daily deeds isn't a matter of will, but a matter of reengineering

Right now we want you to put down this book and go to your favorite radio station/smartphone app/streaming music site and hit play to listen to something you like. We don't care if it's jazz or hip-hop, classical or country. We just want you to listen for a minute or two. (We'll wait.) What did you hear? Maybe you heard a violin or a bass or a lyric about a dude with a pickup truck who drowned his sorrows in a bucket of beer because the love of his life moved to Mississippi. No matter what style of music you listened to, you heard—consciously or not—something that is the underlying secret to improving your wealth and health.

You heard a rhythm.

You heard—you felt—the pace and vibe and beat and engine that created the foundation for the song. Maybe you bebopped to the boom-bap of a pop song. Or maybe you let the soft sound of a cello soothe your soul. No matter how you reacted, it was *there*. And you felt it.

In this whole quest to figure out how to make meaningful changes to your health and wealth, we'll be talking about behaviors, habits, rules, strategies, addiction, willpower, and all the buzzwords that will

signal to you that you can (yes, *can*) break bad habits and form good
ones. But no matter what nomenclature we use, it really is all about
creating a life rhythm—an underlying beat to your life that creates the
foundation through which you form those habits, make decisions, and
create an automatic lifestyle of good health and strong wealth.

Rhythm happens not just in music, but all around us—whether
it's waves crashing, rain dropping, or a sun setting. For many of us,
our rhythm—spending more than we earn or eating more than we
should—is off. And we have to readjust our life playlist to find a new
beat.

That, in a lot of ways, is what this entire book is about. Even if you
know what to do, how can you nudge your life into different patterns,
choices, and habits? How can you go through life hip-hopping to
healthy habits? Thankfully, science has told us not only *that* we can do
it, but also *how* we can do it.

The process really stems not from intangible forces like willpower
and grit, but from tangible changes in your brain that you have to kick-
start and that you can control. Understand, the way we learn to do new
things is through repeated use, coaxing the neurons in our brains to
perform. So a baby hears the word *mommy* six zillion times and the
neurons—because of the repeated use—recognize that *mommy* must
be important. (Darn right she is!) The neurons build an expressway
from one to another so that the baby, once she learns the meaning of
mommy, never has to waste any resources or energy to figure out what
it means. It's automatic .

JEAN
SAYS:

It's just the way
it happens in the
movie *Inside Out*.
What? You haven't
seen it? Download
it. Now.

This is how we learn all information: we are repeatedly exposed to
it, our brain classifies it as a priority, and boom, it's ingrained.

Of course, it also helps you if you can track these behaviors—not
just for data assessment, but also for motivation and awareness. So
what happens when you want to learn something new? You meet your
soul mate, and your soul mate happens to be from Iceland. You've
spent decades of your life learning one language, and now, all of a sudden, you hear the words *Aldur Sönnun líf þitt*. Your neurons say, "What
the heck is that?" Then the neurons hear the words again and again and

again, so your brain figures out this is indeed important, so they have a new expressway to build. On that expressway you readily access the meaning of *Aldur Sönnun líf þitt* (it's Icelandic for "AgeProof your life," for what it's worth).

Now extend the science to not just words and information, but to habits. The principle is exactly the same. You have to teach your brain what expressway to build—and at the same time you probably need to demolish an expressway or two. You need to undo what you've previously ingrained and build something to take its place. You need new neural connection to form a new rhythm to your life. You need chicken breasts instead of chicken fingers. You need IRA, not I-spend-all-day. You need to build your own system of neurological pathways that help you form new priorities—and automatic habits.

This is how it works: During most of our day, the reptilian part of our brain is at work, not the executive-function part of the brain—the part that uses reasons, logic, and decision-making skills (this is the prefrontal cortex). Some research that originated at Duke University shows that 40 percent of what we do every day isn't actually governed by decisions, but by habits. We drive through for burgers because that's what we do every Thursday night before the kids' games. We don't stash enough away for savings because we've never earmarked some of our income for that savings account. Much of the time, we're on autopilot.

Similarly troubling is that we also spend much of the time simply reacting, rather than deciding. In the anthropological scenario of a predator coming into your campsite, you don't call for a meeting with the predator, discuss options with the predator, take minutes of the meeting so that everyone remembers what happened, and then figure out next steps in case it happens again. Nope. Either the predator destroys you or you destroy it (or hightail it to safe territory). Reptilian reactions saved our lives long ago; that's why they trump executive functions, even to this day.

Complicating matters even more is that every real decision we make is first filtered by how we feel about it. That is, emotions drive our decision-making process by triggering a decision, rather than a rational choice. Our emotional reaction is up to three times faster than our cognitive one, so it's only natural that it comes first. This is why situations fraught with temptation are so difficult—strong feelings override facts, and even hard facts don't counteract emotions.

So here's what we want you to do. Take a second and think about what you did today—what you ate, how you spent your money, and other "choices" you made. How many of them were actually choices? And how many of them *could have been* choices, but were done simply because that's the habit you have, or because you let your emotions take over? Your goal here—if you're not satisfied with your health or your wealth—is essentially a three-step equation:

Reptilian habits (bad) → Executive-function
decisions → Reptilian habits (good)

That is, our goal is to have you act reptilian (we mean that in the kindest way). But we want those automatic habits to be the healthy kind, not the destructive kind. To achieve that, you need to employ that executive function—making conscious decisions about what you do. That's because you need the executive-function factors to overpower the reptilian-function ones in order to establish new reptilian behaviors.

It sounds easy—just make a decision to sock more money away!— but we know it's not. In fact, research shows that while many people know what they *should* do, they don't do it consistently. Therein lies the heart of what you're dealing with when you're trying to improve both your biological and financial lots in life. How do you swing the pendulum from one reptilian habit to the other (better) reptilian habit? Through our research—and our work with thousands of patients and consumers—we can say there are ways to swing the pendulum. These are some of the truths for forming new habits—rather, for creating that new rhythm to your life.

It's Not Enough to Decide. Decisions are fine, and we're happy that you've made the decision to read this book—and to learn about the parallels between good health and long-lasting wealth. But reading this book won't make your triglycerides go down and your 401(k) balance go up. Why? Because your neurons don't have a stinking clue that you made a decision. Your neurons need repetitive action. So really, the key to building those bridges is to find your destructive habit and replace it with a new one. Say you smoke, and your reflex is to smoke after dinner. What if you decided to take a walk after dinner instead of having a cigarette? You can decide to get into that pattern. You do it once and your brain is like, "Whoa, Jim, something's off here." You do it twice and your brain is like, "Hey, buddy, c'mon, man, isn't this the time you jam that nasty stick in your mouth?" Do it for two weeks, a month, more, and your brain has learned the new norm.

It's not about simply quitting an action; it's about replacing an action with an action. (Quitting smoking is more complicated than this one action, of course, but substituting one habit for another is part of the addiction-breaking plan.) And while many say it takes three weeks to ingrain a habit, newer data say that it takes a year for your hormone systems to react to your choice, like a new waist size, so it then becomes easier to maintain that new waist size. Meaning: whatever your new habit is, try to create an environment that makes it easy for you (automatic is even better) to stick with it.

It's Better to Play Dominoes than to Knock Down a House of Cards. While there is evidence that some people have success with immediate change-everything interventions, it appears that your chances of success increase when you don't try to knock out all your bad habits at once. So don't wake up Monday morning and decide that you're going to eat quinoa and broccoli, reallocate your budget, and work out three hours a day. Some people can have success with that approach, no doubt. If your personality fits a 180-degree change-all approach, go for it. But when you have competing priorities, it seems that working toward a few—or even one—at a time sets you up better for long-term success.

One of Jean's Money Rules is "Don't diet while you're budgeting and don't budget while you're dieting." Life will always get in the way of making smart decisions, so it tends to be easier on your brain to try to make one or two changes (or replacement actions), and then let those domino into the next two and then the next two and so on. Research suggests that when you gain the skills to change one habit, it's easier to change the next 🗨.

That brings up an important point: it's not just about creating these neurological connections, but also about teaching yourself and developing skills that you can apply from one situation to another— and thus setting yourself up for more success. You have to be aware of your habits, not to be distracted by the stress of life that gets in the way—the rhythm that you are in is key to building habits, as is repetition and awareness that your habits are right on. When you get better at resisting temptation, it doesn't matter if it's a diet temptation or a budget temptation. You've developed a skill: the ability to resist or to automate a substitution. (Tip: tackle the challenges that are easiest for *you* first. Choose things you can automate—setting up an automatic payroll deduction for your 401(k) is something you have to do only once. Similarly, you can establish a running healthy grocery list with an online service like Peapod. Then, you can reorder with just a couple clicks [and without loading your basket up with Oreos].)

Understand the Differences between Motivations. Research has shown that motivation—the impetus to make decisions that turn into actions—really comes in two forms: extrinsic and intrinsic. Extrinsic motivation involves outside forces (maybe a dare to lose weight or a threat from a credit-card agency to shut you down). Those can be very real and very powerful motivators, especially in the short term. But long-term success typically relies on intrinsic motivation, which as it sounds comes from within. That is, are you motivated to do better because it feels right, or you empathize with your future self, or because you want to, and/or because the change itself feels good? The reduced stress of having no bills and no debt feels great, so that's what keeps overspending in check. Many times, successful habit formation starts with extrinsic motivation that morphs into intrinsic motivation.

Not only is that OK, it's probably the way most people are prompted into action.

Value the Step Called Precontemplation. There's a saying developed by writing coach Roy Peter Clark that we love, and it essentially boils down to this: we shouldn't think of procrastination as, well, procrastination, but rather as rehearsal. Rather than framing your delay in getting started as a negative thing, you should value this time that you're revving up and preparing to make changes. You're thinking, you're mulling, you're figuring out how the heck you're going to weave more snap peas into your diet and what you'll do without your $7 coffee every day. This step of precontemplation is not only allowed, it's also encouraged. It's why awareness is so key—creating some metrics that you can track and be aware of provides motivation to make changes. (This is also why having a buddy is so important: it allows you to share, be aware of, and monitor those metrics with someone who can help you stay accountable.) While some of us have a lightning-strike aha moment that scares us straight out of the ice cream tub, most of us have to take time to warm up to the fact that we won't be eating pizza for breakfast anymore. So take some time and let ideas and strategies simmer in your mind. Most of all, think about the reasons *why* you want to make changes—and the benefits you gain. In the end, if you can list more pros than cons, you're likely to take the steps from contemplation to decision to action.

It's Trickier with Food and Money. We'd be remiss if we didn't acknowledge that some bad habits are harder to break than others. While smoking, of course, is notoriously a difficult one to break for many folks (it takes an average of six tries to succeed), our obesity epidemic (two-thirds of us in the United States are overweight or obese, and we've exported this habit very successfully) and debt epidemic (folks who carry credit-card debt owe an average of more than $15,000) show that these problems are incredibly prevalent. There's a reason for that, we believe. You don't need cigarettes to survive. You do need food. And you do need to spend money. You can't just give up food or spending. This is why it's hard—and why failing shouldn't

DR. MIKE SAYS: Although cold pasta and sweet potatoes, etc., become resistant starch when cooled overnight, and act in your body more as fiber than rapid producers of an increased sugar level—see *What to Eat When* or the website WhenWay.com for more info.

cause you to lose hope. It often takes repeated efforts to have success. So you can't make a wholesale change. While you can exchange smoking for walking, you can't exchange eating for walking. You have to eat. Now, of course, we still can use the same principle (greens instead of fries), but that's admittedly harder to make automatic. Yet there are ways to do it, and that's the crux of our next two chapters— establishing priority items for creating healthy habits in the areas of wealth and health.

CHAPTER 3

Here's Your Change

*To improve your financial picture, make these
your top five priorities*

$

S impler times meant simpler decisions. Back when caves were
homes and forests were supermarkets, resource allocation was a
no-brainer. You spent time and energy on the things that helped
you survive and procreate: you hunted for meat, gathered berries, and
summoned enough energy to build roofs, fend off drooling beasts, and
do the hubba-hubba in the glow of the campfire. All with one common
goal: that you and your family survived the next day and into the next
generation. That was it. Your priorities were clear and concise.

Of course, our modern world has made your modern life much
better. Medical advances increase your life expectancy. Technological
advances can take you around the world with ease and speed. Smartphone advances ensure that no matter where you are, you can take
comfort in knowing that there's a coffee shop within 200 feet of you.
Few would trade our modern amenities for the stress and strain that
our ancestors had to endure. But think about what happened to prior-
itization. It became a whole lot harder.

We don't have a caveman to-do list (food, shelter, sex) anymore.
We have a to-do list and a want-this list that reads as long as a James
Joyce novel.

Right? It's not as easy as paying for food and paying for a home and putting the rest in the bank. The demands on your money look a little something like this: You foot the bill for your house and all that goes with it (electric, insurance, gas, upkeep). You pay for your food (what you bring in and what you go out for). You have car bills (gas, insurance, maintenance). You have kids who have necessities (clothes) and not-so-necessities (a smartphone, though they'd argue differently). You have eight nieces and nephews that get birthday gifts. You have a $12-a-day iced-coffee habit. Your wireless and cable bills are the size of some mortgage payments. You're trying to save for college and retirement at the same time. You would like to take a trip every once in a while, not to mention go see a movie, a ball game, or Elton John. Your kid's foot decided to grow a full size in three months. And, well, it never ends ... There's always something else that you need, want, or can't resist.

Everything, in essence, is a priority, because everything you spend money on has some value in your life, whether it's a necessity or it's for your pleasure or well-being. But the reality is that we no longer have three priorities that loom above the others because they're necessary for survival. We have a *bazillion* priorities—some higher than others, but all of them valid. And to complicate matters, those priorities are constantly changing depending on your values, your whims, and your stage in life. This is why so many of us feel the tightening noose of financial worry. It's hard—darn near impossible—to do it all.

(While we'll spend some time dissecting the credit-card business later, it's worth mentioning that the use of credit cards as well as other forms of too-free and too-easy borrowing—hello, instantaneous 401(k) loans—are one big reason we have such a hard time prioritizing. Open-access debt allows us to have it all even if we don't have the means to have it all—creating the slippery slope of spending behavior that can give us immediate satisfaction but eventually leads us into financial distress.)

We see one of the purposes of this book not as telling you that you should spend money on X but not on Y, but rather as helping you to filter out the minutiae so you can have in your mind your clear priorities when it comes to financial decision-making. Think of it as a bit of Esalen-like consciousness raising. Remember, as we discussed a few pages ago, this whole journey is about establishing new habits, but they need to be based on a structure of your priorities. If you have those priorities in place, then the small decisions—should I or shouldn't I buy the hot tub?—will take care of themselves.

Priority 1: Earn a Decent Living

As you know and as we'll explore throughout this whole book, getting financial freedom and security is about a lot of intangible factors—like prioritizing, commitment, impulse control, and things of that nature. But when it comes right down to it, it's as tangible as a concrete floor. Your financial future is all about a simple math equation. How much more do you make than you spend?

Income – Expenses = Do you have enough left over
for a trip to Tahiti, a pack of gum, or neither?

For many people, the key part of that equation is the second factor. We all spend too much money on things we don't really need or want, and our spending outpaces our income. (More on this in Priority 2.) But if you want to live in a modern society (and some don't, and that's OK, too), there are a certain number of expenses that you can't just live without, whether we're talking food, home payments (taking into consideration where you want to live, for safety and schools and ease of commute), insurance, gas, electricity, water, or other essentials. Even if you pare down your budget to the very barest of bones, so that you're paying only for what you absolutely need at the lowest possible rate, you will always have expenses. That leaves you with only one other way to flip the equation—by changing the other factor: how much you earn.

Admittedly, of all the things you can do to influence your financial future, this may be one of the most difficult. Why? It's one of the few factors that—at least on the surface—is out of your control. It's not as if you can snap your fingers and demand that your salary be doubled. It's not as if you can waltz onto Wall Street and ask for a $7 million investment in your app idea. It's not as if you can change careers in the time it takes to refresh a browser.

It's *hard*. But it's not impossible. So if your income is not where you want it to be—to cover your expenses and save for the future—working to raise it should be your top priority. While the good news is that employers are likely to raise salaries every year by about 3 percent, that's not nearly enough to keep up with costs (medical and college expenses, to name just two, have been outpacing inflation for years), or make a serious leap in terms of improving your earnings. By figuring out a strategy to increase your (and your family's) income, you'll provide a financial infrastructure that allows you to take care of the other priorities on this list (not to mention cut down on the dangerously damaging stress associated with financial hardship).

Unfortunately, no matter what we say here and how we say it, we're going to come off like a flippant circus barker: *Step right up, get yourself another job, more money, more money, howzabout a new job here, a new job there!* That's simply because the advice we give might make it seem we're implying you can snap your fingers and double your income, but the reality is that it's a (sometimes long) process that will eventually work in your favor if you make it a priority.

If you're not earning the living that you'd like, you have a few choices:

Negotiate. While this may feel like the most awkward of all your options, it's also the fastest. An immediate pay bump at your current job comes without the headaches associated with some of the other options here. You can do this at the time of performance reviews. (More than half of employers said in a survey that they fully expect employees to ask for increases.) You can request an increase by showing that you can take another job offer that pays more (provided that

JEAN SAYS:

I had a boss early in my career who told me he needed me to go out and get another offer so he could justify giving me a raise to his boss. I did. It worked. But note: My husband, an executive recruiter, says this is a tactic you can use only once with an employer. Otherwise, that employer (rightly) starts to feel played.

you do have said offer and are willing to leave your current job). You can also use data to support your case; do some research to find the salaries of people doing the same job you do at different companies, using industry-standard figures (many industries do salary surveys to get average salaries for occupations). Bosses who are not CEOs need tangible evidence to make salary increases, and the more data you can provide (about your own performance as well as supporting data), the stronger your case. Data > pleading.

Walk. We're not talking about the 10,000 steps a day you should take. You may like your job, the purpose and mission of your company, and the people you work with, and maybe you feel as if you've hit the zone. You do your job well, you're respected, and you're more comfortable than a broken-in pair of jeans. Great. Life and work satisfaction are important to your overall well-being. But if you're stuck in the rut of earning a salary that's not in line with your other life goals, you may have to search for another gig and, if we can borrow some language from LeBron James, take your talents to South Beach (South Beach being a metaphor for "another employer").

Why? The biggest salary jumps you'll make usually won't happen internally, but when you move from one company to another. Some estimate that you'll be able to increase your salary an average 10 to 20 percent when you switch jobs, something that generally won't happen that often if you stay in the same place of employment. Say

DR. MIKE SAYS:

I've had the privilege of leading physician groups for the last 31 years; my style was set by my first boss. If he hadn't been ready to give me what I asked for before I asked for it, I knew I was wrong in asking for it, whether in resources to do the job or in salary. I think excellence in performance should merit more resources, more responsibilities, and more salary. But if your boss doesn't have that latitude, I do agree that comparisons give her the ammunition to succeed for you.

DR. MIKE SAYS:

For a Cleveland guy, this phrase really hurts (though not so much anymore!), but it is true—sometimes to achieve what you want or to get paid more, or both, you need to be willing to take your talents elsewhere. But there is a lesson here—LeBron accepted a lower straight salary playing for Miami to improve his worth and total employment pay and endorsement packages when he came back. Sometimes a lower immediate payout means a bigger payout over the long run.

you make $75,000 and you get a 5 percent increase annually. But you decide to look into another job that pays $95,000. It would take you about five years to reach that salary in your current job. Now go to the job that pays $95,000 and figure in that 5 percent bump: at the end of those five years, instead of being at $95,700 in job one, your salary would be just over $121,000 in job two. To get a bigger base, you often have to leave your comfort zone. How often? Every three to four years seems to be the sweet spot, and that's the average for people in their 20s and 30s. But people in their mid-50s to mid-60s move just every 10 years. The more you grow and earn status in a job, the more flexibility you're likely to have, creating even more job satisfaction (a big plus when it comes to decreasing stress). And here's an additional tip: negotiate hard when you make the switch. Let's say you get 5 percent more on a $40,000 salary when you're 22. That little bump in starting point would mean an extra $170,000 in your coffers by the time you turn 65, just calculated from that onetime 5 percent difference.

DR. MIKE SAYS:

It's not impossible— Tech Elevator in Cleveland, like many businesses around the country, teaches you how to code (and double the salary you make) in 14 fairly intense weeks.

Go Back to School. It's difficult for us to address work issues here collectively, because everyone's in a different situation with a different skill set and different options. But as the world changes, there are more and more opportunities for people to develop new skills that industries have a need for. Maybe you're good with technology. Go back to school and learn how to write code or program computers. Or acquire some other skill that you can turn into a main job or even a secondary one. Good at photography? Start a wedding photo business. One of the challenges, especially as you get older, is that you're not viewed as having skills needed for today's technological advances, and there's only so many times you can say, "Well, in our day…" without being laughed right out of an interview. To stay relevant, you must adapt. Sometimes you can learn new skills on the job, but other times you can seek out after-hours or online educational opportunities to expand your skill set or get certifications in new areas that make you attractive to potential employers.

Take a Side Gig. The traditional work environment has gone the way of the VHS. Nowadays more and more people have flex hours or work from home or cobble together a number of projects rather than have a full-time job. In fact, there are 53 million freelancers in the United States, and, according to some Bureau of Labor Statistics data, seven million American workers have more than one job.

What does that mean for you? Even if you do work in a traditional environment with traditional hours, there are opportunities to earn extra income that give you flexibility to perform when you're not working your main job. Whether you're good with words, computers, photos, plumbing, or something else, you can find side projects that will pay you for your service and expertise (provided you aren't violating any noncompete or other guidelines your main employer has). While it may be hard to work these varied jobs into a budget, they can provide a source of income that you could earmark for savings, or entertainment, or some other line item that you can be flexible with from month to month. There are many online venues to survey for these jobs, whether the traditional ones like Craigslist or newer ones like Upwork.com and Taskrabbit.com, which allow you to advertise your services and find odd jobs.

(Big caveat: one of the big pitfalls here is that once income increases, that somehow sends a signal that it's OK to invest in classic cars or book a weekly massage appointment. For the equation to work, income should increase while expenses stay flat or at least don't increase at the same rate, until, again, you're consistently spending less than you make plus savings, which brings us to Priority 2.)

Priority 2: Pay Yourself First with Savings

Fragile is a glass of wine on the edge of the table. Fragile is a baby's skin. Fragile is an octogenarian's bones. Fragile is trying to ship a picture frame in a manila envelope. You know fragile when you see it—you're one small step from a disaster, big or small. Even though you know what it is, many of you live it every day. In fact, half of Americans are what researchers call "financially fragile." What does that mean? It means you've got so little socked away that you're one small step away from a financial crisis. So you have a busted transmission or a roof leak or a medical emergency and you don't have the funds to cover it, and as a result you have to look to third parties (banks, family, mobsters—some would say that all three of these categories are similar, but not us) to float you some cash to get you by. This is not the situation you want to be in. Yet according to one recent survey by NeighborWorks America, about 34 percent of Americans have no emergency savings. You want to be in a financial situation where you're taking care of yourself and your family—not just to get through every day, but to get through the unexpected days.

One big reason we don't have savings, research has shown, is that we generally lack empathy for our future selves, so we don't consider it a priority. The me of today doesn't know the me of 30 years from now—she is, in effect, a total stranger, which is why today-me has trouble saving money for her. One way to deal is to try to visualize your future self or use an app that does it for you like AgingBooth (or dare we mention it again, the Sharecare App, which also lets you through virtual reality see your future bank account, lifestyle, and each organ, like your heart and its blood vessels, or your brain and its memory centers). When you see that person, you start to develop empathy for and a desire to take care of that future self—which can help you get started saving for the future if you haven't.

One big thing you can do right now as you create your financial priorities: pay yourself first—that is, take some of your income and earmark it for savings. As we said in the last chapter, we'd ideally like you to hit a consistent savings rate of 15 percent (if you can't do that off the bat, start lower and nudge yourself up), meaning you take 15 percent of your after-tax income (including employer matching dollars) and put it away. About one in seven people do save more than 15 percent of their income, according to one survey, so that's your goal—to be one of those people. Think of it as giving yourself a paycheck—one that you'll cash in down the road. This self-payment plan allows you to spread your wealth to different savings silos.

What do we mean by that? Saving isn't just about socking a bunch of money away and telling yourself you'll use it when you need it. It's about saving money strategically, so you can earmark certain amounts to address different kinds of needs. In that way, saving and investing are really about creating a hierarchy, establishing base savings needs and moving up to higher-order ones. The goal, of course, is to cover all bases. When you're just starting to smooth out your financial picture, you want to move systematically through the hierarchy. Once you have one covered, you can—and need to—move to the next. At the risk of sounding too meta, these are the priorities within this priority.

Level	Action	How To
1	Save $2,000 to get out of fragile territory (to cover emergencies)	Automatic transfer of 15 percent from checking into savings with every paycheck. (If you can't hit 15, start lower and nudge up.)
2	Begin contributing to a retirement plan	If you have a work-based retirement plan with a match, try to contribute enough to get the full match. If you don't have a plan, begin funding an individual retirement account (IRA) or Roth IRA through automatic transfers (from the 15 percent as soon as you complete level 1). If you are self-employed, look into a Simplified Employee Pension (SEP-IRA).
3	Continue putting a little money into savings each pay period, at a ratio of 4:1	If you're not yet saving 15 percent automatically, but are saving, say, 5 percent of what you earn, put 4 percent in the retirement plan, 1 percent in the savings account. If you're saving 10 percent, put 8 percent in the retirement plan, 2 percent in the savings account. If you're saving 15 percent, put 12 percent in the retirement plan, 3 percent in the savings account. Once you have a fully funded emergency stash, put it all into retirement or other investments.
4	Accelerate your savings rate each year until you're maxing out your retirement contributions	An easy time to do this is when you get a raise. Windfalls can be a nice boost, too. The average tax refund is about $3,000. Invest that every year for 20 years at 8 percent. You'll have an extra $162,000 for retirement. (You're welcome.)
5	Invest your money via tax-advantaged vehicles: Health Savings Accounts, 529 College Savings Accounts	You can work these contributions in as you earn more and spend less, creating items in your budget. Automating them will increase your rate of savings success.
6	Put money in a brokerage account	If you max out your ability to save in a tax-advantaged way and can still invest more, do it. When you get to retirement, being able to pull from money on which you've already paid taxes is a good thing as it allows the money in your tax-advantaged accounts (IRAs, 401(k)s, etc.) to keep growing.

Priority 3: **Spend Less Than You Make**

Before there were credit cards and loan sharks, a personal economy worked pretty simply: you made money and you could spend that money. If you didn't have enough to cover the cost of something, you couldn't buy it. But as soon as financial life preservers came into the picture (in the form of credit cards and other loans), that equation was null and void. Even if you didn't *have* the money, you could spend the money. While many folks have made some serious profits off this formula, others have been seriously hurt by it: the life preserver has popped, and many are sinking in debt they can't keep up with— because they spend more than they make.

Now, don't mistake us. We're not saying that all loans are bad. In fact, there are many times when they're financially smart (in the case of mortgages, for example, or credit cards that earn you rewards provided you *always* pay them off before interest charges set in). But what we're saying is that you should never, NEVER create a financial environment in which your spending is consistently outpacing your earning. We've spent a whole section talking about budgeting (starting on page 176), but for now there are four important things to remember when figuring out the earn-spend equation.

1. *Be realistic about your earnings after taxes and other deductions.* That number is much lower than your salary, of course. And mentally, you have to know that a $75,000 salary is more like $53,000 in usable funds, and that's before you've paid yourself first. After you're making that truly brilliant move (paying yourself first into tax-advantaged plans, of course, nets you a nice fat tax deduction), it's closer to $49,000. (Ouch.)

2. *Back into your budget.* When you make a spreadsheet of your monthly expenses, don't estimate, ballpark, or guess. And don't delay. Track all your expenses for three months. You can do this by keeping receipts, then writing down what you

spend (pay attention to your cash) by category (groceries, gas, takeout) or using an app like Mint, Level Money, or You Need a Budget. Then use those figures to create your actual line items.

3. *Automatic saving equals more spending freedom.* If you can create automated ways to siphon a predetermined portion of your paycheck into savings, you'll then have the leeway to spend your extra money on whatever you like. That's freeing. And fun.

4. *Do it with a plan.* Recently the Employee Benefit Research Institute found that the biggest difference between people who feel they'll sail on through their sunset years and those who are worried they'll crash and burn comes down to that four letter word: *PLAN.* Three-quarters of those who have a retirement plan of any sort are confident in their prospects. Just one-third of those who don't say the same.

This is not easy. If it were, then we collectively wouldn't have the massive debt problems we have. That's in part due to what we just talked about a few pages ago: you're wired to act emotionally rather than logically, to make impulsive decisions. And most of you are naturally optimistic: you believe there's more money coming in tomorrow to pay off what you consume today. (That, by the way, is a good thing. Optimists are happier, healthier, and more successful than people who weren't born on a sunny day.)

We are not of the mind that you must live without pleasure. In fact, you should budget in pleasure. And you should also budget in room to make impulsive financial decisions that you enjoy. The point is to be strategic about those purchases. We'll spend much of the chapter about budgeting talking about how to do just that.

Priority 4: **Protect Your Financial Life**

If you're a king or a queen, you build a moat around the castle. If you drive or ride in a car, you put on a seat belt. If you play a contact sport, you wear a mouthpiece and a helmet. If you're having sex with a new partner, you make sure the man is covered up. In all aspects of your life, you use protection to safeguard what's valuable to you—whether it's your life itself, or your health, or your assets.

We live in a vulnerable world—not always because of malicious foes, but often because of circumstance. Risk is the price of living (which is why the best-selling and later discredited Charles Givens book *Wealth without Risk* had the most brilliant title of all time). Protection helps minimize the effect of those risks. So one of your priorities could be and should be to build your metaphorical moat around your metaphorical castle—to protect against the invaders, marauders, and hooligans who come in the form of accidents, health issues, natural disasters, and other attackers that threaten your financial picture.

When you see some of the statistics about circumstances that put Americans in financial trouble, we think you'll be convinced that a protection plan should be one of your financial priorities. To wit: 56 million Americans have trouble paying medical bills. About 15 million Americans under the age of 65 will use up their savings paying medical bills. Even with medical insurance, some 10 million Americans will have medical bills they can't pay. About 25 million Americans under 65 don't take the prescription drugs they should, because they can't pay the bills.

And perhaps the most important stat of all: the main cause for personal bankruptcy is medical bills. All those statistics simply reinforce the message we started this book with. Health and wealth are as intertwined as interlocking fingers, and a lot harder to separate.

We'll go into much more depth about your protection options (e.g., health insurance plus others) in chapter 14, but for now, understand that these are the main pieces of your protection plan. But they won't do you a lick of good if you don't take advantage of them.

Savings (acute issue)	Minimum of $2,000 in emergency account
Savings (long-term emergency)	Six months' salary available if you're single, three months' salary if you're in a dual-income family and work for different companies
Health Insurance	Even with insurance you may have to pay large sums in deductibles, but a health insurance policy with no lifetime caps and no preexisting-condition exclusions goes a long way to staving off financial ruin
Disability Insurance	Normally pays about 60 percent of your wages if you're unable to work; especially important if you're in a single-income home
Life Insurance	To help your family have financial stability in case of your death—if you don't have dependents, you generally don't need it
Estate Planning	Will, maybe trusts, a living will, and powers of attorney for those who should make your financial and health-related decisions if you can't do it yourself
Property/Casualty Insurance	Enough homeowner's, auto, and liability insurance to protect you (and anyone you're responsible for) as well as replace your home or car in the event of an accident or natural disaster

Priority 5: Give Back in a Way That's Meaningful to You

Wait, you say. This is supposed to be about *my* priorities. How in the world does giving away my money help my bottom line? We understand. It does seem out of place that on one hand we're telling you to budget this, save that, earmark this, earn that, and on the other hand we're saying that you should give away your money—and not only that you should give it away, but that you should make it one of your top five financial priorities. Let us explain.

First, there are some financial benefits to donating to charities, when it comes to tax breaks and things of that nature. But that's not what's most important. What is important is that you're giving back to something you're passionate about—whether it's about making the world, or your child's school, or somewhere else a better place, or curing a disease that has affected your family, or saving one of the 16,306 species (both plant and animal) currently threatened with extinction. This, of course, can be done with time or money, or a combination of the two. The reason: Doing so has been shown to make you happier. And by being happier, you reduce health risks by lowering stress responses, blood pressure, and other risk factors tied to health problems (which, as we know, can be a financial strain). So, yes, giving back is about being altruistic, but we shouldn't hide the fact that there are some selfish benefits as well.

The bottom line here is the whole thesis of the book: When you do things to improve your health, they will improve your wealth. And when you do things to improve your wealth, they will improve your health. So invest in your passions—by investing your time and money to help others. The dividends are ones that won't show up on your portfolio summary, at least not directly. But they *are* ones that will inspire you, change you, and motivate you to do better.

That's what makes you happier. That's what makes you healthier. And that's what makes you wealthier.

CHAPTER 4

Time for Good Behavior

‹‹◂————————————————————————▸››

*You can strategize your way to a healthy body by making these
your top health priorities*

Y ou'd have to have your head buried in a plate of pasta not to
know the major headlines when it comes to our collective
health. In fact, you can probably boil down all the big type to
something like this: "Studies Confirm: Things Are Bad and Getting
Worse."

Yes, we could pepper you with stat after stat that basically reinforces
the same conclusion. On the whole we're fat, unhappy, stressed, more
likely to see a friend or family member addicted, and saddled with a
whole host of chronic conditions. All told, poor health is a strain on your
body, your family, your finances, the entire health-care system, societal
equality, and even the ability of almost all nations to spend on education and security. You already know that or most of it, or else you'd be
reading fast-food menus instead of this book. But we're not here to harp
on the bad news; we're here to help you figure out how to rewrite your
own health headline, so that no matter what else is going on around you,
yours can read, "Doing Damn Well, Thank You Very Much."

To extend the media metaphor for just another second, the big picture on health issues is rather simple. After all, you already know most
of the five *W*'s when it comes to your health story:

Who: You.

What: Need to get healthy/lose weight/get off
medication/manage stress and/or de-stress.

Where: Everywhere.

When: Now.

Why: Because you want to live a long and happy life
moving around, not shutting down. Because the
money you'd spend on health care is a lot more fun if
you can spend it somewhere else.

But what's missing? The *H*. How. As in, *How the hell do I get it done?*
The *H* is the entire sticking point for so many Americans fighting
obesity, addictions (food, cigarettes, others), and other debilitating
conditions. How do I lose weight? How do I avoid temptation? How
do I quit smoking? How do I have the psychological wherewithal to
fend off the demons that want me to chug gallons of caramel-flavored
coffee creamer? How, how, how?

Now, we don't want to simplify the whole issue of changing health
behavior, because if it were easy, then, well, this book would be missing half its content, because we wouldn't have a collective health problem. It's not simple. In fact, it's terribly complex when it comes to the
moments when you try to bridge the gaps between action and motivation. The truth is that there seem to be a million different options,
diets, and answers, so knowing what will work for you is where the
confusion lies. *My sister-in-law is 100 percent Paleo and she's fit as a concrete statue. My friends swear that kickboxing will help you lose 12 pounds
in three days! Wine doesn't have any calories, right?* So many opinions, so
many conclusions, so many options, so many frustrations.

• • •

If you had to pick one word to summarize how you can make this all
happen, what do you think it would be? *Dedication, willpower, anti-cheese-defense-system?* Nope, none of the above. Success in the health

arena isn't about how hard you try. It's actually the opposite. It's about how *easy* it is to do—to make changes that feel as if they're automatic, that don't require heavy lifting, that don't make you feel pain every time you do x, y, or z, especially if x, y, or z involves vegetables that you think taste like a stapler (unless you have a predisposition to liking staplers). So what's that one word that will help you harness the energy and motivation to succeed?

Substitution.

That is, how can you take something you're doing right now (perhaps not for the good) and turn it into something that will change your health for the better?

The minute you try to *cut things out*, that's the minute you've already failed, because your brain is longing for whatever it was you eliminated. But if you can find a way to substitute a good behavior for an unhealthy one, it's sort of like putting a sock in the mouth of your inner devil—shutting it up and not giving it any ammunition that makes you want to beeline toward the apple pie.

That's why this chapter about changing your health behaviors is about setting up priorities to make smart and easy-to-do swaps in your life. If you can start making these substitutions over the next few weeks, you will find that you can bury your bad habits and embrace healthy ones.

Substitution 1

Swap 30 Minutes of Sitting for . . . 30 Minutes of Moving

In this time-strapped era, it seems impossible to squeeze in something else. Trying to buy an extra 30 minutes in your day is like trying to buy a hot tub at the grocery store. Impossible. So we're not asking you to extend your day or work out at midnight or pry your warm little tootsies out of your comfy bed before you're ready in order to get in a 4:40 a.m. run. What we're asking is that you find 30 minutes during the day when you're sitting and substitute some kind of activity. You do

DR. MIKE SAYS:

The critical periods are more than two hours' continuous sitting and 10 hours of sitting in a day. Both substantially increase your risk of heart disease.

DR. MIKE SAYS:

Some of my patients who were most successful at reversing type 2 diabetes or high blood pressure or even heart disease with lifestyle substitutions are those who replaced the couch in front of the TV with two stationary Schwinn bikes (that use hands and arms) and a small table on which they could place water bottles.

JEAN SAYS:

Or move for 30 minutes *while* you watch your shows. Binge-watching Netflix doesn't feel like such a guilty pleasure when I'm walking or running on the treadmill at the same time!

this for two reasons—for what you're giving up and for what you're getting. Sitting, as you likely know, is associated with getting older faster, increased health problems, and all kinds of aches and pains associated with long periods of inactivity.

But you're also doing it for all the benefits you get from exercise and movement—in terms of weight loss, a smaller waist size, increased muscle tone, a speedier metabolism, cardiovascular benefits, lower blood sugar and LDL cholesterol levels, feeling and actually being younger, and an overall lower risk of disease.

So now the next two questions are...

When Can You Find Time to Stop Sitting? Well, this one is quite simple, actually. You probably have loads of sit time throughout the day that you can give up. Maybe you can do it at work with walking meetings or exercising during your lunch break (and then eating after) rather than sitting and eating. Maybe you can do it at home. Instead of watching two hours of TV, record your shows, move for 30 minutes, and then catch up on the shows. Maybe instead of meeting friends for coffee, you can meet for a walk. Maybe instead of hunkering down to look for funny cat videos at night, you can attend a fitness class with friends. There are many ways—formal and informal—to integrate movement into your life. It just takes an honest assessment of your daily schedule to ask yourself if you really need to be sitting down every time you're actually sitting.

What Counts? Simple answer: everything. Now, while there's data showing that 10,000 steps a day (or step equivalents—see below) is the minimum for optimum health, you can use walking as a starting point or as your main form of activity. But you can also do anything else that counts for those 30 minutes—running, cycling, lifting weights, playing a team sport, dancing, you name it. The point is, most people spend too much time on their butts rather than kicking butt. Best of all, besides the health gains you will get from daily activity, your energy levels will go through the roof— turning a vicious cycle of inactivity and no energy into a super cycle of activity and tons of energy.

Substitution 2

Swap Your American Way of Eating for . . . the Mediterranean Way of Eating

We all know that the number one reason so many of us have health problems is that our diet is, well, pure trash. Yes, there are genetic markers and issues that cause some health problems, but the way we most control our health destiny is through what we put in our mouths every day. Collectively, we have horror-show eating. It's scary, it's gross, and it's not suitable for anyone. But it's also alluring—and that's why so many people have eating issues: they're tempted not just by marketing but by the temporary pleasures that come from a high-volume, especially salty or supersweet onslaught of edible temptations.

The first step is knowing what to eat (that's what we list below). The second step is figuring out how to incorporate healthy eating into your life, especially if your diet has been mildly to majorly trashy. You should find food you love to eat that loves your body back. So the tactic here is to quietly and steadily make substitutions that tip the nutritional scale in your favor. If you eat fried potatoes every day, you create a plan to sub in steamed vegetables for those tater tots three nights a week. If you have dessert every night before bed, you decide that Saturday will be indulge day and every other will end with a big bowl of berries or glass of wine. And you do that in all facets where your nutrition is less than optimal. The key is for you to be honest enough to become aware of all the foods you choose that do not love you back, so you can replace them 🗨. Over time you will gradually change your habits, change your tastes, and ultimately change your body.

Here's how your food dashboard should look:

> DR. MIKE SAYS: The goal should not be to take a purple pill to tolerate those foods for the moment, but to never need a purple or green or red pill, or ambulance ride.

- ➪ Prioritize fruits and vegetables. So many options here, and they're filled with fiber, disease-fighting phytonutrients, and other nutrients. Hearty salads for lunch, fruit appetizers or desserts—you just want to come up with ways to eat more of nature's medicine. If you're one of the "nonvegetable" people, you can try to spice them up

JEAN SAYS: Or sautéed. Microwave (or steam) any veggie just a few minutes (you want it to stay crisp), then sauté some sliced cloves of garlic in a tablespoon or two of olive oil. Plop your drained veggies in and let it cook to your desired doneness. Add a little salt and pepper to taste. Yum.

DR. MIKE SAYS: Of the omega-3s, we have solid data only that ALA and DHA are beneficial to you— DHA for eyes, brain, and maybe joints, and reducing cancer; ALA for heart disease, cancer, and joint health. More on this later in the book, but it is a major difference. So look for the DHA content: you want 900 milligrams a day—in fish oils if you use supplements, or just get four four-ounce servings of ocean trout or salmon a week, plus six walnuts a day for the ALA... At least those are my choices of great-tasting foods that love me back.

with herbs, spices, or low-cal condiments (just about any vegetable roasted with garlic is delicious ; or try dipping them in some spicy mustard).

⇨ Eat lean plant protein and fish. To help you feel satisfied, lean proteins—legumes, beans, nuts, quinoa, edamame, chicken, turkey, salmon, and ocean trout—should serve as the main characters in your meals. We don't recommend red or processed meats or egg yolks because of the carnitine, lecithin, and choline that your gut bacteria turn into items that cause inflammation in your body.

⇨ Healthy fats are good for you. This means olive oil, nuts, and avocados. We recommend extra-virgin olive oil and nut oils, and even canola oil, as your main fats other than DHA omega-3s from fish and ALA omega-3s from flax, walnuts, chia seeds, and avocados . Besides having some heart-healthy benefits, they're also key to helping you feel satisfied (not feeling satisfied means you're more likely to give in to temptation).

⇨ Processed foods are the demons. This is the hardest part for many people, because they're easy. Easy to pick up, easy to fix, easy to shovel down your SpaghettiO hole. But many of them contain one of the five major food felons—simple sugars and added syrups, stripped carbs (any carb other than 100 percent whole grain), and trans fats. Read labels, and get away from any foods that have these ingredients listed as one of the first five items. Better yet, try to avoid foods that have a lot of ingredients listed. That will increase the chance of staying away from bad-for-you ingredients.

Ideally, you want your plates to look like this: some kind of lean protein and loads of fruits and vegetables. You can also have high-quality carbohydrates (like 100 percent whole grains), but the more you can stay away from simple carbs and sugars, the better off you will be. That's because it's those simple carbs that are more likely—when consumed in excess—to be processed in your body as sugar that triggers insulin secretion, and to be stored as fat if not immediately used as energy. The take-home: high-quality foods = a high-quality body.

Substitution 3

Swap Drink Number Two for . . . a Piece of Dark Chocolate

We know how it goes. After a long day at work or with the kids or both, all you want is to unwind with a glass of wine and your favorite semi-reality show. It's nice and relaxing, and, frankly, can take the edge off a stressful day. There's nothing wrong with that; in fact, there's research that shows that a glass of wine or of any alcoholic beverage without added sugar has some protective health benefits—mainly that it helps reduce inflammation in your arteries.

The trouble starts when one turns into two and two turns into passing out on the couch. There's no doubt that many people turn to alcohol (and TV) not only to de-stress but also to desensitize themselves to their other troubles, some more major than others. And while we're not going to venture into the territory of a full-blown alcohol addiction in this chapter, we are going to urge you—if this behavior applies to you—to find a substitute for the second glass of alcohol. This can come in the form of a piece of dark chocolate or some other kind of sweet treat that takes the edge off (such as that bowl of berries without the honey or sweet cream . . . watermelon is a great sweet treat for your health, too). Or maybe it comes in the form of delaying the first glass of wine until later in the evening so you don't have time for the second glass before you go to bed. Best of all, you can sub in your 30 minutes of activity for one of your glasses of alcohol.

Substitution 4

Swap Your Facebook Surfing for ... More Sleep

You work so hard in all areas of life that you're fighting for every minute of recreation. The reality is that digital social networks are a huge source of entertainment and relaxation (or stress, depending on if you're reading Uncle Joe's political rants). On the surface that's good. Social networks increase longevity—and can serve as one of the most important pieces of your health puzzle (see page 103). The only danger lies in spending too much time staring at screens at the risk of sacrificing other healthy behaviors, like sleep.

The data tell us that sleeping less than seven hours a night ages you by sapping your energy levels not just from tiredness but also from damaged arteries that cause your heart, brain, kidneys, even white cells and immune system to work less well, and also causes more inflammation that leads to a greater rate of aging and loss of energy. (And as if all that weren't enough, if you're not getting enough shut-eye you're more likely to have impotence, wrinkles, memory loss, stroke, and a heart attack. More on sleep on page 276.)

AgeProof ESSENTIALS

1. Pick three strategies from the two lists of health and wealth priorities listed in the previous two chapters that you can commit to tomorrow. Prepare for them (learn what is needed to make them happen—like a pedometer and walking shoes, or the phone number of the HR representative and some account numbers to make that savings or retirement pay-yourself-first plan work). Start them. Making an initial commitment and following through will inspire you to do even more.

2. Habits happen with repetition, with automation, with doing one little thing over and over until it becomes so automatic that you don't even think twice about doing it. That's true for bad habits and good ones.

3. Always keep these two things in stock: crunchy vegetables and an emergency savings account. They will provide you protection in times of need. Fill 'em up automatically as much as possible.

Part III
Pressure Situations

The Science of Stress

You have to work against your biological impulses to beat back the greatest threat to your health and wealth

You likely know one major biology lesson about stress: your body has been designed—through a primal need to survive—to instantly evaluate a stressor and then decide which of two ways you're going to engage with it. Do you take flight or stay and fight?

Evolutionarily and biologically, this instinctual choice makes a lot of sense. Way back, when we gathered around the campfire, grilling up the scrumptious catch of the day, you had to react when the tables were turned and some beast wanted to make you *its* catch of the day. So when a four-legged beast growled, grunted, stalked, and then lunged forward for its in-the-wild appetizer, you had to decide whether you'd be better off hauling butt or kicking butt. Flight or fight 💬.

Your body, even back then, knew what it needed to do. Your heart rate increased to pump blood through your body in order to fuel your muscles, and hormones surged to give you a rush of energy, strength, and chutzpah to do whatever you needed to do in order to survive. Above all, there was no shame in either course of action—fight or flight—as long as the outcome remained the same.

If you survived, so did the species.

But fairly recently something has happened in the whole arena of

DR. MIKE SAYS:

Some would say we also have a third response: freezing. We freeze to make the attacker think we are dead. Most animals won't risk the biological danger of catching whatever disease caused something to die before they attacked, so freezing worked to cause the attacker to pass you by.

stress management. Something has changed. There's a much greater emphasis on the flight part of the equation. That is, the common belief now is that you'll feel better—and quiet some of the symptoms of stress—if you can just slow yourself down. Slow your heart rate, decrease your blood pressure, tell your hormones to take a time-out, get your brain clear of all thoughts. If you can do those things, you'll decrease the chance that the harmful effects of stress will take their toll. So we take action by doing the things that soften our stressors. In other words, we take flight.

Warm water in the tub, chilled wine in a glass, a walk in the woods, petting your pup, stretching your neck, child's pose and downward dog... They may not seem like running away, but, because they're all escapist, they're all forms of flight. Are they bad? No. Will they aid in temporary stress relief? Of course.

But here's the thing. In the areas of health and wealth, flight won't ensure your survival.

The only thing that will: Fight.

Let us explain: the great threat to your health and wealth is your stressful response to an event. Plain and simple. High amounts of stress and stressful situations are a major cause of bad things going on with your body; that is, if you perceive yourself being stressed, that leads to all kinds of bad health effects—ranging from overeating and obesity to high blood pressure to fatigue to anxiety to the shrinking of your brain's memory center. Not surprisingly, being stressed also leads to the weaker immune systems that are the root of a whole host of other problems. What is one of the greatest causes of stress? Money. More specifically, money-related issues, as in not having enough, or losing a job, or having older parents to care for, or being too deep in debt. In fact, money makes people unhappy more than anything else in life—except being in the middle of a health crisis.

The bottom line: ain't no bubble bath going to pay off your Visa.

This is why we believe you have to rethink your approach to stress management. While there are soul-soothing aspects to many forms of stress relief, you will never turn yourself right side up with good health or strong wealth if your approach is to take flight by doing things like burying your head in the sand about financial troubles or not going to the doctor because if you just ignore the pain in your abdomen it will eventually go away. Flight doesn't erase the pain; it only delays it.

The answer, therefore, has to be a punch square between the eyes in the form of a strategy that helps you solve the underlying problem. Part of the reason (and here's your biology lesson for today) is this: stress is associated with shorter telomeres—a part of the chromosome that's associated with aging. Shorter telomeres mean shorter lives. Conversely, ridding yourself of the stress that brings on those shorter telomeres could add years to the clock (or make the ones you have more pleasurable).

That could mean taking medication or making lifestyle changes. That could mean seeking help from a professional financial planner. That could mean creating a budget and making difficult choices about what you're no longer going to spend money on.

Stress management, at least as the term is used in pop lingo, is not the same as life management. So if there's one message that should come through in this section, it's this: avoidance will not make your situation any better. That said, there are a couple of notable exceptions. In volatile economic markets, it's been better to take flight and ignore them, waiting out the ups and downs, which will be better for you in the long run than trying to guess every little twist and turn, which will drive you bonkers. Similarly, getting on the scale daily, rather than watching trends and making adjustments accordingly, can be bad for your sense of well-being and level of stress.

We also don't want to give the impression that all of traditional stress management is bunk. In fact, many people use meditation to help de-stress, and this can be very useful, mainly because it helps provide clarity of thought; decluttering your brain makes it easier to make smart decisions. (People use exercise to get similar results.) So in that way, meditation can be a vehicle to the ultimate destination: making smart and strategic decisions about the areas that are causing you the most stress.

In the following chapters, we'll look at the major causes of financial stress—and the major health effects of stress—to guide you through the tactics that will help you face stressful situations head-on.

CHAPTER 5

We Can't Stress This Enough

Being frazzled is no fun—and no good for your health.
But don't worry: we've got some solutions right here.

In this day and age, so much about medicine and science has zero shades of gray. An X-ray can tell you if your bones are broken. A blood-pressure test can alert you if your levels are too high. A quick swab to the back of your throat can determine whether that scratchy pain is strep or not.

Just black or white. This or that. A test can determine where you stand, and then professionals can help you determine the best protocol to fix the bone, blood, or artery to your heart or brain, or to remove many common cancers or treat bacterial infections, or whatever problem you have. Yes, there is a financial price, but most of these are standard treatments with safe and reliable outcomes—there is always some risk, but much less than even 40 years ago—and payments that are now efficiently taken care of by standard insurance plans that pay 100 percent of what you owe if you go "in network" (more on this later, page 261).

We've come a long way in this regard, as better diagnostics and better treatments have extended life expectancies and the quality of many, many lives. That said, there are still many questions that modern medicine has yet to answer. Perhaps some types of cancer or pain management come to mind. Another thing that falls into that category is the subject of this section: stress.

See, at this time, there's no gold-standard test to determine whether you're in the danger zone of stress levels. There's no one-size-fits-all pill that will melt your stress away. You can't have your stress surgically removed. And you can't really go on an antistress diet (win seven mother-in-law arguments in two weeks!).

Instead stress—at least the way you personally experience it—involves quite a bit of art in addition to the science. That's because we all perceive events in different ways. Some people thrive on pressure and don't really acknowledge things that would send other people through the roof. Some people go bonkers if the traffic light takes five extra seconds to turn green. Those personality and perception differences (that is, differences in how you perceive the event, and, if it causes you stress, how long the stress lasts) make it difficult for the medical establishment to help you manage your stress, and they make it difficult for you to pinpoint the effect of stress on your life.

But this is what we do know: no matter how ambiguous the whole stress arena may feel, stress is a major source of health problems. And we also know that stress about finances and stress about relationships are the major contributors to your overall stress levels. The other major causes, which of course relate to and interact with finances, are health, sadness, and work pressure. Case in point: very powerful and very common sources of stress are relationship issues with family, friends, and colleagues. They can involve some unresolved upset from the past, an ongoing power play, disrespect, or a range of other issues that are not always a big deal in any given moment, but that, if not dealt with, rapidly accumulate and drain your mental energy to an unproductive level and to the depths of unhappiness.

It's also worth noting that major stress is only one form; when we have chronic low-level stressors, that can have the same effect—things that don't seem all that important, but that hang over your head like a storm cloud that never blows over, play a role in the constant drip of negative effects of stress.

In the next chapter we discuss the major causes of financial stress and how to handle them (you'll learn that handling the stress directly is really the only way to "manage" it). In this chapter we're going to discuss some of the biology and health implications of stress—and how some lifestyle changes can help combat the negative medical effects.

The last thing we should emphasize before diving into the specifics: Stress sometimes gets a negative rap—it's talked about as something that you always want to eliminate. But stress is sort of like fat in this way. Yes, you want some, but you don't want a lot of it. If you have too much of it, it's going to damage your body. But the goal isn't to get rid of all of it. You need some fat in your body for brain function, for energy, and for other purposes. In the same way, you also need some stress. Without it you probably wouldn't take precautions to take care of yourself. Think about it: if you didn't have *some* level of worry about finances, you wouldn't feel the need to protect yourself by making smarter financial decisions (building that emergency stash, buying life insurance) until it was too late. Stress actually can help you make smarter decisions and protect your body, your life, and your assets. So our goal when it comes to the health aspects of stress isn't to shed stress entirely. The goal is to figure out which stressors are really damaging your health, address them, then come up with strategies that make everyday stress feel like a normal part of your life—not an "Oh, woe is me" part of your life.

If you're like most people, you probably respond to stressful events in ways that are related to that specific type of stressor—you fight, fly, or freeze. Once you develop an awareness of how each form of stress really affects you and how you respond, you can develop a strategy for actively dealing with that stressor and its consequences. You become an active manager of that event rather than a passive, powerless recipient of its effects. So that awareness is the first step, then developing a plan, then the discipline of practicing that plan enough that it becomes automatic for you.

When you reach that überlevel of stress management, especially when it comes to getting your finances in order or feeling in greater control of your relationships, the effect is huge: you're happier, healthier, and more productive, and everything seems to fall into place. So while there's no magic number you're after in terms of your stress levels, that doesn't mean managing your stress is any less important than managing your blood pressure. So hop in a hammock and hear us out on the biology, psychology, and technology of stress.

What Your Body Does

While we don't think you need to know every piece of anatomy in order to be motivated to make and to sustain lifestyle changes, we do believe that having some understanding about how the body works gives you a little more power to control it. (The same can be said for finances, right? Once you understand how IRAs, retirement income, and various investments work, they're not so scary, and you can make smart decisions, rather than just ignoring those words and worlds because you don't understand them.)

So we all know the layman's way to describe our responses to stress. They can take the form of anything from fatigue and depressionlike symptoms all the way to your-head-feels-as-if-it's-going-to-explode. You want to punch the dashboard. You want to cry. You want to have a glass of wine (or three). You want to cry in your glass of wine.

Here's what's happening inside of you: immediately, when you're faced with an event that causes you stress, your hormones change to pump more blood sugar to your body, your blood pressure rises, and your heart rate increases. (Mentally, stress serves the same purpose as pain—it's a biological smoke alarm letting you know something bad is going on and needs attention.) When the barrage of stress is constant—the way it is in today's world—your systems can never settle into a relaxed state, meaning that your altered hormones, readiness for a fight, and elevated blood sugar and blood pressure (and associated symptoms) stay that way. And that's what chips away at your health, causing heart problems, depression, anxiety, back pain, indigestion, other bowel problems, headaches, sleep problems, and a whole host of other issues.

Those hormones are powerful little buggers. Essentially, they act to trigger one big chain reaction of biological and chemical events that makes you want to run away and start over, or rip your hair out and shove it down the throat of the next barista who spells your name wrong on the side of your coffee cup. This biological process involves what is called the "stress circuit" and your nervous system, and is slightly different for the different causes of fight, flight, or freezing. Here's how the general process goes down:

- When faced with a stressor, your brain (via the hypothalamus at its base) releases CRH (corticotrophin-releasing hormone). That hormone sends a message to the pituitary gland, which releases another hormone called ACTH (adrenocorticotropic hormone) into your bloodstream.

- ACTH waves over to your adrenal glands to release cortisol (you may know this as the stress hormone) and starts the production of norepinephrine and epinephrine (you know this as adrenaline).

- All together, these chemicals trigger the processes that involve your heart and blood. Cortisol, for example, promotes an increase in sugar into your bloodstream to fuel your muscles.

- Now, that said, we need to modify the science we've described to make it more accurate (and, unfortunately, make it more complex for a moment). Your body secretes slightly different mixes of chemicals and hormones that cause your different feelings in response to different stressful events: for example, cortisol and epinephrine and testosterone are released to augment irritation or fight; anxiety is associated with similar cortisol but less epinephrine and testosterone, and associated with freeze; and flight brings on cortisol and epinephrine but less testosterone than fight. Your physical response correlates with the type of reaction to the stress, not just the intensity of your response.

- When the stress stops, the cortisol travels to the brain to stop the production of CRH—and stop the game of dominoes.

What's the key phrase in all of this? *When the stress stops.* When the stress stops, that's what stops the cycle. You need that to happen, because the overflooding of your system with all these hormones is what causes the health problems we mentioned a few paragraphs above (excess glucose in your blood leads to arterial disease and diabetes, by the way). Besides all those issues, the overabundance of stress hormones actually inhibits growth hormone, which you need to keep your brain sharp and your muscles strong (to prevent injuries and rev metabolism), and to live a healthy life.

In layman's terms, we'll look at two stress types: mind stress and gut stress. Mind stress is more cognitive. It's when you realize that you need to drive for 30 minutes to a meeting that starts in five minutes. We calculate the gap between what we need (30 minutes) and what we have (five minutes), and we get stressed. Gut stress is different. For example, the notion that because you will be walking into a meeting room 25 minutes late, everybody will be looking at you, judging you… that makes you feel uncomfortable and anxious. Or you can experience both. For example, for some people the idea of separating from a spouse may trigger mind stress associated with financial concerns, whereas for others it may be more about the gut stress associated with the fear of being alone. Most people tend to have both types of stress, although a recent study showed that men are more likely to be under mind stress and women are more likely to be under gut stress.

So the point in all this is that even though stress is hard to objectively evaluate (and we all experience it a bit differently), that doesn't mean that the effects of chronic stress are some squishy piece of psychobabble. Your body was well designed to handle stress in short bursts the way our ancestors did, but not so well designed to handle years of living paycheck to paycheck with five figures of credit-card debt. That's really the reason that the only answer to stress management for some types of stressors is addressing the stressor, not evading it. You have only so much mental or physical energy—you can use it to love, to be social, to be productive, or to deal with what stresses you. Ignoring what stresses you only shifts the stress to the back of your mind—where it continues to drain your mental energy. Yes, one of the biggest issues with stress is that it drains your mental battery even if you are not fully aware of it. Dealing with it is the only way to deal with the energy drain. We suggest you become aware of what events trigger a response in you and what domino effect they trigger in you, and then prepare in advance with practice so you can avoid the health (and, yes, financial) effects of responding with fight, flight, or freeze.

What You Can Do

When you think of traditional stress-relief methods, they probably fall into one of two categories—healthy or unhealthy. In the first category, you have things like massages or lavender-infused baths, both of which have benefits for your body and psyche. (Nothing like working out some muscular tension in your neck to help loosen things up.) In the unhealthy category, there are all kinds of things we do to make ourselves feel better temporarily, whether it's overwatching (gaming and TV) or overeating or overdrinking or overspending or putting them all together—overeating while overwatching and so on. All of them, as you know, will hurt your health in the long run, even if they do take away the short-term sting of your stresses. We, of course, don't advocate unhealthy methods for stress management. And we're all for healthy methods of stress management, as long as you fully accept that they might help you feel better, but don't necessarily work to wash away what's causing you trouble.

Therefore, the answer to stress is the answer that we already talked about earlier in the book: be aware of what will bother you; be aware of your response; and plan and practice an automatic response. (We cannot overstate the importance of awareness.) Being aware of the kind of events that cause you stress is like knowing your playing field. Strategizing about what's bothering you usually won't work if you haven't already prepared for and practiced a response or two. That response can be to tackle the issue, and that issue solution may require planning and strategy. The actual action is: "Facing the problem, and working on solutions." That's what works, and that's what stops the hormonal soup from bubbling over in your body.

That said, we do think you always should have a prepared, automated approach and everyday plan to manage stress. During stressful times we fall back on automatic habits, and the more stress you have, the less likely it is that a new cognitive strategy can be rolled out on the spot and work. We need repetitive habits that become second nature. You need to spend time building awareness, then building and practicing your automated response. You open an out-of-the-blue huge electric bill and look at a deficient bank account statement and might respond by picking a fight with your spouse. But if you have awareness of the issues, you can develop an automated habit for dealing with them, such as taking deep breaths every time you get frustrated that you're caught in traffic or reaching for a bag of carrots every time you get frazzled and want the chips. The more you turn learned response into automated habits, the more successful you will be, and the less events will age you.

After all, you can't solve every problem right away. It takes time to chip away at credit-card debt. It takes time to repair bad relationships. It takes time to handle family angst. So it is useful to think about stress management holistically—to think about your general approach to handling life's hiccups and hurdles. We like to think of it as a five-spoke approach, with all the spokes really coming from the same hub: putting you in the best position to make smart, rational decisions that will help you achieve your goals and reduce the health problems associated with stress.

The strategic spokes of stress management:

Awareness. This requires you to think about what caused you to feel stressed or powerless in the past, and how you handled it (or not). You might respond differently depending on your preexisting emotional state, but if you have had any of the three responses, flight, fight, or freeze, you can become more aware. (This area is where the Sharecare App really helps; see page 9. Denial is not an option when you see a nongreen signal.)

Preparation. One of the problems with stress is that it seems it's always the unexpected demand pushing us over the top, when we already have a lot to deal with. Unexpected bills or expenses. Unexpected pressures at work. Unexpected actions from our kids ("You got a dolphin tattoo on your forehead?"). We think we have most of life pretty well managed, but what we don't see is what hurts the most, because we're taken off guard—we feel and sense we are powerless. This feeling is especially prevalent in the area of money, but it's also a source of stress in other areas, such as family, work, and relationships.

So the trick here is to spend some time developing an emergency plan—an automated response, a habit—for when specific stresses occur. A stop-drop-and-roll for life. Now, that doesn't mean you always expect the worst, but it means—as odd as it sounds—that you learn to prepare for what you can't prepare for.

Stress is about feeling powerless, more than dealing with the unexpected. The most obvious example of dealing with powerlessness is creating and maintaining an emergency savings account that has nothing to do with monthly budgets or other savings plans (or even keeping a few extra dollars at home to buy things should a bank Internet holiday be forced by a hacker). This money is earmarked for the bleep-happens line item of life. You can also apply the same principle to other areas. Have you figured out what you might do if the boss piles on another deadline when you think you can't handle any more? What happens when your 16-year-old announces she's joining the circus? What if your spouse walks in one day and doesn't want to be your spouse—or vice versa?

Maybe you were aware enough to anticipate that and developed a plan so you have the power to face life alone; while you lack the power to stop your daughter from ruining her future, you can make it a habit to use your power to control your attitude about this and other things. Thus preparation can give you control, so the main cause of stress, feeling powerless, can be substantially reduced. Now, there's no way to make a contingency plan for every possible life scenario, but it is worth taking a look at some of the big life issues that could happen and asking yourself if you're prepared for them—and, if not, what you have to do to get prepared. And note: Being prepared also is a good mantra for all aspects of your health and financial life. It means you'll know how to respond—in an automated way—to all kinds of scenarios, even if you don't know now what they will be.

Your To-Do List. What does your to-do list look like? Do you keep a digital list or a piece of paper with lots of notes? Or do you try to scrunch it all in your brain, hoping that you'll remember to shuttle the kids, finish the project, pack the bags, book the airline tickets, send in the taxes, and do all the zillion things you need to do—by yesterday? No matter what form your to-do list takes, your goal is to cross stuff off, right? You want to take care of one task and then another and then another so you can—for once—enjoy a guilt-free night bingeing on *Game of Thrones.* That's how most of us live—and how most of us have to live, with so many responsibilities to so many people. Part of your logistical plan should be to back up your to-do list in case the cloud gets electrified or a torrent floods the cell and the fuse box.

While the goal is to turn your to-do list into a did-it list, some strategic thinking goes into how you approach your list. Some research suggests that the best way to approach your tasks is to crank out the easy stuff first and save the decision-making tasks until later. Why? Because it seems that we have only so much decision-making energy in a day, and if we use it all up early in the day on big tasks, we actually won't have any stores available when unexpected things come up later.

But we also know that juggling tasks is a very personal decision. If you're better off saving the easy stuff for last, that's fine, too. Just be aware that perhaps your brain is wired to do it the other way around—and if you find yourself unable to manage everything, try a different tactical approach to managing your day. You can make yourself more productive, financially safe, and younger by being aware of where you find your power.

Spiritual and Physical Action. Will a deep breath get you out of debt? No. Will a deep breath keep you from throwing a fit? Maybe. Will a deep breath help you in your approach to managing stress? Absolutely. Your preferred stress management technique may be a physical action that helps you face the event or manage it—it may be using physical energy or it may be using spiritual energy, but it is knowing oneself and being aware of, practicing, automating, and using what works for you. Different people respond to different choices, be they music or aromatherapy or sensory actions, or spiritual actions or physical ones.

We know it's easy to write off deep breathing as some kind of how-to-book hocus-pocus. But there's real science here. Taking a deep breath through your nose triggers the release of nitric oxide, which has a calming effect and opens up your blood vessels. (Think about why this helps. When your blood pressure rises in stressful situations, it's because those arteries constrict, making it harder for blood to pass through. So when those arteries open up, your blood pressure lowers, and you feel much calmer.) Thinking about how you really feel and understanding your feelings lead to that awareness of triggers and anticipation, which leads to learning how you can neutralize the response, which then can lead to practice. That's when the neutralizing response becomes so automatic that it's like the chopsticks you played after a year of piano practice. Tough the first time, so automatic the 80th that your neighbors could hum it.

The second way deep breathing helps is by giving you some mental clarity, which can help you make specific decisions to solve your stresses. Whether you choose to do deep breathing by yourself in a meditative way or perhaps in a yoga class or in the few minutes after the knucklehead cuts you off in traffic, the fact is that deep breathing serves as a method by which you clear your mind of clutter and piece together smart, rational approaches to your issues.

The Swagger Factor. We all know how stress can feel—as if we're the nail and life is the hammer. We get pounded and pounded and pounded, and there's nothing we can do to stop it. That's the tough part about life: there's so much we feel we have no control over, and there's a lot of frustration and angst that simply happens in all of our worlds.

While it's not easy to just change the way you think, we believe that the awareness we've been talking about building can help you reframe your approach to stress. Instead of feeling as if you're the passive recipient of the world around you, you should recast stress management as power or energy management. That is, if you can take control of your health and energy, you will now have the swagger and ability to handle the problems that come your way. It's when you're tired and down that you get caught up in the vicious cycle of stress—you're unhappy, so you eat pie, so you get a sugar high, so you're happy, but then you crash, can't handle the next task, want more pie, then gain weight, then get depressed because of it, then eat more pie because you're depressed, then can't make decisions because you're bummed, and so on and so on.

But what happens if you can flip that vicious cycle and make it a victorious cycle? One that's filled with energy and swagger and a general *je ne sais quoi* about the way you handle your stuff? All of that really is about harnessing the energy to handle the day-to-day and month-to-month bumps that come up.

And for us, and we think for many, that means learning how to say NO—no to those things that would go on your B, or C, or D, or E to-do lists. No, so you get enough physical activity and sleep and protein and water so that you feel naturally up, and can stay that way. So that *you* can be the hammer and your stresses can be the nails.

We know it's not easy to explain and it's not easy to change. Which is why sometimes the best way to become one of those people is to fake it till you make it. Act as if you've got it covered, others will believe you've got it covered, and eventually you'll come to feel that way yourself.

We're not suggesting that you just flip a switch and decide to be human hype video; we are suggesting that all the health tips and strategies in this book aren't only about living longer and avoiding several knee replacements. They're also about infusing your life with joy and energy, not so you can be oblivious to your problems, but so you have the chutzpah to handle them.

CHAPTER 6

Feeling Spent

⫷←————————————————→⫸

*The biggest way to combat financial stress is through
a windfall of information*

$

I f you or someone you love has struggled with weight, you know
the answer to this question: What is the most comfortable pair of
pants/shorts/skirt you own? Almost always the answer involves
an item of clothing with an elastic waistband. Something that has
some stretch. Something that allows your clothes to fluctuate as your
body does the same. Something that allows you to walk, sit, hang,
slouch, breathe, and live in your comfort zone.

It may seem a little odd that this chapter about financial stress
starts with a discussion of clothing, but the elastic waistband is at the
heart of what financial stress is all about.

See, credit cards are the financial version of stretchy pants. They
offer you some give—to perhaps live beyond your limits. They give
you a false sense that things are the way they should be. They allow
you to feel comfortable, even if it's not good for you in the long run.
Because eventually, if you stretch enough, you're going to put the
waistband under more and more tension until something pops.

It's the new way of living—charge it now, be comfortable now, get
what we want now, extend, extend, extend. The problem: that comfort
zone can be a mirage—in truth, you actually don't have as much wig-

gle room as you thought. And when that waistband pops—when you see the damage that has been done, that you can no longer manage—then the stress that comes with being under financial duress becomes one of the biggest burdens you can carry.

As we've discussed, the intersection of medical and financial stress is one of the major reasons we've written this book. Financial stress can damage your physical and mental health, and being unhealthy can damage your finances. When things go wrong, it's the most vicious of circles—you're sick, you incur a lot of expenses, you can't keep up with the bills, so you get more stressed, which makes you sicker, which means you have more expenses, and so on. More than one-third of Americans say paying for out-of-pocket medical costs is, for them, a significant cause of stress. So one way to handle financial stress is to deal with your health issues by handling that portion of your budget in a smart and cost-effective way.

But that's only one part of what causes financial stress in people's lives. Many other factors contribute to this major issue. Unemployment. Underemployment. The fact that, until 2016, incomes in America were stagnant for almost two decades while prices continued to rise. More than $1.3 trillion in combined student loan debt. The list goes on. And it takes its toll. According to the 2015 *Stress in America* report from the American Psychological Association, 72 percent of Americans report being stressed about money at least part of the time, and 22 percent say they're under extreme stress for financial reasons. And that's not even considering that financial problems create relationship problems, and relationship problems are a huge source of stress. Bottom line: you can't, or at least you shouldn't, talk about health and relationships without considering the impact your finances are having.

When it comes to solving the problems, however, the solutions diverge. In the health arena, you can change your lifestyle choices tomorrow and start seeing results fairly soon. Let's say you overhaul your diet, start an exercise plan, and do any number of other things to improve your health. It may take months before you reach your goals, but your genes sense the changes you make, and the changes within your body start almost instantaneously. It wouldn't be uncommon to see some changes in weight, waist size, and the overall way you feel the very same week. With a financial overhaul, we can't quite say the same thing. It's not as if you stop spending $15 at lunch every day and all your credit-card debt goes away the next day. Financial change often requires a little more patience to get the feedback that things are working.

So what does that mean? In order to deal with the major stresses that happen with your finances, you have to have two things—patience and trust. You have to have the patience and trust to know that by employing the strategies that will keep you financially fit, you will end up in the right place, even if it's not immediately apparent.

This is especially difficult in this day and age. One of the reasons we're so financially stressed is that there are so many moving parts. In days past you earned an income, had a budget, and got a pension, and life was sort of financially simple. But now employment is fluid, and we as individuals are taking more of a role in investing, retirement, and expenses—for good and bad. And worse, we don't pay attention—not until a financial stressor smacks us in the face. So part of this harkens back to our advice a few pages ago: the best way to deal with financial stress is to fight it head-on—including with preventive measures that can keep stress from biting you to begin with.

Our goal here—when it comes to directly tackling financial stress—is to create a new comfort zone. One that feels right not because of any artificial wiggle room that you create, but because you've set parameters and adopted habits that enable you to live in a place that is truly safe, financially.

To get you there, we'll help you take a look at the major financial stresses that people experience, in order to isolate the ones you're experiencing specifically. Then we'll give you tactics for how to handle them—with knowledge and action, not to mention patience and trust.

Stressor 1: The Mind-Numbing Question: "Will I Outlive My Money?"

It's easy to picture the idyllic retirement: the beaches, the hammocks, the new hobby or business you can't wait to start, you get the idea. It's also just as easy—though not as pleasant—to picture the ugly side of retirement. Many of us constantly ask ourselves these questions: Have I saved enough for retirement? What happens if I live longer than my money lasts? Who will take care of me if and when my health fails? We want to think retirement is going to look exactly like the first picture, but we also know deep down that if we don't do things right, the reality can be dark, cold, and scary.

Compounding all this: it's hard to think about the long term if you're worried about the short term. If you're having trouble paying bills or you're spending too much, it's easy to say, "I'll worry about retirement later." Later becomes a few years, then a few decades, then "OMG, I haven't saved boo and I'm 58 next year."

This fear is driven in part by the fact that life expectancy is going up, and you hear a lot of talk about Social Security going away. So the possibility of living 20 or 30 years past retirement isn't just a fantasy, it's very much a reality now. And that means you have to account for that in your retirement strategy—how much you save and for how long. For what it's worth, the Social Security Trust Fund is not going to run out. But by 2037, if nothing has been done by our government, the trust fund will be able to meet only about 75 percent of its obligations to payees. Our feeling is that our government will eventually address this. But if you're a skeptic, or prefer to be cautious, when you're running a retirement plan projection, count on receiving only 75 percent of what your Social Security statement says is coming your way, and save more to make up the gap.

So you essentially have three strategies for not running out of money in the future, and they're really quite straightforward:

- **Work longer:** Nobody says you have to retire at 62 or 65, so if you love your job or can find another one, you can extend your income. (You can also redefine what *working* means, maybe creating flexible income as a consultant or in part-time jobs to continue bringing in money without the burden of full-time work if you don't want it.) The more years you can continue to draw an income, the more years you can put off starting to pull money from your retirement plans and starting to take Social Security. Both of these are good things.

- **Spend less/save more:** Take a look at what you're earmarking for retirement (and company matches) via 401(k)s and other retirement accounts. If your current trajectory isn't where you need it to be (see page 32 for details about projecting what you need for retirement), you may have to increase your contributions to your retirement accounts. The earlier you start saving and the more you put away, the more security you will have. A small sacrifice today (maybe you need Netflix or Amazon or Hulu but not all three) will decrease your overall stress levels by giving you the knowledge that you're putting away enough money for later. The other way to save more is to increase your earnings—by working a side gig or changing jobs—and use that added income to boost your savings, not your disposable income.

- **Earn more on your investments:** You do have the option to increase the risk you are taking on the money you have saved (and thus potentially get a greater return on those investments). We are not fans of this strategy unless you're currently not taking enough risk with your investments. Although you could certainly make more, you could certainly lose more as well.

Stressor 2: "I Have Too Much Debt."

Plastic works well for many things—storing milk, building electronics, combing your hair, you name it. But when it's in your wallet? That can be trouble. Sure, credit cards are convenient (it's easier to pay at the pump with a card than go in to pay cash, and if you pay them off in full every month, that's fine). Sure, they may afford you some necessities or luxuries that you need or want from time to time but that don't quite fit into your monthly budget. And sure, you can reap rewards like frequent flier miles by using credit cards. But we all know that using a credit card also means borrowing someone else's money now and then paying interest (often at a high rate) on that money until you pay it back. The banks make the money—your money. So when those credit-card balances start to get out of control, that's when your stress usually mounts—because your expenses (and the accompanying interest) outpace your earnings.

When you have more debts than you can comfortably handle, that's when stress sets in. You are always worried about where the money to pay that next bill is going to come from. That creates another series of dilemma dominoes. Without enough money to cover your bills, you worry about your ability to see the doctor, deal with small life hiccups, pay for the extras your children so often want.

Plus, debt is a savings killer (which then adds to the stress of Stressor 1). When so much of your financial energy is going toward repaying your old obligations, you can't get ahead for the future. That puts both your credit and your relationships at risk. ("Consumer debt is an equal opportunity marriage destroyer," researcher Jeffrey Dew wrote in a report entitled *Bank on It: Thrifty Couples Are the Happiest.* That means it doesn't matter who you are or what your income; debt is trouble. Even if you make a half million dollars a year, outspending your income is still outspending your income.)

It can be difficult to see your way out of deep debt, but having a plan for how you're going to pay back the money you owe will get you going. Try the avalanche method of debt repayment. It's the fastest, cheapest way out of debt:

1. Lower your interest rates as much as you can by transferring balances, refinancing and consolidating (more on this on page 180).

2. Take all your extra money and throw it against the debt with the highest interest rate while making minimum payments on the rest.

3. Once you've gotten rid of that debt, throw all your additional muscle against the one with the second-highest interest rate, and so on.

If that isn't working fast enough, you may need to resize your life or increase your income, creating a new budget model that allows you to put more money toward debt and perhaps sacrificing other things.

Stressor 3: "Uh, I Have Insurance, and This Procedure Still Costs Me $3,000?"

Part of the mission of this book is to reduce your risk of developing chronic diseases and to improve your chances of having a strong and healthy body for a long, long time—that is, living younger. But there's another bonus: slowing the rate of aging means that you'll develop fewer issues that need medical attention than the typical person (whose risks increase threefold every 10 years), and that will save you money. Your health can also pay off financially.

It's no surprise to anyone here: even if you have health insurance, you're going to be paying an arm and a leg (hopefully not literally) to cover medical costs. About 8 percent of the average consumer's annual spending went to pay for health care in 2014 (two-thirds of that to health insurance, the rest to co-pays, prescriptions, etc.). That's a 20 percent increase in spending from 2012, and it has done nothing but substantially increase since 2014. Now factor in what happens if you don't lead the healthiest of lifestyles or you have genetic predispositions to certain conditions or bad luck strikes you and you're involved in an accident that puts you out of commission. Life happens. And it's not always pretty. And it almost always costs a lot of money to get you back to where you want to be. That's the nature of our health-care system (and this isn't the time or place to have the discussion about what can and should be done to lower costs). For the foreseeable future, the fact is that health problems come with a price tag. Research from Fidelity Investments showed that a 65-year-old couple should plan on needing an extra $275,000 in retirement to handle health-care costs alone.

So what's the play here? This one isn't easy, because unlike with cable bills and mortgage payments, there's no way to perfectly budget for medical expenses. Some years and months may look a lot different from other ones. And if you have a spouse or a family, you're planning for lives other than your own. But what you can do is rethink the way you *frame* health-care costs. Many people take the deal-with-it-if-it-comes approach, but the smarter strategy is to earmark some of your savings budget (and retirement portfolios) specifically for those health-care costs. Simply being aware that the costs are coming and that you have money slotted for those expenses will give you some very crucial peace of mind. And, in fact, when you break it down, even that $275,000 doesn't look as daunting as it does as a lump sum. For that 65-year-old couple, it's roughly $5,000 a year, each. Creating a line item to deal with it is a step in the right direction. One way to do this? When you get rid of a payment—whether it's a car payment, a credit card you've retired, or a college-savings contribution you no longer have to make because Junior has (finally) matriculated—add that amount to your retirement savings or, if you have one, your HSA (health savings account, page 268) knowing that you're doing it specifically to bolster the amount you have to keep you in good health.

Stressor 4: "We Fight About Money. All. The. Time."

The sexy answer to the question, "What do couples fight about?" is, well, "Sex." But even when couples are having sexual difficulties, it's not as if they get into knock-down-and-drag-outs about it (unless it involves sex with someone else). The nonsexy answer to the couple-fighting question is the real one—and the harder one. Money. Couples argue about who spends what on what, why we need another [fill in the fun toy] for the [fill in the room of the house], and how in the world we're supposed to pay the bills when all the money is going toward that money pit of a [boat/closet/eating-out habit] we have. It should also be said that oftentimes money is the proxy for other issues. If you have a fight about money, it may be one person's way of saying that the other person is selfish or controlling; so sometimes even bigger issues about the relationship are at stake.

The fights are never fun. And never funny. That's because you're often trying to equalize two different sets of needs, desires, and values—in the complex family and/or couple environment. And because the stakes—debt and divorce—are so high, the tension is real. And real important. One study from the National Marriage Project found that the more frequently couples fight about money, the more likely they are to divorce. And compared with disagreements over other topics, financial disagreements last longer and generate more negative conflict tactics, such as yelling or even hitting, especially among husbands.

In addition to eliminating debt and building assets (which highly correlate with longer-lasting marriages), couples can minimize fights about money by giving each other some financial autonomy. Each person in the marriage—whether or not that person earns money outside the home—has to have some money to manage/spend/save as he or she wishes. One spouse's controlling the entire budget (or giving the other an "allowance") is way too parental and unromantic.

And it's important to remember that just because you marry doesn't mean you both want the exact same things at the exact same time. The other thing that helps alleviate fights is agreeing on the big goals so you can work toward them together. This *is* the romantic part of money management: envisioning your future, whether it's thinking about your first home or your retirement home, the place you want to spend your anniversary, or how great you'll feel when your child graduates without debt. So, if you haven't done this in a while, sit down with your better half and ask (preferably with a glass of wine in hand), "What do we want our money to do for us this year? In five years? In 10?"

Stressor 5: "My Job Is Unstable."

Just as food is the fuel to run your body, money is the fuel to run your life. If you have a steady stream of fuel coming into your life, you can run efficiently, provided you don't burn it all up (see Stressor 2). But without that fuel, everything stops. You can't pay bills, you can't save for tomorrow, you go into debt, and if that lack of fuel drags on you, you run the risk of bankruptcy, which creates many other problems. We all know: unless you're wealthy from family money or a lotto drawing, you need income to keep the fuel pump primed. So it's no surprise that having an unstable job (or losing your job) is a major financial stressor. You can cut all the expenses you want, but unless you're going to live in the woods and hunt squirrels for meals (or move back in with your parents, which might—believe it or not—be worse), you need income to pay for the daily necessities.

The surprising thing, perhaps, may be that today's economy, while better than it was in 2008, isn't all that much better for job stability— or at least for assuaging the fear that jobs are at risk. The University of Michigan's consumer confidence survey showed that people were just as worried about losing their jobs in 2015 as they had been in 2009. Now, some of this fear is very age dependent. If you lose your job in your 20s or 30s, it's easier to regroup, perhaps go back for some additional training, and try another path. It's a different story when you're in your 40s or 50s. You've got the mortgage, the kids heading for college, the dueling car payments. And job *in*security—like so many of the financial factors we isolate in this book—is closely tied to health. A Washington State University study found that threats or perceived threats of layoffs caused workers to pay less attention to safety and subsequently experience more injuries and accidents at work. Another study from Texas A&M University found that people fearful of losing jobs were less likely to seek support in a corporate wellness program. Yet another vicious circle. It's difficult to address particulars, because people's jobs, companies, and situations can be so different, but there are some patterns that we know to be true, and you can use these lines of thinking to help give yourself perspective on job stability.

- Get an honest assessment of where you stand. Not knowing whether your job/company is truly at risk is worse than knowing the lay of the land. It's better to approach your manager and ask about your status, reassuring him or her that of course you plan to be at the company as long as you can. That doesn't mean you're ensured a job, but getting honest feedback (or reading it in your boss's nonverbals, then really checking with your boss to make sure you are reading those nonverbals correctly) may give you an indication of whether you should be working your contacts and looking for another job before someone else decides for you.

- Assess your potential outside your company. If it's been more than a few years since you updated your résumé, did a little networking, and went on an interview or two, it's time. You don't have to switch jobs, but getting a sense of your worth on the open market is key to understanding your value at your current job as well.

- Consider being part of the gig economy—that is, piecing together income from a variety of sources in gigs rather than full-time work (about one-third of our workforce now participates in some form). Our new entrepreneurial environment means increased sources of revenue (albeit short-term or part-time revenue). Now, this does present its share of challenges, in that you may not know when and how often income will come in, and it can fluctuate from month to month (as well as year to year), making budgeting and planning tricky. But the upside is that you can create more income opportunities and more control of your life than you would have in a job where your salary is stabilized. If you are working several gigs, it's helpful to try to gauge how long that work will last. (Giggers—or anyone with a fluctuating income—can create a monthly budget by taking an average income over six or 12 months and using that as a baseline income. Any income above your baseline should go into a savings account to close the gaps in low-income months.)

Stressor 6: "College Costs What?!?"

For kids college means a lot of things. Wearing the school colors to the game, meeting people who will become friends for life, having plenty of fun, taking great classes to prepare for the field of their dreams. For parents who want to help give their kids the opportunity to set themselves up for their future careers, college means something entirely different: "Holy [bleep], this costs more than a house!"

College tuition rates have risen at about three times the rate of regular inflation (7 percent versus 2.2 percent on average) for decades. And frankly, parents don't want to saddle their kids with huge amounts of debt by having the kids take out loans (undergraduates come out of school with an average of about $33,000 in student loans, and much, much more if they go on to graduate school). When kids amass that debt, it means they marry later, buy homes later, and move home more frequently while they're getting their financial footing—a fact that often prompts another holy-[bleep] moment.

Now, it's important to remember that retirement savings should come before college savings because there is no financial aid for retirement and there is financial aid for college. (Or, to put it another way, you can't borrow for your retirement.) But many parents disregard that logic and try to save at least something for college. If you don't have the financial means to save for college, and you don't qualify for aid, you need to have open and honest conversations with your children about expectations—because part (or much) of the financial responsibility for college is going to be theirs. They should also know that they can minimize their borrowing costs by keeping their grades up, sticking with an activity (whether it's curling, chess, or clarinet) in which they really excel, and casting a wide net when applying so they can find a school that wants them—and will therefore offer them merit aid—as much as they want that school. The discussion about in-state public versus out-of-state or private school is also important, as is talking about the fact that two years at a community college followed by a transfer to a four-year school that will accept those credits can cut the price of a college education in half.

AgeProof **ESSENTIALS**

1. The way to manage most stresses isn't to run from them. It's to face them head-on with practiced strategies, tactics, and problem-solving techniques. Only when you eliminate the stressor (not ignore it) will your body benefit.

2. A budget—and emergency cash cushion—helps heal all nonrelationship wounds.

3. Stress is like ice cream—more than a little is bad for your health and it comes in all flavors. But the only way to figure out how to cope is to recognize what kind of stress is starting to chip away at you. Awareness is the first step of the process of fighting stress.

Part IV

Team Works

The Science of "Us"

They're private and personal, yes, but health and wealth have to be team sports

In this world of social media and sharing, of likes and favorites, of posting a photo of your favorite chili recipe, it seems that *everything* we do is public: monumental moments ("We're engaged!"), insignificant moments ("Puppy pooped on the porch"), and everything in between ("If you support [politician of choice], you're a dingdong"). Your world infiltrates the worlds of those around you.

Still, a few bastions of isolation remain—the things in your life that you tend to keep private and celebrate or struggle with on your own. From our perspective, those three islands of privacy are the doctor's office, your financial statements, and your bedroom. Now, you can certainly make the case that close groups of friends may share secrets about their sex lives, and we've all certainly seen more and more people publically announcing health issues and victories. But traditionally, these three areas—money, health, and sex—are ones that we all consider to be intensely private and personal.

That's OK. That's the way it should be. You don't need to announce to your followers and friends that you took out more life insurance, or that you do or don't have the BRCA mutation, or that the trapeze is now safely installed. But here's the thing: when you consider

DR. MIKE SAYS:

I have a medical team I use for myself (whether I need a podiatrist or a dermatologist or a pharmacist or a dentist), many of whom I also use for referrals, as each is a true superstar in his or her field, and each pays attention to details and discusses care plans with me.

JEAN SAYS:

And I have a financial team—a financial adviser, accountant, and attorney—for the very same reasons. But my spouse is an important team member, too.

something to be private and personal, you automatically assume that also means solo 💬 **Q**. That closing of the ranks—that going solo—is, we believe, a mistake. It can pay off big-time to involve the members of your team—your family, your trusted advisers, the friends you make time to see in person (as distinct from the ones you can't remember meeting except on Facebook).

Unfortunately, it just doesn't happen. So often, people are afraid to involve others in issues dealing with those three areas. (OK, we'll leave the sex stuff to those experts and just focus on our main areas of expertise.) People think that the mountains they need to climb when it comes to climbing out of debt or trying to break an addiction are mountains they have to climb by themselves with no support, no advice, no assistance. Why? Because they're embarrassed—embarrassed that someone will judge them or think less of them because they drink 12 sugared sodas a day or spent 10 grand on window treatments for the guest room that nobody uses. And that's tough, we know, because we're all proud, social creatures. We all want people to like us and respect us—and *not judge*. So we fear telling people our problems and stories if we think people are going to roll their eyes, musing, "Oh, it's your own fault for getting into this mess. What did you think would happen when you eat a pint of ice cream for breakfast every morning?"

Bottom line: It's totally understandable that we hang the privacy sign on our doors. It's just not OK.

So the question is: How do you change your handling of your health and your wealth from an individual sport to a team sport?

We think it helps simply to look at team structures all around you—whether in sports, business, or entertainment. Almost every successful endeavor we can think of has a team structure. Bands don't just have musicians; they have road crews, producers, agents. Moviemakers aren't just the actors, but also the directors, the sound editors, the makeup crew. Golfers have caddies. Quarterbacks have offensive linemen, receivers, and equipment managers. Corporations have leaders, workers, support staff. The team works because everybody serves specific roles with a common goal.

That's the way you have to think about your health and wealth goals.

You are the CEO of your body. You are the CEO of your bottom line. But who else is going to help you get where you want to go? Who's going to provide the missing pieces of the puzzle to get you to move forward? Who's going to be your makeup crew, your caddie, your roadie? Who's going to steer you and support you? Who's on your team, and what roles will they play?

The *what* is key, but do not be mistaken, the *who* is more important. You want to make sure your team members are top-notch, have the time to be devoted to your issues, and will keep everything you share with them as confidential as it needs to be. So your choice of team members may be more important than anything else (save whom you chose as your partner in life—who, by the way, is an important member of both your health and your wealth teams).

By taking ownership of the direction you're heading in, you will not only empower others, you will also empower yourself—by acknowledging that the help of other people doesn't make you weaker, but stronger.

As we'll explore in the next chapter, your team isn't made up just of professionals. It's made up of a mixture of pros, relatives, and friends— some of whom are integral parts of your team from day to day, and some of whom play roles more intermittently. We don't want you to think you need to hold weekly meetings with 50 people to announce that your blood pressure dropped by a point. The whole team strategy is all about two things: one, opening yourself up to treat health and wealth as shared endeavors; two, knowing whom to have on your team and the roles that they can and should play.

There's strong evidence to support this approach. For one, the basic biology of human interaction shows it. When you bond with others (and connect with them in meaningful ways), your body releases oxytocin—this is a feel-good chemical related to better health. (Now, we're not saying that you want to snuggle up to your accountant— unless your significant other is said accountant. But we are saying that creating connections—even if they're mostly intellectual in nature—does contribute to the increase in this good-for-you hormone.)

Further evidence involves what are called mirror neurons. These are structures in your brain that essentially trigger it to make you act like others around you; you "mirror" their actions, such as by yawning when you see someone yawn, even if you're not tired. So when you surround yourself with people who are doing things you want to do (perhaps including a personal trainer or a friend who's notably frugal), you're triggered into copying those behaviors. Some of the groundbreaking research into this phenomenon showed that good (and bad) health habits can spread almost like a virus among social communities—that people reflexively start adopting the habits of their networks. This is one of the main reasons you read headlines about how it's better to have a circle of friends who have healthy habits, because you're more likely to follow their lead—not because of any peer pressure per se, but because you naturally conform to the group's actions. The same can be said for financial habits. If your social circle frivolously spends money without thinking about the bigger picture, you're more likely to follow in their free-spending footsteps. You absorb the atmosphere of the relationship through mirror effects in the brain. How does a doc know if you're depressed? She feels it herself when she talks to you.

. . .

DR. MIKE SAYS:

Or, as I like to say: choose your advisers wisely, your friends carefully, and your partners with even more care. Values need to be discussed before rings. Values about finances and beliefs about lifestyle and work, and sexual compatibility.

This is all just a scientific way of saying that your body and brain want you to have strong networks that will help you 🗨. From the research, we see that there are really two types of effective teams—each of which can play a role in your quests for more money and a healthier life. There are teams that compete and teams that support each other. Early research (from way back in 1898, involving competitive teams in cycling) showed that teams with internal competition actually performed better. (Think about how the members of those Tour de France teams work with each other and against each other at the same time.) This suggests that goal-setting and working with and against each other simultaneously can be effective for achieving collective goals.

How might this play out on your team? Think about how weight-loss competitions at places of employment tend to work—people get excited, they're public about goals, they want to show they're driven to lose weight, and, well, they also want to *win*. Of course competition can backfire if it gets too emotionally charged, but it is worth noting that elements of competition aren't necessarily bad parts of team dynamics.

Certainly the most common reason team dynamics work is the other element: support. Plenty of studies support this. In one weight-loss study comparing a program that uses social support (Weight Watchers) with a self-help group, the social group lost three times the weight than the other group. (Weight Watchers, as you may know, uses weekly weigh-ins in small-group settings as one of the pillars of the program.) And here are three more interesting examples: Users of the MyFitnessPal app who shared their food diary with friends in the app lost twice as much weight as users who didn't share. Married couples who joined health clubs together yet worked out separately had a 43 percent dropout rate over the course of a year. Those who went to the gym together, regardless of whether they focused on the same type of exercise, had only a 6.3 percent dropout rate. And perhaps you'll remember the four twentysomething sisters who made national news when they decided to buckle down together to dig their way out of nearly $200,000 in combined student, credit, and car loan debt. They did it in under two years!

Now, we know that constructing a team isn't easy, especially if you don't have any potential members, or just those who come and go—like a general doctor once a year or an accountant in April. As we show you how to construct a team over the next pages, consider some of our overall principles for putting an effective team in place:

You Are the Leader, but You Are Not the Only Voice. As we said, you are the driver of all your health and wealth decisions. You decide whether you're driving forward, going in reverse, or stuck in neutral. You tap the brakes. You press the accelerator. You decide which way to turn. And you decide if you're heading to the world of your dreams or

DR. MIKE SAYS:

This step and person is the key. You want someone to be honest and to make sure the difficult issues and changes are dealt with so you stay on track. In health, after you eat an entire box of chocolate chip cookies, you don't want someone who questions if you saved a cookie for him. You want someone who helps you figure out what triggered that eating, and helps you work out a plan so that trigger either never happens again, or, if it does, calls forth a different (healthful) choice in the future.

down a dead-end street. But part of assembling a good team is trusting your team and its members—that means trusting that they can advise you which way to go and maybe alert you that a truck is heading in your direction.

Oftentimes you will have to rely on the advice of others, even if it's hard to hear. For example, let's say you've assembled a team of people to help you care for an aging parent, and you're doing this from far away. You've got a care manager in place who is the leader in some ways. That person may have to raise unpleasant issues—the nursing home is raising prices, dementia is getting worse—rather than shielding you from them 🗨. This involves what Harvard University professor J. Richard Hackman calls a "compelling direction." Have you articulated your goals—big and small—so that every member of your team can give advice and make decisions to foster your long-term goals, not just in-the-moment desires?

Find an Equal. Oftentimes your team is going to feature people who have more acronyms after their names than a government agency. That's good. You want experts. But perhaps the most influential member of your team will be an accountability buddy—someone who pushes you, hugs you, helps you, hears you. Now, make no mistake; your buddy is not a cheerleader. This person is a listener who helps you clarify your goals, checks in on your progress, explores what went right when a goal is met, and explores what went wrong when it isn't. For this reason we don't think this buddy should be a best friend or even a spouse (and certainly not your mother), who could be too kind to be

DR. MIKE SAYS:

For the over one million people who have taken the free RealAge program repeatedly and who have made their RealAges substantially younger, the buddy was key.

useful. Keep in mind: although you have to be able to open up with teammates and talk with them honestly, the people on your team should be people you trust more than people you like 🗨. (You can even find people online to fill the role of accountability buddy, if you don't have anyone in your life who is the perfect fit; more on page 112.)

The Two Most Important Body Parts Are the Mouth and the Ears. Talk as much as you listen. Listen as much as you talk. Relationships seem to work best when people contribute roughly equally to the conversation. This whole process works only if you do a little of both. (Face-to-face is best, but digital communication in which you're actually talking can be a substitute. Text and e-mail as a last resort.) You have to be clear about what you want and need from teammates, but you also have to be open enough to hear what they're saying. Are you hiring a financial adviser to manage your portfolio or to take a look at your entire financial life and weigh in? Do you want an ob-gyn to handle most of your big-picture primary care issues? Do you want a trainer, and, if so, do you want a cheerleader or a drill sergeant? If you are not clear, it's impossible for your teammates to deliver. This means you have to own the things—you have to organize and articulate your goals to the people who are to do the things—that you're not good at yourself. People can't help you if they don't know where the holes in your system are. And here's the other thing that people discount: you should connect the members of your team with one another—to spread ideas around Q.

Don't Be Afraid to Push—or Have Someone Who Will. Professor Hackman makes the point that every team needs a "deviant"—someone who is going to push boundaries. We like this point a lot, because it speaks to the notion that sometimes we all need a kick-start or a new perspective or just a voice in the distance that tells us that we should rethink the way we do things. That doesn't mean that this so-called rebel has final say (or is even on the mark); it just means you've opened your mind to new possibilities. While maybe you don't want your primary doc or your financial adviser to be the deviant, there's nothing wrong with having another accountability buddy who can serve this role.

In the next two chapters, we'll be showing you whom you should include on your health and wealth teams—and how to make sure everybody is working together, so that they can all assist you in reaching your life goals.

Q JEAN SAYS:

In my financial life, my financial adviser is connected to my accountant, who is connected to my attorney. They are all connected to my husband (even though we keep our finances largely separate). It helps tremendously because even though we have different accounts, my husband and I have joint goals. When we are all talking together, we can address questions like whether my husband and I should be putting our surplus resources toward prepaying the mortgage or investing for the future, and whether we've put away enough (combined) that we no longer need disability insurance.

CHAPTER 7

Your People Portfolio

*One of your greatest investments will be choosing the makeup of
your financial team*

When you were younger, you were involved in all sorts of
teams. You had sports squads or sororities. You had the-
ater casts or bandmates. You had your packs, your groups,
your rabble-rousers, your group of crazies who bonded together over
a common goal—win the game, nail the opening-night performance,
make life hell for your poor math teacher who couldn't turn his back
without having a spitball fired his way.

As you grow older, you probably have fewer opportunities to think
in terms of teams. Yes, you consider your family your ultimate team.
Yes, you think of your work environment as one big team or a group
of small ones. And, yes, you may even have a book club, rec softball, or
a you're-too-old-for-this-but-are-doing-it-anyway rock band. The reality, though, is that most people don't think in terms of the pack mentality anymore—especially when it comes to finances. Many people do
exactly what we talked about a few pages ago: they don't want anyone
looking in their metaphorical wallets or purses, and they don't share
their financial situations with anyone.

That's a mistake.

If you can put together a team of professionals (and, in some cases, nonprofessionals) who are there to assist you with all your financial goals, you have increased the probability that you will make the money you need (and more), establish financial security, and have the freedom to enjoy what you want in life.

Now, we're not suggesting that you employ a financial entourage—folks who need to be involved in every transaction, or who scold you if you buy a pack of gum when you could be socking away that buck or two. We're talking about creating a system of professionals, serving various roles, who can advise, guide, think, protect, and inspire.

A couple of things to keep in mind before we get into the nitty-gritty of your teammates:

Get Specific with Your Goals. No matter what kind of team member you're looking for, you have to articulate goals—what you want from your teammates. For example, "financial adviser" can mean a lot of things to a lot of people. Do you want someone to just manage your portfolio or to look at your entire financial picture? Do you want quarterly check-ins? Do you want a phone call when the market takes a surprising turn? Do you want to deal with the adviser him- or herself rather than talking to associates? If you're not clear, then it's impossible for your teammates to deliver—and nobody wins.

Get Social. While you probably won't invite your doc out to dinner or suggest martinis with your dentist, the financial team is a bit different. Get to know the folks who are helping your financial picture. According to some research, two of the best predictors of a team's productivity turned out to be energy and engagement outside formal meetings. It makes sense: if you're able to talk about the news or new restaurants or what your families are up to, you'll find it easier to talk about harder topics like whether you're spending too much or not saving enough. MIT research found social time is "deeply critical" to team performance—and this can apply not just to formal work teams, but to the informal ones you're creating as well.

That's why we believe it helps to think of your financial team as being like your health team, a structure that you're probably much more used to. They're not typically people you need more than a few

DR. MIKE SAYS:
We could get to know you better if you did.

JEAN SAYS:
Actually, Mike, I do socialize with a couple of my doctors—and feel that I'm better off for it. It also makes it easier for me to open up with them when the topic gets a little tough. (And of course I like hanging out with you.)

times throughout the year, but they're people who can assist in their own specialized areas. Here's a look at who your financial teammates are, what they do, and how they can help.

Your Money Buddy

The buddy system is a well-tested one when it comes to health. Many people share their weight-loss or health goals with a friend or family member (let's both lose 20 pounds by March!), and attack them together—using the support to motivate, to push, to hug, to hold each other accountable. Research shows that this kind of social connection works. So why shouldn't we extend that same line of reasoning to the financial world? On the surface it may seem uncomfortable to put together some sort of debt-reducing contest or tell a friend about the goal you set to fund half of college up front so your kid won't need as many loans, but communication with your buddy doesn't have to be very detailed. That is, you don't have to disclose all your financial secrets; you can work in general terms. How?

Let's say one of your goals is to reduce credit-card debt. You can report to your buddy the percentage of debt you knocked off each month. There doesn't have to be a revelation of every item on your credit-card bill (oops, new shoes!), but there can be a system to use the strengths of the buddy system—support and accountability. The point: when you go at issues solo, you're more likely to ignore them or perhaps even continually make bad choices because (shhhhhhh!) *nobody needs to know*. A buddy is that little (and very real) voice that coaxes you along—with just enough oomph to keep you moving in the right direction.

Perhaps this is the best part about a financial buddy: it doesn't have to be someone you know. You can find one online at sites like Linkagoal.com or SparkPeople.com or Sharecare.com; on those sites people use financial management as a common goal, as well as the traditional areas of weight loss, diabetes reversal, and many other health opportunities. Digital support and accountability may not be the *same* as in-person support and accountability, but it's still effective .

DR. MIKE SAYS:
In fact in our ClevelandClinic Wellness.com e-mail-based e-coaching program, we find participants want to know their coaches better, and bond with them.

Financial Adviser

For starters, it's important to remember the second word in the title of this team member—*adviser*. This person is not a fortune-teller. This person is not a personified lotto ticket. This person is not an ATM that will dispense money whenever you want (unless you are a pro basketball star, and even the greats have to have limits, as the career is often short, and the bank account gets liquidated too easily). This person is meant to steer you in the right direction, to protect your assets, and to help you increase those assets at a rate that's aligned with your goals and values.

That said, this is also one of the most confusing roles out there: What do they do? What credentials do they have? How do they get paid? And how can I tell good ones from bad ones? Part of the confusion is that financial advisers aren't like doctors—anyone can claim to be one. There's no one standard certification or credential. That makes picking a financial adviser difficult.

But confusion shouldn't mean you ignore the opportunity. The right financial adviser can help you increase your money and plan for the future at a much better rate than most people can do on their own—not only because of his or her expertise, but also because of the accountability that comes with talking through your financial picture with a pro. For starters, the best way to narrow down the list beyond a Google search is to ask for recommendations from people you trust who are—in assets, or perhaps profession—similar to you. (This is the best way to choose any team member, really.) This will give you a starting spot. Once you narrow it down to some possibilities, then you can look at the major issues or questions. Here's how to navigate:

The Big Picture

Before you engage in any kind of professional relationship with an adviser, it's vital that the two of you be aligned in your goals and understanding of what services the person or firm may provide. Some advisers deal only with investments, while others are more holistic and deal with all financial facets, including taxes, insurance, and college planning. No matter where you end up, though, every initial conversation should start with a question from this person: What are your goals? Your adviser can't suggest a one-size-fits-all plan for you. He or she must know what you want before suggesting what to do. The goals should drive how your money is managed and used. And there's another intangible factor that should play into your decision. It's one that we really can't outline for you, but one that you just *know*. Do you feel comfortable with this person? Open, honest communication is crucial in this relationship, and if you can't bring everything to the table—the good, the bad, the "I put a hot tub on a credit card"—then you're not going to get your money's worth. Importantly, that goes both ways. A financial adviser is no good if he or she isn't willing or able to say no to you—or to tell you when they think you're about to make a stupid, expensive mistake.

Finally, one word about fiduciaries. Starting in April 2017, under a pending ruling from the Department of Labor, any financial advisers, insurance agents, and brokers advising you about your retirement (and selling you products to help you get there) would be held to a fiduciary standard—which means they have to put your interests before their own. If there are two suitable investments for you and one has a high commission and the other a lower one (or no commission), the fiduciary must choose the one that costs you less. This is a win for investors. But note that it applies only to retirement advice. If you've got a plain-vanilla brokerage account—one that doesn't have the tax advantages of an IRA or 401(k) or other retirement account—your broker is not held to that standard. The advice he or she gives you just has to be "suitable," which, according to the Securities and Exchange Commission (SEC), means the financial adviser "must have a reasonable basis for believing that the recommendation is suitable for you." The language—and therefore the protection—isn't as strong.

Pay Structure for Financial Advisers

Years ago, if you had a financial adviser, chances are that person was a full-service stockbroker, who earned commissions for buying and selling investments for your account. Today many financial advis-

Questions You Should Ask a Potential Adviser

Your Question	What You Want to Hear
How will we stay connected? Will we schedule meetings? Will I meet with you or associates?	"Let's talk about that." You want to hear that the adviser is going to work according to what you're comfortable with—not his or her preference. If you want to meet often, that should work. If you'd rather just have yearly check-ins, that's fine, too, although you should consider coming up with a list of scenarios (e.g., an investment imploded) in which the adviser will reach out to you in between.
Do you work with other clients like me?	"Yes, like x, y, and z." (Note: Your adviser doesn't have to name names, and in fact shouldn't without permission from those individuals. General descriptions are fine unless you're asking for references—see below.) It's especially helpful if the adviser works with people from your same company and so will know benefits and retirement plans and structures. If you own your own business, you want someone who is skilled at setting up plans for entrepreneurs.
Do you have references?	"Here they are." Always important to get a sense of how this person works with perspectives from other people. BTW: It's not enough to get references; you also have to call them.
Do you also own shares in or a part of the investment you'll recommend to me?	"Yes" or "No, and here's why." There are reasons the answer to this question could be no—different goals, different time horizon. But knowing the answer is yes provides a certain degree of satisfaction.
How did you handle 2008?	"I talked with my clients about how they were positioned to weather down markets, and the fact that we knew this period would eventually come, and encouraged them to stick with their plan." You want to know that your adviser has the ability to lead you through both boom times and recessions. How often did he or she communicate with clients? Did he or she change course in a meaningful way? How did he or she handle clients who insisted that they wanted to dramatically reduce their exposure to equities?

ers charge a percentage of your assets under management. That model, too, is starting to change with the advent of "roboadvisers"—computerized systems that manage your investments based on goals and risk parameters that you input—which are significantly less expensive than human advisers (but, it should be noted, aren't going to pick up the phone and talk you off the ledge in a 2008-like market meltdown). We may be heading into an era where advisers charge for advice separately from implementation of that advice. Stay tuned.

Is one model better than another? As you'll see below, they all have pros and cons.

Kind	Pros	Cons
Percentage of assets under management: Typical wealth manager model (based on total portfolio amount). Note that some of these advisers call themselves "fee-only advisers." They are, but their fee is for managing assets rather than for devising a plan. See below.	When you make more money, the adviser makes more money, which gives them an incentive to do well. A typical fee is 1 to 2 percent. Fees tend to fall when you accumulate more assets (ask about discounts for bringing other family members into the tent).	There may be a steep threshold (minimums of $500,000 or more are common) to get some advisers to take you on as a client. Also, advisers looking to boost the size of your portfolio may take outsize risks to make that happen—to your detriment.
Fee only: Based on an hourly rate or flat fee for the plan	Advisers don't make money for recommending particular products, which gives them the opportunity to be extremely objective.	Some of these advisers will charge you an added fee for fulfilling your plan (managing the money for you); others give you advice and leave it to you to follow their instructions (which you may or may not be up for doing).
Fee based: Fee for setting up the plan (or a percentage of assets under management), plus commissions for buying and selling particular investments	This can provide convenience for clients—and an opportunity for them to save money by purchasing certain investments themselves.	All the potential conflicts of interest you get with a commission-based adviser with a complicated fee schedule to boot.
Roboadvisers: Automated investing services that create an asset allocation and portfolio for your needs based on your age, risk tolerance, and other criteria you plug into the Web interface	Significantly cheaper than human financial advisers, robos generally charge 35 basis points (about one-third of 1 percent) or less.	Not comprehensive. Robos don't ask questions about your estate, for example, and offer only limited accounts (if you want a SEP-IRA because you're self-employed, for example, or a 529, you may be out of luck). Also, fairly new and therefore largely untested.
Commission: Typical old-school stockbroker model. Makes fees for both buying and selling investments (stocks, bonds, mutual funds, etc.).	Consumers often feel as if they're getting advice for free. Of course they're not; the fees are buried in the cost of trading in and out of the products themselves.	They may lose objectivity and put you into lesser-quality investments that pay them more. They may also encourage trading more than you need to (or churning). On the flip side, having to pay a commission can sometimes discourage clients (i.e., you) from making moves you should be making.

Credentials

It's easy to get lost in a sea of acronyms—it can all feel like gibberish that doesn't mean a thing. But those acronyms do matter—they reflect the kind of training an adviser has had. A quick cheat sheet to help inform your decision:

CFP. Certified Financial Planner. CFPs are held to a fiduciary standard whether they are giving advice about retirement or something else. To become a CFP requires obtaining a bachelor's degree for course work that includes finance, fulfilling a continuing education requirement, passing the CFP exam, and having at least three years' experience. To find out if a planner is a CFP, go to CFP.net and search by name. CFPs also have to disclose conflicts of interest to their clients.

RIA. Registered Investment Adviser—the registration being with the SEC or the state. RIAs are held to a fiduciary standard. RIAs also have to file a form (called Form ADV) every year that gives you a lot of information about them. Part 1 tells you about the type of clients served by the adviser and the adviser's firm, about the firm (who owns it, how much in assets it has under management, how many people work there), and if any of the firm's advisers have securities violations, felonies, or disciplinary actions within the past 10 years on their records. (Note: If you find this information, either get a satisfactory explanation from the adviser or just move on to a different adviser.) Part 2 is written by the adviser him- or herself. The adviser has to give this part to you before you become a client, and then again once a year. It contains information about the fees the firm and adviser charge and also—importantly—about partnership agreements with other businesses. This is key. If your adviser is recommending you buy a particular insurance policy, and will be compensated if you do, you want to know about it. To get this document, it's easiest to go to the website of the Financial Industry Regulatory Authority at FINRA.org and use the BrokerCheck tool.

Registered Representative with a Series 6 (for selling, among other things, mutual funds and variable annuities) or 7 (for selling, among other things, stocks and bonds) and a Series 63 (to gauge understanding of state securities laws). All brokers (even those who are not RIAs) must be licensed to sell investments (many CFPs have such licenses as well). Generally these folks get a job with a broker-dealer that sponsors them to take the exams, at which point they register with FINRA. You can check them out using FINRA's BrokerCheck tool (see above).

Insurance Agent. They also give investment advice when they sell life or disability or long-term care or health insurance. Indeed, insurance pitches these days are often geared to paying for college or supplementing retirement. These agents are licensed to sell insurance products by their state, which generally requires that they have some education and take an exam lasting one to two hours. An adviser licensed to sell insurance products may or may not be licensed to sell other investments, which may not or may limit the sort of advice he or she can give.

CPA. Certified Public Accountant. CPAs sometimes double as financial advisers (more on CPAs in a moment). They are also held to a fiduciary standard.

CFA. Chartered Financial Analyst, also held to a fiduciary standard. Many equity research analysts are CFAs, but some financial advisers are as well. Like CFPs, CFAs have college degrees, then go through a rigorous series of courses in topics ranging from investment selection to portfolio management to the tax efficiency of various assets. They then take a six-hour exam every year for three years.

☞ Six Things You Should Cover in a First Meeting with a Financial Adviser

---

Your first meeting with a financial adviser shouldn't be a one-way conversation—with that person spouting off about credentials, philosophy, and company history. You should be doing plenty of talking as that person finds out about what *you* want. Here are some other things that should be covered in any introductory meeting.

⮕ Risk tolerance: This depends on your stage of life, your goals, and your investment personality.

⮕ Asset allocation: How will your investments be distributed among investment classes—stocks, bonds, etc.—to balance risk and reward?

⮕ Income distribution and tax consequences at retirement: What are you socking away and what are the tax implications when you're ready to withdraw?

⮕ Incapacity management: What happens if you're unable to make financial decisions?

⮕ Legacy planning: Divorce, children, and other factors can make this complicated.

⮕ Retirement timing: Looking at assets and your goals, an adviser will need to know your ideal time for retirement—and then help you make adjustments to meet this goal, or suggest ways to tweak it.

Resources for Finding a Financial Adviser

plannersearch.org: To find members of the Financial Planning Association

NAPFA.org: To find fee-only advisers who are members of the National Association of Personal Financial Advisors

letsmakeaplan.org: To find advisers who are Certified Financial Advisers

GarrettPlanningNetwork.com: A network of fee-only advisers willing to charge by the hour

---

Estate Planning Attorney

We like the endings of good books and good movies, and, if the team we're cheering for is winning, the ends of big games. But there's one ending that few of us want to think about—our own. (Though if you follow the health advice throughout the book, there's a good chance you'll be putting off that ending for a long, long time.) But it is something that you do need to address if you want to protect your assets for your family. The person to help with those issues is an estate planning attorney. This is someone you need to deal with not multiple times each year, but rather once every few years. (Though circumstances can change, and you do want a good relationship so you can easily make changes as you wish.)

When you're hiring an estate planning attorney, you're looking for a lawyer who can help you put together a basic estate plan—a will, a living will that tells doctors and hospitals about whether or not you want life support, durable powers of attorney for health and finances—as well as advise you on whether you need more sophisticated trust documents to protect the people you love, your assets, or both. The easiest way to find one is through—you guessed it—a referral (a financial adviser will likely have the names of several good ones). In your first meeting, you want to get an overall sense of the cost of developing a plan ($1,000 to $2,500 is fairly typical, unless your situation is especially complicated) and of how the office is run. In that meeting, ask the questions on the next page.

Tax Team Member

Taxes are like teenagers' selfies; we don't like them, but we know we have to put up with them because they're not going away anytime soon. We don't like thinking about them. We don't like seeing them come out of our paychecks (even when we know they're being used to pay for government-funded services we believe in). And we sure as heck dread the day when we have to submit them. But we do know this: we have to take care of them.

The question we all must answer: Go it alone, or seek professional help?

Doing taxes with tax software is cheaper, no question. Many sites allow you to start your federal form for free, but there are typically

Questions to Ask Any Estate Planner	
Your Question	**What You Want to Hear**
How often should I revisit my plan?	"Every three years or when you have a big change in your life." Such changes include marriage, children, divorce, and substantial inheritances or other changes in assets. You'll want to ask about the cost of changing the plan.
Are you able to advise me on my legacy (for instance, gifts or an impact that I'd like to use my money to make once I'm gone) in addition to my estate?	"Absolutely!" More and more estate planning attorneys are stepping in to help their clients create "ethical wills"—a written statement to help pass values, not just money and possessions, from one generation to another. They also advise on charitable bequests (and the trusts you can use to make them) made not just at death but also during life.
Do I need a revocable living trust?	"No." Although, in some situations having a revocable living trust—a document often marketed as a means of protecting your assets from probate—can make sense. You might want one if you're a very public person, and you don't want the media prying into your business after your death, or if you own property in more than a single state, which makes probate more complicated. Otherwise the answer is no. And an attorney who says you need one might be padding the bill. This is a good question to use as a barometer of integrity.

charges for state forms, and more complicated forms like Schedules C and E. You should expect to spend up to $100 for software and about three times that to hire someone just to complete the 1040. If you have additional forms to complete, that'll cost more. But doing your own taxes—even if you use software—can take up to 16 hours for a 1040, according to the IRS, including the time it takes to gather all your documents. If you use a tax pro, you still need to gather your documents, but you'll save time. Aside from time and money (both of which are valuable), the biggest difference between dealing with a person and dealing with a website is *advice*. A person can be helpful if you need help with compliance (making sure everything is done right) or tax planning, whether it's for estate planning reasons or because you own a business, are heading toward retirement (and thinking about which assets to use when), or are going through another life change (a move, a divorce, receipt of an inheritance). But here's the thing: not all tax preparers are accountants, and not all accountants prepare taxes. So if you decide to go the pro route, make sure you know the differences, and can choose the right type of person for you and yours:

Tax Preparer. Tax preparers with big-name firms are generally trained by those firms in how to prepare taxes. Each must have a PTIN (preparer tax identification number) and register with the IRS, but they may not stick around after tax time. Ask any person you're considering using what happens if you get a letter from the IRS after tax season is over. When you call the office, will your local preparer be available to help? Or are you going to be routed to a call center (across town or across the country), where you'll deal with a stranger? Ask some of their clients to verify. It's optimal, although it may not always be possible, if the person who prepares your taxes is actually familiar with your financial situation. Also, before you use a tax preparer, check out the reputation of the firm and the individual with the Better Business Bureau, and make sure there is no negative chatter online.

CPA. A Certified Public Accountant is licensed by the state to act as a public accountant. (Public accountants are hired as independent third parties to examine the financial statements of companies, nonprofits, and individuals, and to make sure those financial statements accurately reflect reality.) CPAs have college degrees, they pass an onerous exam, and they generally have to pass an ethics exam as well as fulfilling continuing-education requirements. Only about a quarter of what CPAs study is tax related. CPAs are also fiduciaries. They have to keep your best interest in mind at all times. And they can sign off on an audit, because they're impartial third parties. If you go the CPA route, you want to know—do they specialize in personal taxes, small business taxes, corporate taxes, etc.? And how much work have they done with people whose careers and financial lives mirror yours?

EA. Enrolled Agent is a status awarded by the IRS to someone who becomes credentialed either by working at the IRS (as a former employee) or by passing a three-part exam. Some enrolled agents are accountants who decided to take the EA exam instead of the CPA exam because they are interested specifically in tax work. For that reason, although they're generally considered a step down from CPAs in expertise and they charge a little less, when it comes to finding someone to prepare your taxes, we like 'em and we think they can be a bargain.

Tax Lawyer. There are attorneys who have training—sometimes even master's degrees—in taxation. You'd typically want to hire one if you need to for business reasons (because your business is buying or being bought by another). Hiring one to do your personal taxes is expensive—and overkill.

Questions to Ask Any Tax Specialist	
What to Ask	**What You Want to Hear**
Have you handled this fill-in-the-blank special situation before?	"Yes." If you do a significant amount of freelance work, have an interesting residency status, own real estate in multiple places, have other people (in various states) working for you, or have any other special circumstances, make sure this is not the first time the tax pro is seeing them.
Are you up to speed on the requirements of my state, city, town?	"Absolutely." This is particularly key in a year in which you've moved (or if you're a snowbird and split your time). Federal income taxes are the same no matter where you live. Not true of states, cities, etc.
Will working with you enable me to file my taxes on time?	"Yes" or "No." But there should be a good reason. Some tax pros automatically put a good many of their clients on extension. An extension for filing is not an extension for paying; you may prefer being done with taxes by the April 15 due date, barring special circumstances.
What documentation do you need from me?	"Here's a list." Any reputable tax pro will ask for verification of your income (W-2 forms, 1099s, etc.) and verification of expenses (receipts, credit-card statements) in order to prepare returns. Pay stubs themselves are not sufficient. Be wary of preparers who are willing to ballpark expenses, too.
How are your fees structured?	"Here is a written schedule of my fees." Prices will usually depend on how complicated your return is—is it just the basic 1040 or are there schedules involved (B for dividends and interest, D for capital gains and losses, E for rental income and losses, for example)? Be wary of anyone who takes a percentage of your refund; he or she may act too aggressively on your behalf.
What happens if I get audited?	"Count me out. I take off for St. Barts on April 16th." Kidding. "I've got your back. If you hear anything from the IRS, contact me immediately." This is a situation you want to deal with as much as you want to run with the bulls in Pamplona, of course. But you want to know that your tax preparer (a) will be around and (b) is prepared to deal with this. Specifically, you want to know if your tax preparer will be the one responding to queries from the IRS, if the tax preparer can represent you before the IRS, and, if there are mistakes in your return and it needs to be amended, who pays for that.

Other Team Members

In our complicated world there are people to handle complicated issues, and the team members listed in this chapter aren't the only ones you can use. For example, a financial counselor can help with areas other than investing—like budgeting, saving more, spending less, getting out of debt. Many financial counselors are credit counselors, while others teach financial education or work on military bases. But there are also counselors who work with individuals. You can find one through the website of the Association for Financial Counseling and Planning Education at AFCPE.org. Financial therapists (yes, these exist) can help with financial troubles in relationships. The Financial Therapy Association has a zip code locator at FinancialTherapyAssociation.org. The website of *Psychology Today*—psychologytoday.com—also allows you to search by discipline.

CHAPTER 8

Inside Your Health Huddle

《◀────────────────────────────▶》

A strong medical team can help heal you—long before
you need it for illness care

I f you've ever had a health problem (who hasn't, right?), then you already know that the medical system is built with a team structure. Just look at a typical ER scenario. Uncle Joe says he's having chest pain and Aunt Mary doesn't want to chalk it up to the habanero-laced chili that Joe had last night. So she calls 911, and that's the first domino that falls in the intricate system of dozens of people all doing a series of very specific jobs.

Look at all the folks who touch Uncle Joe from the minute Mary makes the call. A dispatcher sends out the paramedics. The paramedics do vitals (and sometimes do an EKG and sometimes put an aspirin under Uncle Joe's tongue), and rush Joe to the ER. A triage nurse assesses the threat level and takes more vitals. Technicians run tests. (All the while Mary is questioned by a financial specialist about insurance if she is not needed by Joe's side.) An ER doc evaluates Joe's pain and medical history, then makes judgments based on those earlier diagnostics and what she learned from Joe. Then, depending on the severity of Joe's problem—and assuming that he needs more than a Pepcid and a resolution to start avoiding habaneros—he could meet any number of radiology technicians, maybe even a radiologist, interventional cardiologists, surgeons, anesthesiologists, nurses, and assistants who (in addition to Joe's own stem cells—see page 202) will help fix whatever heart issues caused the emergency in the first place.

Most of us are used to thinking that medical teams are reactionary—that of course we need people with various specialties to help heal us when we have pain, or a fever, or both. The common idea is to have a team available when we're hurt, sick, or confused about a medical issue. In fact, we expect that kind of specialization.

But here's the question: Why are so many people averse to thinking about having proactive health teams in addition to reactionary ones? Why don't you think of your approach to health as building a web of people who have expertise that can help you anticipate problems and keep you from avoiding the path that Uncle Joe just took? Why can't you think of health teams as not just fighting the crimes of disease, but also preventing them in the first place?

The fact is that you can. You can stop thinking that your doc is simply the person you see when you throw out your back, can't hear your spouse, or have chest pain that won't go away with Tums. Health team members aren't just problem solvers; they're also problem avoiders. Think of your doc as the head coach on the football team you manage, the manager of the downtown restaurant you own, and the captain of your ocean liner. Choosing just the right people is key, for they keep you out of trouble, and help you navigate trouble if it arises.

Now, we're not saying that you should pop in for teeth cleaning every two weeks or that you need to call up your primary care doc to ask whether she prefers that you put spinach or kale in your morning smoothie. What we are saying is that you should take some time to strategize about developing a health team that can serve both roles well—that can treat problems when they arise *and* offer guidance and work with you to craft a plan to improve your health now and in the future.

Like most teams, your health and medical tribe will have people who serve various roles—and you'll have some flexibility, too, to figure out who's necessary when, and when to call in others.

Choosing this team is key—just as with your finances. You want to find people and systems who can discuss your personal goals and background, not those who have a one-size-fits-all mentality about whatever specialty they're in. That's because, when it comes to your health as well as your finances, you are the quarterback, the lead singer, the pilot, the chairman of the board. You are the one who has to make decisions and stand in the spotlight. You have to take control of your situation, ask questions, make choices, add the kale, manage the stress responses or eliminate the stressor, do the exercises, get the shoes that fit right, and alert your health team honestly about issues. Everybody else is there to block for you, to play the bass line, or to assist in navigation.

Most times your primary care physician (see below for why we advocate a doc here) can suggest team members, but you are the one who has to work with each person, so you need a team that fits your personality and problems. Choose your head coach and your team wisely, and you could sail safely and avoid needing illness care for many years. Pick an incompetent boob who talks a good game, or even a well-respected professional who specializes in treating illnesses and not in keeping people well, or who is hopelessly overbooked and can't find the time to squeeze you in, and your boat may sink needing major repairs. We've seen it happen. We've been called in on salvage operations.

But make no mistake: Your primary care doc and those who are assisting you? They can help save, improve, and extend your life.

We like to think of your health team as a tiered system. There are those on your primary team—your go-to people who should be regularly integrated into your life. And then there's a whole cast who serve as your secondary team—those people you may see only once or twice a year (sometimes less) or if you have a specific issue, but who are important in keeping your ship seaworthy nonetheless.

Basic Medical Team Philosophy

Before we get into the ins and outs of who's on your health team, it's important to go over some basic tenets of thinking about your health.

JEAN SAYS: I apply the same standard here as with financial advisers. You need to be able to talk to your gynecologist/ urologist and financial adviser with equal ease. Otherwise he or she might be the best doc on the planet, but he or she isn't the right one for you.

DR. MIKE SAYS: You'll often educate your primary care physician or caregiver by this process. I love learning, as do most docs, so keep teaching us without our having to travel to Seattle to attend an expensive course. Thank you very much.

JEAN SAYS: Mike, thank you for saying that! I always feel a twinge at telling my doc I'm going for a second opinion.

That's because medicine is a complex system with a lot of moving parts, and it's not always clear who does what, what you should do, and how the pieces connect. So here are some things to remember, as you build and think about your team:

Your Team Never Goes Away. But you can always add and subtract members. At any given time—especially up into your 90s—you want the best possible team for diagnosing and treating unclear issues. If someone isn't giving you what you want, you can—and should—make a trade. Sometimes picking your doctor wisely means walking out of a doc's office if he or she isn't the best choice for you.

Today many primary care physicians have developed expertise in particular specialties, like thyroid autoimmune dysfunction or gynecologic infections, while continuing to practice as primary care physicians. As you develop particular needs and conditions, matching yourself with the best doctor for you has become a far more complex—but also far more rewarding—mission than it was just a generation ago.

A Team Doesn't Operate with Blind Loyalty. When you consider that 30 percent of initial diagnoses are wrong, you know you need to remember that second opinions are a major part of the health-care system. Your team should know and respect that you will sometimes seek alternate opinions, and you should feel exactly zero ounces of guilt when you do. So later in this chapter we'll give you some questions to ask while you're channeling your Joe Friday (remember, you want more than the facts—you need the facts *in context*, that context being any doctor's compatibility with your situation and availability to serve your needs).

Your Team Members All Need to Connect with Each Other. Every member of your health-care team should be able to access your medical records (which you, and you alone, give each team member permission to see) in an easy-to-read format, so they all have quick access to your history and to information about your medications, illnesses, activities, and more. This is one of the reasons all your team members should know that they're part of your team, especially if they're affiliated with different health-care organizations, so they can all access your records. The advantage of shared access is that it can cut down on expensive mistakes, delays, or overlaps in treatment ("Why are we taking those same X-rays again?"), as well as making decisions more accurate. You need to check to make sure your team has access to your medical records, and you have to take the lead to make sure they communicate with each other.

You Need to Speak Up. In health care you are going to be dealing with a lot of trained professionals—people who have had decades of schooling and experience. So by definition they'll know more than you do about a particular health issue. And they may not be shy about showing it in the terminology they choose to use. But you know your body Q. And you need to speak up when you don't understand or you feel something isn't going right, or you just feel your body isn't healing right. Some research shows that fewer than 50 percent of patients speak up when the caregiver is unclear about treatment or diagnosis. Bottom line: you absolutely need to get involved in your care—by writing notes, asking questions, being assertive, bringing someone along who can be a second set of ears, and not being afraid to talk about anything with your team.

> **JEAN SAYS:**
> Ugh! This is a huge problem in the world of finance, too. My feeling has always been that you shouldn't buy what you can't understand—that goes for both health and finance.

Health Team: The Starters

These people are your MVPs—most valuable providers. They're the ones you will rely on most throughout your life, so you want to take special care in making sure they're the people you want helping direct you in your care.

Primary Care Provider

Think of your primary care provider (PCP) as your gateway into every health issue you may ever have. This is the person (or group of people) who dictates your health destiny in many ways, because his or her evaluation of your needs or issues is your first line of prevention and defense. So you need to think of this person not solely as the one who writes a scrip if you have strep throat, but also as the one who has a huge web of influence over every health issue and question you have.

That's why trust and connection aren't just things that you value in your romantic relationships, but also what you should value in this one, too (minus the roses and emoji). This main member of your team plans with you what you need to do—note the *you*—to stay well for the next year and coming decades. You and not she: that means that although the plans are created for you with her help, you are the one who eats the foods you choose, takes the half a multivitamin morning and night, and deals with the stresses, not she. She tends to your routine needs, like treatments for ear infections or flu shots—either herself or through her team. And she knows when to refer you to other caregivers, including other physicians if you need a specialist—and helps you choose those providers.

Note: We do not usually think women should choose an ob-gyn as a primary care doc, but women should have one as an essential member of their team. While most gynecologists screen for weight and blood pressure (92 percent do this), studies show that few counsel successfully on stress management, food choices, portion sizes, physical activity (four components that are essential for maximum health with minimum work), inflammation, avoiding toxins like BPA/S (bisphenol A and its substitute bisphenol S are endocrine disruptors to avoid for you to have a healthier life, both in the data and in our opinion interpreting the data for you), reducing LDL cholesterol, or many other important aspects of your health. The role of your primary care doc is to provide you with enough information and motivation to make healthy choices, plus to refer you to the best specialists and team members when the need arises. We often use the term *primary care physician* or *doc*, but feel free to substitute *primary care practitioner* to include a nurse practitioner or other pro if you know that person has appropriate skills and connections to make it work, and meets the criteria below.

Your primary care provider, an internist or family practice physician or nurse practitioner, is whom you see for general checkups, for education on how to stay healthy and well, and for diagnostic tests and assessments to see how you are doing and, when you're sick, to uncover the cause (for which your primary care provider will then suggest courses of action). Your primary care provider should have an electronic medical record (EMR) that you can access and that you allow others, like a doc in the box in your favorite vacation spot, to access when needed.

So how do you find one of these great primary care providers? If you're looking for a new PCP, befriend an ER nurse or an ICU nurse. These registered nurses get a battlefield view of doctors at their best and worst. They know who is sharp and respected, who stays on top of things, who sees patients in the ER or ICU. They're aware of who uses the best consultants and who guesses correctly most of the time. To make friends, visit an ER during off-peak time (midmorning on a Monday is best). You can politely approach the charge nurse at the time and ask if she (90 percent of US nurses are female) can see you for a few moments. (This seems difficult, but really isn't, and people want to help.) A good script: "I have to choose a new primary care provider who has privileges at this hospital, most ideally one who is particularly good at treating diabetes [or whatever is your or your family's most common disease of concern]. I've been doing some research to try to find one, and I know most are great at this hospital, but I wanted to just ask you, knowing how much you know, which specific PCPs you would choose if you were in my position."

Your first visit with that potential new PCP should include some time for you to get to know each other. Make sure you feel comfortable talking about the details of your health and lifestyle with this person.

You might ask ("Yes" is the right answer for most of these):

- **Are you board certified?**

    The American Board of Medical Specialties recognizes two dozen areas of medical specialty. Note: if you'd rather not ask, you can check if the doc you are going to interview is certified by calling (866) 275-2267, or going to ABMS .org. Doctors who are certified have passed tests given by their specialty society, which is evidence of skill. To be fair, it is optional to be certified, so there probably are many great docs who aren't and have never been certified. But it is one way to ensure quality.

- **Are you accepting new patients?**

  You want an active physician or PCP with plenty of patients. Just as you'd rather order salmon in a busy, crowded restaurant instead of one that is empty.

- **Do you practice in a group with other PCPs, internists, or family physicians?**

  Yes, and they all should be board certified.

- **Do other doctors or nurse practitioners use you as their primary care provider?**

  Yes, and some will probably talk to you about why they chose that doctor.

- **What tests will you do at regular office visits? How often will you order these?**

  Good answer: "I adjust the tests based on your needs and national standards, and administer them often enough that you can be motivated by your progress."

- **What days are you not here? Who covers on nights and weekends?**

  A specific doctor who has equally strong credentials and training. Or specialists that this provider or doctor will keep in touch with daily. In the hospital, your PCP should generally talk daily with the specialists who will care for you.

- **Does the PCP covering have access to my total medical records?**

  Yes!

- **Do you accept my insurance plan?**

  You have some options if your insurance plan isn't already part of your doc's or PCP's program 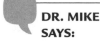.

DR. MIKE SAYS:

If your desired doc's office doesn't accept your insurance, but she is really your top doc choice, don't give up. Call the insurer and ask if it would consider adding this doc to its list. If the company won't, ask why. Sometimes if even a few patients call and ask an insurer to add a doctor, it will. Likewise, ask your desired doctor if you can convince her to start accepting that insurer. And every year when you renew your health insurance (a lovely period in November called "open enrollment" by many employers), call your doc's business manager and make sure she intends to keep accepting your choice of insurance plans. When we docs are not members of a large health-care provider, we are persuaded by just a few factors. If dropping a plan will create big problems for two or three regular patients, that carries weight. So speak up.

It's no good if the doc or PCP only accepts cash. While this is more common among some concierge practices, most of those (such as at the Cleveland Clinic, Mayo Clinic, Northwestern, etc.) charge cash for the once-a-year big visit, but accept insurance payments if you require more tests or hospitalizations or procedures during the year.

- **Do you have someone who will review my physical activities with me and teach me the right exercises to stay young?**
- **Do you have someone who will review stress management with me?**
- **Do you have someone who will review toxins to avoid and can teach me how to make my home toxin-proof?**
- **Do you refer to a nutrition educator or a dietitian, and/or a private chef?**
- **Do you have a special interest in the medical problems I have, or in my family's largest risk factor?**
- **Do you or your staff use telemedicine-on-demand visits, where I can see someone that day for something minor like a sore throat or a bug bite?**

Another good answer (besides "Yes") could be that they're in the process of learning about this, and plan to have it operational within three months.

Before you leave the office, ask the staff about other details, such as how long a wait patients usually have, billing policies, and basic office maintenance.

Throughout your life you will be referred to specialists to help you manage your conditions. The specialists and team members your PCP chooses are key. Choose a strong primary doc (or primary care provider), and there's a good chance that person will know the top specialists.

Accountability Buddy

Time and time again, we'll go to this major mantra: you control your health destiny and your rate of aging through the choices you make, through the things you do (or don't do), through your ability to resist the smell of cinnamon-sugary blocks of baked dough in the mall. And you know what? Your primary care provider will not be available via speed dial or FaceTime or text message to help you walk past those gooey calorie bombs. But your buddy will.

You need that one person in your life who can be that angel on your shoulder when you need it. This is the person with whom you celebrate your achievements and to whom you confess your missteps—because this person can give you the exact right amount of what you need, whether it's a hug or a pep talk or even a metaphorical slap on the wrist. Choosing this person isn't always as easy as it may seem. For example, your spouse may be the natural choice. Oftentimes men successfully use women as their buddies, but the reverse doesn't hold up. Women don't often click with husbands as buddies because admonishment from a partner—even if warranted—just doesn't play well . And you don't always want your best friend to be your health buddy, either. Maybe there's some natural competition, or maybe your lifestyles don't quite mesh (if she's super healthy or super unhealthy, it may not be the best fit).

JEAN SAYS:

Trust us on this, it feels like criticism even if you don't mean it that way.

The best person is really someone who *gets* you, perhaps is slightly ahead of you when it comes to health goals, and can provide equal amounts of care, direction (education as to what works), and sternness. So it's worth taking some time to think about who this person can be. And when the time comes, you simply say, "I really want someone to be here with me as I try to reach my goal. This is what I need—just someone to listen, let me check in with them every day, and nudge me when I need it. I'd really like you to be that person. Can you help me? Can we help each other?"

The reality is that most people want to help; it's very satisfying to help someone steer his or her life in the right direction. So the difficult part isn't asking, because most will say yes; the difficult part is really identifying who's the best buddy for you. (Don't forget to look online. Sometimes the best buddy can be a virtual one.)

Pharmacist

Why do we put this person in your starting lineup? Because this person can have more of an influence on your well-being than you think (at least than the typical person may think—though we know you're smarter than typical, since you're reading this book). And a good relationship with your pharmacist may not only save a trip to your doctor, but can also save you some serious trouble—medication errors occur in at least 5.2 percent of patients. Pharmacists are the most underused resource on the health-care team today—but we want to change that for you.

Pharmacists are highly trained professionals who must know about the chemistry of the products they dispense and what effects, both good and bad, medications have on the body. Therefore they can also tell you whether and how any medication you take could or will affect your blood glucose levels, for example. They alert you to the potential side effects of any vitamin, supplement, or drug you are going to take. With each new supplement or prescription, they can review your medication profile to see if any of your current medications might interact with your new one Q.

It is important to find a pharmacy or pharmacy system you like and to stick with it. This way the pharmacist at that pharmacy can keep an accurate and up-to-date profile of your medical history, allergies, and medications. How about Express Scripts, CVS Caremark, and other mail-order pharmacies? They can save you money because you're ordering three months' worth of medication at a time (though many retail pharmacies now offer three-month scripts as well, with competitive co-pays).

Ob/Gyn (for Women of All Ages after Puberty)

An obstetrician-gynecologist is essential for women over age 13, not just for pregnancies and deliveries, but to deal with all issues involving the female anatomy. A gynecologist can also give you great advice and guidance about pregnancy (please do take a prenatal vitamin with DHA omega-3 for three months before conception, as that decreases

Q JEAN SAYS: And your pharmacist is a huge ally in your ongoing battle to save money on prescriptions. If your doctor has prescribed something that's not in your insurance plan's formulary, a call to the doc from your pharmacist can uncover an alternative that is.

the risk of autism and autism spectrum disorders by 40 percent, and congenital defects of other kinds and childhood cancers by more than 65 percent), as well as about issues involving hormones and hormone replacement therapy as you go through menopause.

But more than that, you need an ongoing relationship with a gynecologist because so many issues involving hormones and the prevention of infections and cancer of your breasts, bladder, kidney, and vagina require a weighing of benefits and risks—and that requires that your ob-gyn know you from more than just a visit at age 50 or so.

Urologist (for Men over 50 Calendar Years of Age)

A urologist is essential for men over 50—that's when issues relating to your prostate kick in and guidance on avoiding symptoms from an enlarged prostate and avoiding prostate cancer should become routine. Many prostate-related issues (anything from treating an enlarged prostate to prescribing hormonal supplements like testosterone cream) require a judgment call regarding the benefits and risks of treatment. That argues for a real doctor-patient relationship and for in-depth discussion about your preferences, just as a woman should have with her ob-gyn. Most men over 50 should see a urologist as part of their yearly routine.

☞ Four Great Questions to Ask When You're About to Be Given a Test or Treatment

⇨ What difference will it make? Will the test results change our approach to treatment?

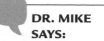

⇨ How much improvement in terms of prolongation of life or reduction in risk of this problem is the treatment actually going to make 💬?

⇨ How likely and severe are the side effects?

⇨ Is the hospital a teaching hospital? (A *JAMA Internal Medicine* study found that mortality was much lower at teaching hospitals.)

DR. MIKE SAYS:

Remember, AgeProofing is all about techniques and practices to live longer better.

Health Team: Role Players or Free Agents

These are the people who can be major contributors to your team, but they fit into an "optional" category that you use once a year or more often if necessary. We believe that all these folks are necessary and can help you achieve your health goals, but they're optional because picking them can be somewhat out of your control. Why? Some of these practitioners don't accept insurance, so any expenses would be out of pocket. In those cases you have to see how these health-related expenses fit into your budget. It is worth noting that paying now can help prevent major costs in the future. (As you now know, health-care expenses are a major driver of financial problems.) But you also need to be realistic about what you can afford.

Culinary Coach

These days you see plenty of food experts on TV—showcasing some of the world's weirdest delicacies or teaching you some kind of culinary secret that will have you committing suicide slowly but likely in a way that will cause you much pain and disability. But there's a lot to be learned about healthy food in your quest to live long; that's mainly because food is your number one vehicle to a healthier life. While you control what goes into your mouth, it is worth considering including someone on your team who can help you navigate all the edible pitfalls out there in the world—and teach you about food as medicine, and find foods you can establish a relationship with (you love 'em and they love you back). This person can be a registered dietitian (RD), nutritionist, or cook educator—all of whom can educate you about ingredients, nutrients, and portion sizes. A lot of data now shows that what you eat and how you eat it can set the stage for such problems as inflammation. For example, just eating more than four ounces of red meat a week changes the bacteria in your gut to produce TMA and BB (don't bother learning what they stand for), which cause inflammation and a greater likelihood of brain rot, heart attacks, strokes, kidney failure, and probably cancer than does a blood pressure of 190/105 or a bad LDL cholesterol of 220. Using spices to make any food taste sensational and preparing veggies enough different ways to stave off salivary boredom are two other skills worth adding to your culinary arsenal. A chef trained in culinary medicine can teach you how to do both these things in a jiffy.

An RD is trained in nutrition and has passed a national exam (and may also have a master's degree Q). If you have diabetes, you want to be sure to work with an RD who has training and experience with diabetes. Your dietitian helps you figure out your food needs based on your desired weight, your lifestyle, your medication, and other health goals (such as lowering blood fat levels or blood pressure). Even if you've had diabetes for many years, a visit to the dietitian can help. Dietitians can help you learn how the foods you eat affect your blood sugar and blood fat levels. Some of the things that your food expert can coach you on are:

- balancing food with medications, supplements, and activity
- reading food labels
- planning meals
- planning for eating out and special events
- finding good cookbooks
- making food substitutions
- finding food choices you love that love you back

Q JEAN SAYS:

My BFF (and running partner) just got her RD with her master's in nutrition—and I watched her sweat through organic chemistry, statistics for nutrition, and all sorts of other tough classes. Trust me, it's rigorous.

While most medical insurance policies and plans do not pay for preventive nutrition and cooking courses (many will pay if you have prediabetes or diabetes, but we'd like you to get counseled to avoid that and osteoarthritis, rather than wait for these problems), we think the $30 to $100 per hour routinely charged by pros in the field will save you many multiples of that in co-pays and time lost for illness care. Food choices, appropriately prepared, can be easy and fast and prevent as well as treat many illnesses. Since food is so difficult to learn, we think your phone should have your culinary medicine chef on speed dial. And we truly believe such a person should be a routine part of your care team.

Phys Ed Teacher

Don't cringe at a flashback of your sixth-grade dodgeball-loving gym teacher. Since expenditure of calories (that is, physical activity) is the other part of the inflow-outflow equation (see chapter 9), you may want to consider adding an expert in activity to your team. Some people work well with trainers; some people prefer group exercise. And others are perfectly fine doing some kind of activity on their own.

Of course you know the advantages of regular physical activity: it can help lower blood sugar, help control blood pressure, and help control your weight. It can also improve your blood fat levels, reduce stress, and improve your overall fitness level. As we'll discuss, we recommend a walking plan if you're new to activity, but as your health improves, you'll want to add in more elements of activity. Even if you do cardio on your own (walk, run, swim, etc.), most people need guidance on form for resistance exercise and need help to make sure they do not injure themselves with either overuse or poor alignment during workouts. That is where a pro comes in.

The best person to help you and your doctor plan your fitness program is someone trained in the science of exercise who knows proper technique for both resistance and cardio exercise. Your doctor can help you look for someone with a master's or doctoral degree in exercise physiology or for a licensed health-care professional who has graduate training in exercise physiology. Certification from the American College of Sports Medicine is another sign that a person has the basic skills needed to plan a safe, effective exercise program. Always get your doctor's approval for any exercise program.

While some medical insurance policies and plans do not pay for preventive phys ed, many companies are defraying the costs of gym memberships and related costs. (Most Medicare Advantage programs offer SilverSneakers for free; sign up even if you usually use a gym in your home. Wherever you travel, there is likely to be a SilverSneakers program that allows you to exercise even when visiting your faraway grandchild.) If your insurance plan doesn't offer a phys ed program like SilverSneakers, we think the $20 to $100 per hour routinely charged by pros in this field (just as in culinary medicine) will save you many multiples of that in other health costs. Physical activity prevents illnesses.

And something to keep in mind: This is an area where you can save money and employ your buddy. A workout partner can be just as good as a professional in many cases, because the accountability to each other will get you moving—which is the main point, after all.

Counselor

If something—your work, your marriage, your house's roof on its last legs—has you more frayed than a 10-year-old shoelace, then you know that stress can play a role in not only your psyche, but also your overall health. Not everyone needs some type of counselor or therapist to help with life's problems, but it is worth considering if you have had prolonged stress that is affecting your work, your relationships, and your life in general.

You can go a couple different routes to get some professional help to manage stress and tension. Some options:

* A clinical psychologist who works directly with patients can have a master's or doctoral degree in psychology and is trained in individual, group, and/or family psychology. A few sessions with a psychologist might help during a time of

special stress. Over the long term, a psychologist might help you work on more persistent problems.

- A psychiatrist is a medical doctor who can prescribe medication to treat physical causes for emotional problems. Psychiatrists also provide counseling.

- Marriage and family therapists can help you with personal problems in family and marital relationships and problems on the job. These therapists should hold a master's or doctoral degree in a mental health field and have additional training in individual, family, and marriage therapy.

- Social workers may be able to help you find resources to help with your medical or financial needs and should hold a master's degree in social work (MSW), as well as having training in individual, group, and family therapy. Some social workers may even be able to help you cope with many concerns related to illnesses, including problems within the family and with workplace situations. LCSW stands for licensed clinical social worker. This means the social worker has passed a state exam.

While many medical insurance policies and plans DO pay for counseling for illness care, most do not pay for preventive stress management. But this, too, is often a bargain, as you can use online programs mostly (see below). The $40 to $300 per hour routinely charged by pros in this field is likely to be extensively needed only if you need illness care.

You can also try some do-it-yourself programs if you like—for one, the Stress Free Now program from the Cleveland Clinic (www .clevelandclinicwellness.com).

Your Educated Buddy

This person is exactly like your other buddy—she's available for a quick phone call or text if you have a question or need some support. The difference is that this person has some health education—is, for

JEAN SAYS:

OK, Mike, I have a buddy like this. But I always feel that if I call to ask a medical question she'll think I'm taking advantage. (Although, on the flip side, I don't mind when my pals call to ask me about their life insurance needs.) How do you feel about being the educated buddy for a friend?

DR. MIKE SAYS:

I love the opportunity; if you can't be there for friends, whom can you be there for?

DR. MIKE SAYS:

Look for micronized zinc oxide, and nothing else, in the sunscreen.

example, a nurse educator, who is trained in helping people make changes in health habits, stay on a physical activity plan, work through stresses, make good food choices, and more. Often these people are called "care coordinators" but you want them for more than that— to help guide preventive care. And you want them more available than two phone calls a month—we think they should be available to you by e-mail or phone anytime. This person—often a registered nurse or dietician or pharmacist—can also help you manage medications and work through issues when you're sick. It's like having your own personal coach there to help you manage all aspects of your health .

Such a buddy is increasingly available free of charge or with small co-pays, especially for patients with chronic illnesses related to obesity such as osteoarthritis, diabetes, and hypertension. Your primary care doc can get you one. We have an online coaching program that has been shown in studies (now peer reviewed) to help participants make important changes (see eCoaching at ClevelandClinicWellness.com). But most medical insurance policies and plans do not pay for preventive education.

Health Team: On the Bench, but Routinely Used Once or Twice a Year

Dermatologist

Although dermatologists have long been patient advocates and have stressed the importance of sun avoidance and protection, yours can do much more. Screening for skin problems can be done digitally to speed up the process, but in-person appointments can give dermatologists the chance to talk to you about such things as proper sunscreen, proper use of that sunscreen, proper skin care with acne, allergies, and atopic dermatitis, avoiding trigger factors in rosacea, and adopting a diet low in saturated fat and high in healthy fats to decrease the incidence of nonmelanoma skin cancer.

Dentist

This isn't just about having bright whites to flash at the party. These regular visits are about keeping you healthy as well. That's because gum disease is a leading cause of body-wide inflammation and even a cause of diabetes. The excess blood sugar in your mouth makes it a good home for bacteria, which leads to infection; other issues that can be caused by periodontal disease include substantial increases in inflammation often associated with premature labor, heart attacks, strokes, impotence, premature wrinkling, kidney disease, and even brain rot. That is why we believe that seeing both your dentist and your dental professional (for a cleaning) every six months is important for preventive care. Elephants die when they lose their teeth; we hope you thrive with yours intact. Be sure to tell your dentist about other wellness and health choices or events that you're making or that are happening to you.

Eye Doctor

When eye problems are caught early, there are very good treatments. The eye doctor is usually an ophthalmologist. You should see your eye doctor at least once a year to check for any changes in your eyes. If there are changes, the doctor will treat the problem or refer you to another doctor with special training in that area.

Podiatrist

Since foot problems are so common, and misalignment is a substantial cause of hip and knee arthritis, especially in those who are physically active, we think a podiatrist, and an orthopedist trained in assessing and correcting joint and bone alignment, are other essential pros you should include on your team. These health professionals are trained to treat problems with feet and lower legs. Podiatrists have a doctor of podiatric medicine (DPM) degree from a college of podiatry. They have also done a residency (hospital training) in podiatry. Sores, even small ones, can quickly turn into serious problems. Any foot sore needs to be checked by your podiatrist. Do not try to fix these yourself, because you could cause an infection. And since feet often have less than optimal blood flow, infections there can bring about disasters. So do inspect your feet daily for signs of trouble.

Most important, orthopedic specialists and podiatrists can spot foot and ankle misalignments that can lead to back, hip, and knee problems. They can also keep an eye out for corns and calluses, which can lead to more serious problems. Seeing one of these guys (yes, usually men) once a year can often delay back or joint problems for several decades.

AgeProof **ESSENTIALS**

1. Health and wealth are private. Private doesn't mean solo. You are only as AgeProof as the quality of your team.

2. Employ the buddy principle. A confidant (probably not your spouse) may be the most valuable person on your team. To hug you. To scold you. To fortify you.

3. You are the CEO of your body and your bank account. Ask questions. Check references. Make smart decisions about whom you want to add to your team.

Part V
Survival Instinct

The Science of Inflow and Outflow

Why you're not designed to have a balanced body or budget—and how you can make sure that you do

Many things we talk about in this book really come down to a simple equation: what goes in versus what goes out. This is true for money (how much you earn versus how much you spend), and this is true for many health issues (how much you consume versus how much you burn). Easy to understand, right? If you chug milkshakes by the gallon and rarely exercise, your body will store the excess as abdominal fat, which then triggers a whole host of health problems 💬. And if you spend more than you earn and build up debt (which will probably lower your credit score), you sacrifice money you could be building up for your future and, perhaps, inspire a visit from a crowbar-wielding thug who wants you to make good on your loans.

But here's what might surprise you: your brain and body have absolutely zero interest in making these equations work in your long-term favor. In fact, we could argue your brain is actually working against you—making it incredibly difficult to manage the relationship between inflow and outflow.

You'd think that your body—as majestic and complex as it is—would know how to create a sort of biological equilibrium, that it would all just naturally sort out between inflow and outflow. Eat what you need, burn off the rest, live happily ever after.

DR. MIKE SAYS: Of course the quality of what you eat matters—you want the calories to be nutritious and love you back to make you younger rather than to age you. So amount in your inflow and outflow matters, but so does the quality of your choices.

As far as your body is concerned, there is no happily ever after.

As far as your body is concerned, there is only thinking that belongs as phrases on a coffee mug: *Seize the day! Live in the moment! You only live once!*

To understand what we mean, rewind your mind. Think about society that existed long before baristas and iPhones and HDTV and every other modern amenity we take for granted.

This is how it looked: Caveman and Cavewoman hunted and gathered their food. They gorged on what they found, in case it would be days before they'd find more food. They spent the night by the campfire and then did a few, ahem, other things to keep warm and satisfy other hormonal urges. The result of that hubba-hubba: Cavechild. Cavewoman—knowing that Cavechild couldn't eat berries and venison without teeth—nursed Cavechild for a few years while Caveman protected the clan from trolling beasts. Then, at some point, when Cavechild had made it past the first few years of vulnerability, and after they had taught Cavechild some survival tricks, well, there was no dire need for Caveman and Cavewoman, meaning that they were expendable, be it by natural or animalistic disaster. The species survived, even if the parents didn't.

Here's the evolutionary abstract of that story: Evolution cared only that you lived till Cavechild could live without you. So you needed to live only until you were about 30 to ensure survival of the family. It wasn't necessary that you last to 40, 50, or 60, let alone 70, 80, or 90. That's the way mankind existed for 10,000 years. It wasn't until the last 150 years or so (with the development of modern agriculture and small weapons and, let's be honest, antibiotics, anti-hypertensives, and statins) that we started going against the grain of what our bodies were programmed to do.

Satisfying immediate needs and desires (that is, giving in to temptation) is our biological instinct: survive the day. That means you eat what you want to eat, and you do whatever it takes to feel good in the moment, not caring about the future. The reptilian part of your brain—ingrained with that instinct from generations upon generations of working that way—still trumps the executive part of your brain (the part that makes decisions based on logic and problem-solving). It still functions as if it's natural for you to eat whatever you want to—and spend whatever you want to—today, because you need only to survive to age 30. According to this lizard logic, there's no need to worry about adult-onset diabetes or maintaining the premiums on a long-term-care insurance policy, because, frankly, you were never going to be much of an adult. You were a baby-making, generation-extending machine who expired when your job did.

We don't explain all this to give you a built-in excuse: "Sorry, it's my biological destiny that I must eat four red velvet cupcakes today. Whoops, bought a new smarter-than-smart TV this morning because of my reptilian brain." We explain it to validate that this stuff—creating medical and financial equilibrium—is *hard* because you're swimming upstream. You're fighting your instincts. You're trying to make decisions about your future, even if your body doesn't give two flips about it.

So where does that leave you? Great question. Because what you're trying to do is outsmart your instincts. The key is that you have to do it without feeling as if it's a fight. Once you frame it as a struggle to over-power this biology, you're likely to lose. If you try to mandate a 24-7 chicken breasts diet, you will likely falter at the first sign of caramel. If you decide you're going to do work with Gramps's 1942 typewriter instead of springing for a new computer, you'll eventually cave—and will probably end up bingeing on a lot of unnecessary goodies while you're at it.

The winning ticket: Don't try to outmuscle your biology. Outthink it. The answer is to fight fire with fire. Fight the automated instinct with healthful decisions that become automated.

What we want you to do is trash the concept of willpower—the thinking that if only you are strong and tough enough to resist the allure of a new love seat, then you are worthy of a robust retirement fund. Much research, in fact, shows that avoiding unhealthy behavior isn't about the traditional notion of brute force and natural willpower, and that you can actually train yourself to effectively deal with in-the-moment temptations that come your way. We believe the answer is not about will, but about automation.

Instincts—good ones and bad ones—are automated. Your countermove is to create your own automation to achieve the results you're looking for. How? Well, there are lots of examples that we'll go through in the next chapters. But think about things like automatic payroll deductions for your 401(k). These take the thinking and decision-making out of the process. You click a box once and you're done, rather than having to wrestle with whether you want to put $1,000 away for retirement this month or spend it on a to-die-for antique mirror you saw when you walked down Main Street. Admittedly, it can be a little trickier for health issues, but there are ways to automate behavior—making sure you're going to have one of the same three choices for a healthy breakfast every day, for example, rather than rummaging through the pantry and ending up with a blueberry Pop-Tart that expired in 2012 as your only option.

One of the things we've learned from our collective 75-plus years studying health and wealth is this: humans can't be trusted to do the right thing.

You can't outsmart your basic biology with willpower. You have to do it with structure, with technology, and with automation.

The next two chapters are about managing the inflow-outflow equation by using these things. In the end, your brain wants you to seize today, but you'd better be prepared to also seize tomorrow.

CHAPTER 9

The Energy Equation

⟪⟪ ⟶ ⟫⟫

Your body's fuel—pumping it in and burning it off

The first physics lesson you ever learned—before you even knew what physics was—was probably this one: what goes up must come down. It's the principle of gravity. Throw a ball into the air over your head, and it's going to come back to hit you in the head if you don't get your hands up to catch it. Jump from the top of the fence you just climbed, and you're going to land on earth (likely with a broken ankle or two). What goes up must come down: It seemingly applies to everything in life.

Unfortunately, when it comes to your health, what goes up doesn't automatically come down.

Like your weight. Or lousy LDL cholesterol. Or levels of toxins. Or blood pressure. Or blood sugar. Or inflammation.

When any of those indicators goes up, it's just going to stay up—and potentially keep going higher and higher. There's no Einsteinian equation that mandates that the extra weight you gained over the holidays will melt off come January 2. Oh, it would be nice if your body automatically sought this kind of equilibrium to keep you at a perfect weight, but as we discussed a few pages ago, there are evolutionary reasons your body doesn't want to equalize.

So where does that leave you, a product of today's expanding-waist society? Trying to figure out how to create your own biological formulas to optimally balance the amount of fuel you ingest with the amount of fuel you burn. When you can create a balance between the two, that's when you achieve optimum health, a longer life, and jet-packs of energy to seize every day.

This—we would argue—is the most fundamental of all of the health strategies and tactics we talk about in the book. That's because food—for better or worse—drives what's happening not only in the way we look on the outside, but also in the way (almost) everything functions on the inside.

Before we discuss the inflow and outflow of energy in the body, it's important to have a quick biological discussion about the way the energy system works—and to clarify a few possible misconceptions you may have about it.

The way we measure energy in the body is via calories (you've heard of those, we suspect). Calories are the unit of measurement for the energy you extract from certain foods, as well as the energy you burn off through living and moving. In oversimplified terms, the process works like this: When you eat a meal, your body and bacteria in your intestines break down the energy in the food to be absorbed into your bloodstream. It usually ends up as blood sugar. That blood sugar is shuttled via your bloodstream to power your various organs, systems, and muscles. Makes sense, right? Your heart, brain, and other organs need energy to do their jobs. Those are the caloric expenses that you have zero control over.

You do, however, have control over other caloric expenditures, like when and how much you exercise. When you move your body more vigorously—say when you run, dance, or even have sex—your body parts need more energy and blood delivered to those areas to perform the tasks you're asking of them. That's how the energy you ingest via food gets burned off; it's used to rev your various biological engines.

Now, if we lived in a perfect world, the system would work

seamlessly: you would ingest only what you needed to burn and burn off what you ingested. All systems go, you live at the perfect weight, woo-freaking-hoo. But your body doesn't work like that. While you do get rid of some of the energy you have via the digestive and waste system, the extra energy you consume and *don't* burn off gets stored as fat. That's because your body is a smart little bugger. It knows that if you ever need more energy than what is readily available via the food you ate a few hours ago, now broken down and circulating in your bloodstream, it can rely on that extra fat you have, draw energy from it, and help you move the way you want to move. (That's your reptilian heritage helping you out, by the way. Remember, it wasn't sure how long it would be until you'd eat again.) If it helps, think of your fat sort of like a savings account; you deposit and draw from it for energy.

In the past (as recently as 80 years ago), having more fat was helpful, as we and the entire world were calorie short. But times and agricultural methods have changed, and coffee and everything else is available on every other corner. So now, unlike savings accounts that have actual money in them, your fat surplus isn't a bonus anymore.

While we've just simplified the energy system, it is important to discuss one important nuance. The general equation involved in creating some kind of equilibrium is calories in versus calories out, but that should not send the message that every calorie is treated equally. Your body processes the different major- or macro-nutrients—protein, fat, carbohydrates—differently. While all nutrients eventually do get converted to sugar, some calories (like protein) are earmarked for helping out your muscles, while other calories (like sugar) go directly into your bloodstream and turn right to fat if they're not immediately used. Some nutrients change the bacteria in your intestine to cause inflammation in the rest of your body. Some also have hormonal effects that change the amount of energy you use. So throughout our discussion of calories, resist the temptation to think that simply counting calories is the secret to good health. Calories are the mechanism for measurement, and they drive the energy exchange in the body, but that's

DR. MIKE SAYS: In addition, your body has a circadian rhythm to help you be more active during the day. You become more insulin resistant as the day goes on. That means calories eaten in the morning are used more efficiently than those eaten after 2 p.m. So eating the same number of calories before 2 p.m. results in more weight loss or less weight gain than calories eaten after 2 p.m. So eat dinner for breakfast and more early, less later. See the book *What to Eat When* for more info.

JEAN SAYS: Just as, by the way, it is hugely beneficial to make sure that your financial assets are diversified.

not something you should try to game. Eating five saturated fat– and sugar-laden muffins in a day as your only source of nutrition may keep you under a daily calorie count, but it will do nothing to help your health—and everything to hurt it 💬.

The last thing we'll say before we get into the details of inflow versus outflow is this: in almost all cases, you will not have enough outflow to keep up with too much and too poor quality of inflow. Translation: food (the inflow), not exercise (the outflow), dictates the majority of our health outcomes. And that—if you want to get the most out of your life—is where you should direct most of your attention.

Your Health Inflow

If you look at the energy systems in today's world, there's a whole lot of talk about diversification 💬. Oil, gas, nuclear, wind power, solar power, and so on. For a variety of reasons—ones that are way out of the scope of this book—it can be beneficial to have alternative sources that provide energy.

But when it comes to the human body, there are no alternatives. We get our energy from food. Period. End of story. That's what powers your brain, your heart, your muscles, and everything else. There's no alternative fueling source. You don't stick your mouth up to the sun or idle by an oil tanker and get calories in any alternative ways. If we want to live, we must eat.

Therein lies the problem: not only must we eat, we *want* to eat.

When our society shifted from basic food choices (meat and berries) to the Frosted Flakes and Cheetos of the world, food became less about fuel and love of your body and more about satisfying short-term reptilian demands. How could manufacturers develop flavors and tastes that provided a rush to our brains—and, in turn, inches to our waistlines? Well, they did it quickly, efficiently, and cheaply—and now we're looking at a society that thinks green foods include a Shamrock Shake.

We're in a food crisis, and most of that stems from the fact that we eat too much processed food, too many sugars, and not enough real and healthy foods. And to be complete, we eat too much unhealthy fat and not enough healthy fat. So if we really care about the inflow—that is, the nutritional pipeline by which our bodies run—then we must take into consideration the quality of everything we consume. And while eating right can be a challenge—especially when you're faced with many temptations—the methodology for fueling your body is actually quite simple. To get started, there are really two things you need to know about your power sources: what to eat and how to eat it.

The Whats

The vital rule of nutrition is this: the best foods you can eat have the fewest ingredients. We don't want to make it complicated, and we don't want to pepper you with all kinds of rules, programs, and constructs for how to eat. So the simplest way to think about it is this: you should know what the good foods are, and know what to avoid. And if you eat the good foods 90 percent of the time, you've tipped the scale—quite literally—in your favor .

The goal here really isn't to try to stick to any calorie count or set limit; it's to eat a makeup of foods you love that love you back—good foods so you feel satisfied and have absolutely zero urge to go nose deep into Nana's clam sauce. We've got an easy way for you to remember what to eat:

> **LUV-U Foods***
>
> **L**ean protein, with an emphasis on plant-based protein (even nonlean seeds and nuts)
>
> **U**nsaturated fats (especially odd omegas like DHA omega-3 and extra-virgin olive oil (omega-9))
>
> **V**egetables and fruits
>
> **U**nprocessed grains

---

*Yes, that means these are good.

DR. MIKE SAYS: Yes, I believe in trying to get to 100 percent, but even I select four days for exceptions—my birthday (with cake), our anniversary (with chocolate soufflé), Thanksgiving (with everything), and one other day (with fried French toast or equivalent).

JEAN SAYS: Oh boy, are we confessing here? Most days contain exceptions for me. I keep Hershey's Bars in my freezer and break off a piece or two most nights after dinner. My other big weakness is a good doughnut. When I come into contact with one (at Federal Donuts in Philly, perhaps, or Doughnut Plant in New York City) I don't even try to resist. Otherwise I aim for moderation...most of the time.

DR MIKE SAYS: Go for 70 percent dark chocolate, Jean.

And avoid:

SSSSnake Oil Foods*

Saturated and trans fats

Simple sugars

Simple syrups

Stripped carbs (that is, processed carbs stripped of their whole grains)

JEAN SAYS: Mike, how many days do we have to be off the cookie batter (or whatever) to retrain our bodies into thinking of carrots like cookies?

DR. MIKE SAYS: Two weeks trains your brain, but data now says one year causes the old brain circuits to be reabsorbed and new ones hardwired.

The LUV-U foods have been shown to have a whole host of benefits. Vegetables and fruits contain phytochemicals and other disease-fighting compounds, not to mention fiber, which helps keep heart disease at bay. Plus, those vegetables and fruits have a ton of vitamins and minerals and can really satisfy a sweet tooth (once you teach yourself that sweetness really can come from veggies and fruit and not just from cookie batter).

Unsaturated fats help lower levels of harmful LDL cholesterol and triglycerides, decrease inflammation, and raise levels of good HDL cholesterol in your blood, and unprocessed grains (100 percent whole wheat and whole grains) are good for fiber, lasting energy, and satiety. Lean protein—in the form of non-mercury-laden fish (especially salmon, ocean trout, anchovies, and sardines), skinless white meat chicken, and skinless white meat turkey, and especially plant-based proteins like beans (any type, prepared just about any healthy way), quinoa, chia, nuts and seeds, and many greens like spinach and kale—also provides lasting energy and satiety, as well as contributing to repairing muscles when they're broken down. If you regularly balance your meals with these foods, you're well on your way to pumping your body full of high-octane fuel.

On the flip side, you want to stay away from the SSSSnake oil foods. If any of the first five ingredients on any package is or contains these

---

*They may look appealing at first glance, but they're not what they're cracked up to be.

ingredients, reject it. That means any saturated fat, trans fat (partially hydrogenated vegetable oil), added sugar, non-whole-grain carbohydrate, or added syrup. We also reject the food if one of the first four ingredients is salt, egg yolks, or any type of red meat (it contains saturated fats, but is bad for you more because it changes the bacteria in your gut to produce inflammation in you).

Saturated Fat. This includes most four-legged animal fat, such as milk fat, butter, and lard, and tropical oils, such as palm and coconut oil.

Trans Fat. This includes partially hydrogenated fats, vegetable oil blends that are hydrogenated, and many margarines and cooking blends. The USA has joined Canada in banning all synthetic and added trans fats in the food supply.

Simple Sugars and Syrups. These include brown sugar, dextrose, corn sweetener, fructose (as in high-fructose corn syrup), glucose, corn syrup, honey, invert sugar, maltose, lactose, malt syrup, molasses, raw sugar, and sucrose.

Stripped Carbs. Enriched flours and all flours other than 100 percent whole grain and 100 percent whole wheat. These include enriched white flour, semolina, durum wheat, and any of the acronyms for flour that is not 100 percent whole grain or 100 percent whole wheat—they should not be in your kitchen.

· · ·

We won't list tons of foods that fit all these categories, because we believe you probably know—either through research or instinctually—where foods fall. For example, you obviously know that green beans are good. Ranch dip? Not so much. Avocados are great, and guac with only avocados, tomatoes, onions, peppers, and spice is terrific. Add sour cream and you make it a food felon. Nothing wrong with an apple, but when you disguise it in a costume of piecrust, butter, and sugar, it's not exactly health food. Skinless white meat chicken is good. Chicken soaked in batter of grease, sugar, and salt is bad. Egg whites are great. Egg yolks aren't healthy, as they contain lecithin and choline, which in large amounts change the bacteria in your intestines to produce a small molecule that you absorb and that produces inflammation in your arteries, kidneys, and immune system, and probably in your brain.

The Hows

OK, so maybe you *know* the good foods to eat. The harder questions are how you integrate them into your diet, how you make sure they make up the majority of the food you eat, and how in the heck you stay away from the tidal wave of junk that's hurled at you in commercials, in supermarkets, in office break rooms, everywhere you look. It's tricky because of the very fact that we're inundated with choices. And research indicates that the more choices we have, the less smart the decisions we make about those choices turn out to be ⬤.

So what we're after is to figure out systems that work to make eating well easy. It's not about struggling to find a turnip soup recipe ⬤. It's about working to find things you like—and then frameworks for how you eat them. That way eating healthy is just what you do, not something you have to work for. It's more automatic. The four keys to changing the makeup of your nutritional inflow are these:

Experimentation. Do you like quinoa? Do you know what quinoa is? Do you even know how to pronounce *keen-wah*? It doesn't matter if we're talking quinoa or macadamias. For you to figure out how to love eating healthy, you have to discover the healthy foods you love. That takes time—and a willingness to try something (not just once, but several times, since your taste buds adapt and it may be a few times before you "take" to a food—remember how long it took your infants to take to carrots). Some of our favorite under-the-radar foods are mango, pomegranate seeds, chia seeds, jicama, Broccolini, lots of squashes, any vegetable you cannot pronounce the name of, and many spices.

Substitution. Most diets work like this: cut this, cut that, cut a little more of this, cut a lot more of that. If you follow these rules, then voila! You've lost 15 pounds before you know it. The problem with diets that have lots of rules and restrictions is that dropping something from your diet leaves your brain searching for something to replace it (and

JEAN SAYS: And the less happy we are about the choices we make. Think about being in a restaurant with an extensive menu. No matter what you order, it's really hard not to think someone on the other side of the table did it better.

DR MIKE SAYS: Nancy (my wife) does have a great leek soup recipe and I love the Periodic diet tomato-onion-corn soup—and both love me back.

that's when you turn to other no-no foods in desperation). Addiction research tells us that the best way to handle dropping an addiction to something unhealthy is by replacing it with something healthy. That's because your brain needs to be occupied with action. So if you decide you're going to give up soda, it's not enough just to "give up soda." You have to add in tea or coffee or ice water with lemon to satisfy the brain's desire to do something that you've always done. So yes, your goal should be to eliminate those SSSSnake oil foods from your diet, but to do so you need to take very specific steps to add more LUV-U foods in.

Preparation. You wouldn't dream of making a speech without preparing remarks. You wouldn't think about going on vacation without packing your stuff. You wouldn't dare go on a first date without Googling the heck out of your new suitor. We spend all our lives preparing for whatever tasks lie ahead. Except eating. When it comes to eating, so many of us just grab whatever is in front of us, or we rely on the convenience of drive-throughs, or we say, "What the heck, let's order a pizza tonight." Zero prep. And that's our collective downfall. If we can spend a few minutes every week thinking about meals and making a shopping list, we will have eliminated the in-the-moment temptations that come up all around us. Yes, it takes a little time and energy, but that time and energy are better spent on getting ready to eat well—which will give you more energy in the long run.

Automation. The holy grail in all of this is one simple concept: automation. How can we just eat right naturally without giving it another thought? Through a regular shopping list and a regular rotation of recipes. You choose two or three meals you love and eat one for each breakfast, and do the same for lunches and snacks Q. For example, for breakfast you could have oatmeal and berries or an egg-white omelet with veggies and without cheese, or a 100 percent whole-wheat English muffin with walnut butter and avocado. For lunch you could have a salad with tons of veggies and a grilled chicken breast. You vary only for dinners.

By knowing what healthy meal you're going to order when you go out, without relying on scanning the menu. By making a week's worth

JEAN SAYS:

Oatmeal with raisins and cinnamon is breakfast for me. Cooked oatmeal, not instant. Half cup oatmeal, one cup water, three minutes in the microwave and I'm good to go. Plus, you can always find it in an airport. And I never get tired of it.

of lunches on Sunday so that all you have to do is grab one and go, rather than fall prey to the "Let's order Chinese food" coworker. Automation is the secret to restoring order when it comes to feeding your body what it really needs. That's especially important when you consider that many eating habits are based on childhood associations—you may seek comfort food for stress relief or maybe because it acts as a surrogate for emotional warmth you're missing. High stress generates emotional fatigue—meaning you experience a drop in sugar and increased anxiety, and may be more likely to reach for foods that cause sugar to rise. You want to get that reflex so that when you do feel stress, your habit is about a healthier kind of comfort food.

JEAN

SAYS: I do two things—maybe three—that help when it comes to saving time and money on groceries and eating a healthier diet. I plan meals for the week. In part this is because I love to cook—but I don't love to make decisions about what to make for dinner. So every weekend I ask my husband, "What do you want for dinner this week?" He might answer, "Something with eggplant, your chicken marsala, a soup, spaghetti and meatballs." I build my shopping list around three or four dinners, knowing that we'll have a day or two of leftovers. That allows me to figure out how to make the dinners healthier at home—before I get to the store. If you are in the meat aisle and Googling recipes, you're sunk. So before I go to the store, I can decide that the meatballs will be turkey meatballs, and the eggplant a baked eggplant parm. Second, often I don't go to the store at all. I'll do my grocery shopping from home using Peapod.com. I don't make impulse purchases, because the food isn't staring me in the face. And because I'm a returning customer, the app saves my old lists—which saves me time.

DR. MIKE

SAYS: Switch to veggie meatballs, and that dish will love you even more!

☞ How to Shop the Supermarket

The key to a perfect trip to the supermarket: if you don't buy the food that's bad for you, you won't eat the food that's bad for you. Your shopping strategy:

⇨ Shop the perimeter. The junk food is in the aisles.

⇨ Read labels. No SSSSnake oil foods in the first five ingredients.

⇨ Don't go when you're hungry—this, by the way, will save you money, too. (If you must, take some nuts or fruit and eat on the way.)

⇨ Foods with fewer labels and ingredients are generally better than those with lots.

▷ Shop for produce first. It'll fill your cart and make you less likely to fill it with junk.

▷ Fresh and fresh-frozen veggies, or fresh salmon from the Alaska salmon run, or even frozen salmon from the overage of that salmon run, or ocean trout: make them a priority.

Your Health Outflow

With a car, you fill your gas tank, burn the gas, and then, when you're close to empty, you fill up again. You use what you need, then replenish when you run out. Your body—via your eating—fills up much more often. Interestingly, your body is also in a constant state of outflow. We expel what we don't need, or we store it to (presumably) burn later. The common form of outflow that we're all familiar with—expelling waste—happens as a natural part of the digestion process when your body takes unwanted nutrients or nutrients that are waste to the bacteria inside you that you don't absorb, passes them through the digestive tract, and moves them along and out to your porcelain destination of choice. Your intestines are a complex system and the most dense part of your immune system, letting you unconsciously filter and sort (with the help of the bacteria that inhabit your intestine) what to expel and what to store. That waste product is only a fraction of what you expel as part of the inflow-outflow process. The other part comes in the form of calories you actually burn off—through your body's furnace, which takes either sugar, or fat, or glycogen (the stored form of carbohydrates) to power your body's systems.

That calorie-burning process really happens in two ways. One is the way that you really have no control over—the calories you burn just *being*. Even if you spend all your time on the couch with a *House of Cards* binge, you're still burning calories naturally as your organs move and churn and work. Since you have very little control over this part of your metabolism (your natural metabolic rate), it's worth spending more time on the area that you do have control over—that is, how much you can burn off during movement and activity, and even after you stop exercising in some cases (the other part of your metabolic rate). Remember that you burn more during activity because as your heart rate increases and your muscles are being asked to work more, your brain knows it needs to send energy through your bloodstream to power those systems. Simply, the more you work or the harder you work, the more demands are put on your body, and the more energy you need. So to do that work, you burn off the calories that come directly from food and are immediately available, or the calories that are stored in fat.

As a reminder, you won't be able to out-train a bad diet (a bad diet means you will either get obese or have other aging health effects, or both). For this system to work best, you do need to base your diet around the LUV-U foods we just talked about, not cheesy meat burritos. When you eat well, you maximize the effects of the outflow to help you lose fat, drop weight, and gain energy. Plus there are approximately seven zillion other reasons to engage in regular activity, including evidence that four types of physical activity that slow or reverse your aging (any physical activity, resistance training, jumping, and cardio—see below) also improve your mood, decrease stress, reduce injuries, drop lousy LDL cholesterol, increase healthy HDL cholesterol, decrease inflammation, insulin resistance, and blood sugar (and the risk of developing problems associated with them, like cancer and memory dysfunction Ⓠ), and so much more.

JEAN SAYS: And dramatically reduce the amount of money you have to spend keeping yourself healthy and beautiful inside and out.

So when it comes to creating energy balance, paying strong attention to outflow—burning energy through activity—helps you get and stay younger. These are the major principles that will help you (1) get into an exercise program you enjoy if you don't have one already, (2) maintain that or another exercise program for life, and (3) enjoy all the benefits that come from having an effective activity plan.

Form a Foundation. The simplest form of activity we have—walking—is also the most effective. Even though it's not a huge calorie-burner per minute (averaging five calories a minute as opposed to some cardio play like squash and competitive swimming, which can go up to about 16 calories per minute), it provides the base of activity throughout the day. Research shows that walking 10,000 steps a day (which is easy to track nowadays with pedometers, wearable technology, and smartphone apps) helps give you about 50 percent of the maximum age-slowing effect that all physical activity can give you, improves your health, helps you manage your stress responses and your weight, and contributes greatly to an overall wellness program. For those just starting a program, it's also the easiest to engage in—meaning that it's not a daunting task (as some exercise is for novices) and it's something you can build into your day (meaning you don't have to sweat, shower, and change clothes to do it). The first step is building to and staying with 10,000 steps a day. Do it.

Create a Recipe with These Ingredients. You know what's good? Vegetable soup. Lots of flavors, lots of variety, mmm. You know what's not so good? Cabbage—or any other one-vegetable—soup. Bland, boring, yuck. When it comes to a long-term activity plan, you want a nice, robust vegetable soup. You want some variety, you want some different flavors, you want to feel satisfied. But here's the thing: You're not just creating variety for the sake of variety to keep you from getting bored (though that is an added advantage of a varied workout routine). You want variety because it's that multitool approach that's best for your health. Besides walking, or general physical activities—10 minutes of gardening equals 800 steps; 10 minutes of swimming is between 300 (treading water) and 1,200 (active strokes) steps—include these elements in your program (add gradually):

Resistance exercises: Here you're challenging your muscles by pushing and pulling against some outside force—gravity. That includes moving dumbbells, resistance bands, weight machines, or even your own body weight (push-ups and squats count) against gravity. Doing these kinds of exercises increases your strength (without making you look like a muscle-bound superhero). That strength helps prevent injuries, increases your metabolism (to help burn more fat), and is

DR. MIKE SAYS: I've added steps to my day just by parking farther away, taking fewer elevators, and going for a walk after dinner—that 10,000 a day is rarely missed. The way to build is to start wherever you are now (yes, use a pedometer) and never do fewer steps today than you did yesterday. Soon you'll hit 10,000.

associated with all kinds of better health outcomes. Adding these exercises after you have hit 10,000 steps a day but before you start more intense cardio activities helps you prepare for cardio and avoid injuries. Doing about two strength-training sessions a week for 15 to 20 minutes each makes your RealAge about 1.8 years younger. You'll also burn more calories when you aren't consciously using your extra muscle mass (i.e., while you're just sitting there), and more muscle mass means more outflow of calories.

☞ Why You Need Muscles

When you hit some magic age, not only do hormone changes make it harder to maintain muscle mass, but something seems to make metabolism slower (like older cars getting fewer miles per gallon). It seems to happen at about menopause in women and at a similar or slightly greater age in men. While no one knows what the real causes of these changes are, they can lead to an evil cycle: more fat makes your hormones less active, so they're less able to maintain muscle, which means it's harder to burn fat. But getting thinner turns this into a virtuous cycle: less fat mass means more effective and active hormones and a more effective metabolism, which means more muscle building and less fat. To achieve that, increase resistance exercises as you age. You can help negate the effects of slowing metabolism and hormones with only 30 minutes a week.

Cardiovascular exercise: Three times a week, you want to do an activity in addition to walking that raises your heart rate to at least 80 percent of your maximum for about 21 minutes at a time. (Calculate your max heart rate by subtracting your age from 220, for men; it's 208 minus 88 percent of your age; for women 220 minus your age. In both cases, use your RealAge if you know it.) This can include running, cycling, swimming, dancing, rowing, playing singles tennis, or doing any other type of sport like this (sorry, sex could count, but you're likely not elevating your heart rate that high—and definitely not for that long!). Since this is intense exercise, we recommend perfecting the walking for two months and then doing resistance exercises for an additional two months before adding cardio. This sequence (walking before resistance before cardio) also helps avoid injuries. And if you have not done cardio since Reagan was president, check with your doc to make sure it is safe for you. Besides the calorie-burn benefit that you get (remember, you're burning more calories as blood pumps energy to your working muscles), these types of exercises also strengthen your heart, which, as you can guess, is a prime factor in staving off heart problems, and improves your metabolism 💬.

DR. MIKE SAYS: Recent data indicate that a two-minute stationary bicycle warm-up, followed by all-out activity for 20 seconds, followed by a two-minute slower period of activity, followed by a 20-second all-out period, followed by a two-minute slower period of activity, followed by a third 20-second all-out period, followed by a three-minute cooldown, may be equivalent in metabolic benefit to the longer period of cardio. While that one minute of intense exercise (in three 20-second doses) may be equivalent metabolically, the regimen of 21 minutes three times a week has stood the test of time and repeated studies on your overall disability and death rates—it improves your length and quality of life, or as we say, makes your RealAge—the actual age of your body—younger.

Jumping: Bone remodeling consists of two stages: resorption, when cells called osteoclasts dissolve old bone, creating small cavities; and bone formation, or remodeling, when cells called osteoblasts build new bone by filling those cavities with calcium. Usually bone resorption and bone formation occur around the same time and are balanced. When they're not balanced, you lose bone mass. In addition, bone remodeling happens through electricity in the form of low-energy waves that put stress on the bone. To form bone, you need that charge—and that comes from weight-bearing exercise and building muscle that stresses the bone. You can get it from jumping (20 jumps on a hard surface like a driveway morning and night seems to get the best results in the two studies we have). This is one of the secrets from the book title. It is part of the method to ensure you live longer—by AgeProofing yourself—without breaking a hip. Because breaking a hip is often associated with a rapid decline in overall health (from a number of factors, including a higher risk of developing infections), this is one of the major fears that people have about aging. Check with your doc for an OK to do this if you have back pain or knee problems.

Stretching: Fact is, you'll burn more calories cleaning your home than you will stretching. So that's not the reason to do it. The reason is that you want to work on your mobility and body suppleness. Being flexible allows you to more easily do other physical activity and maintain a strong musculoskeletal system so, again, you won't break a hip. Plus you just *feel* better (and younger) when you're loose. Aim to stretch by doing yoga 10 minutes a day—and that helps you meditate and breathe properly, so you can manage your responses to some stressful events. But if you can't do 10 to 15 minutes , just try to remember to get up and do a quick stretch for 30 to 45 seconds (touching your toes is fine) after you've been sitting for every long period.

DR. MIKE SAYS: I do sun salutation and downward dog, plus a few others, in the shower each morning—that's one way to fit it in.

Our guess: once you start doing a regular stretch/yoga routine, you'll want to do more and more. These poses and stretches elongate your muscles—and also give you a set time to work on deep breathing (which is also associated with managing your responses to stressful events).

Do What You Love. What's the best exercise you can do to burn more calories, fry more fat, and get in the best shape of your life? Some may say squash or swimming. Some may say CrossFit. Some may say yoga . The reality: They all can be really good, if you perform them consistently and with good form. So do you know what the best exercise really is? The one you love. Because if you love it, you're going to stick with it—and perhaps even do it when you think it would feel kinda nice to be butt-down on the bed watching *Law & Order* reruns. So even though we outlined the optimum list above, you should make it a mission to experiment, to try new things, to be bold and hang out with a friend who swears by SoulCycle or Orangetheory or whatever the exercise du jour is. Maybe for you it's walking your dog in the morning and at night—and heck, you can even fit in intervals with a dog who likes to go fast and then take a few minutes to sniff around. If there's one sentence that's an absolute truth about physical activity, it's

JEAN SAYS: Running for me!

this: *You never regret having exercised.* Getting there is the hard part, so if you can find the activities you most enjoy, then, well, you answered the question at the beginning of this paragraph.

Don't Go Crazy. Temptations come in all forms, be they with marshmallows or mates. Here's one that comes when you start to get fitter and fitter: to become some sort of exer-crazy person—that is, someone who goes to extreme after extreme when it comes to training. Run longer or faster, or take on a crazy challenge, or just do more than what's necessary for optimum health and fitness. While there's much to be admired about these physical beasts, they also are rolling the daredevil dice because this is exactly when you increase your risk of injuries. Why does that matter? Because when you're injured, that's when you fall out of a routine (and can't perform the activities that will keep you healthy). And that's not even mentioning the health risks of the actual injury. While this doesn't apply to everyone, it is worth thinking about. Most of us don't take part in enough exercise, but there is a segment of the population that gets too much. That's not a license for not exercising, but it is a reminder that ideal health isn't about the most exercise and the least food. In fact, more than two hours of exercise in a row, even after maximum conditioning beforehand, causes you to exceed the free radical–buffering capacity of your cells and end up aging yourself. Focus instead on creating your own natural equilibrium between inflow and outflow to help your body find a balance that it won't naturally find on its own.

CHAPTER 10

Addition, Subtraction, Multiplication

‹‹•————————————————›››

Make more, spend less, and watch your
wealth grow exponentially

$

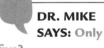 **JEAN SAYS:** I'll admit it. I bought five. And I had a very elaborate plan for what I was going to do with the money after I won.

DR. MIKE SAYS: Only five?

From the point in time that humans had bounty to covet, many have fantasized about the windfall. Pirates want treasure chests, villagers want to seize the castle, and heck, even leprechauns ride the rainbow for a pot of gold. Modern-day desires aren't all that different. They just come in the form of hoping to hit the record-breaking Powerball numbers (c'mon, you bought tickets—just like us), or an idea for the next Facebook or Spanx, or a lucky pull at a Vegas slot. We dream of the pot of gold. There are even scientific names for the phenomenon—*rescue fantasy* and *Cinderella complex*—but whatever you call it, we all occasionally dwell on the well-heeled fairy godmother who is going to come in and save us.

Unfortunately—and we all know this—these dreams are mostly just that: dreams. Entrepreneurs have goals that involve dreaming big—yes, you need to dream big and have a plan to make it work. That's ambition—it has pragmatism behind it. Wishing has no plan. The odds of receiving a change-your-life windfall of cash are about the same as those of (successfully) tightrope walking across Niagara

Falls (which only Nik Wallenda has done)—and much less than those of being attacked by a shark (1 in 11.5 million), dying from a bee sting (1 in 6.1 million), or being struck by lightning (1 in 3 million). #justsayin

But that's OK. Just because your fortune likely won't come in the form of 04-08-19-27-34-10, that doesn't mean you can't create your own stash of cash. It takes more than luck, of course. The fact is, there's money to be made, and money to be saved, and once you invest it your money *will* grow. It takes strategy, smarts, patience, trust, and a plan to work on your own inflow-outflow formula.

In the health equation we discussed in the previous chapter, we talked about the calorie being the main form of currency. In your wealth equation, your main form of currency is, well, currency.

The equation is simple:

Make more money. Spend less money.

Do that and whatever's left can be used to create opportunities in your life, perhaps with a mixture of spending some of it now (to increase life satisfaction in your present) and investing some for later (to ensure that you have life satisfaction in your future). That's what AgeProofing is all about: living longer better (including by not running out of money or worrying about doing so). In this chapter we'll discuss that exact formula—how you can increase your income and keep spending in check.

In the old days, that simple equation was as easy as it was crude. You made money, and you could spend only what you earned. So if you didn't make enough to pay for bread or a roof or a horse and buggy, then you didn't get bread or a roof or a carriage straight out of *Downton Abbey*. But with the advent of credit cards and unsecured personal loans, we could borrow on the money we didn't have. Those new advances, while tempting and helpful , created equations that often had negative numbers on the other side of the equal-sign.

JEAN SAYS: For the record, I'm not anti–credit card (as my wallet will attest). I'm a believer that they are great tools for people who have the ability to use them wisely. Not everyone has that ability.

DR. MIKE SAYS: How would I travel without a card to charge airline and hotel charges? But I was taught early to pay the charges off 100 percent, before the card companies add charges that would require a magnifying glass to find in the agreements I signed.

JEAN SAYS: You'd use a debit card!

That's the crux of our collective financial problem today: many of us spend more than we earn.

Consider these stats:

- A 2015 Nielsen survey showed 40 percent of Americans are living paycheck to paycheck. Although 55 percent of these people make less than $50,000 a year, 24 percent make between $100,000 and $150,000. Housing, food, and communication devices are the big sinkholes. Lifestyle purchases, like meals out, are also contributing.

- About 43 percent of households "revolve," or don't pay off their credit-card balances in full each month, according to the most recent Survey of Consumer Finances from the Federal Reserve. The average household with credit-card debt owes more than $15,000, and the average interest rate is about 15 percent, which means that just *carrying* that debt costs about $2,250 a year.

DR. MIKE SAYS: Wow. Fifteen percent, and the banks pay only 1 or 2 percent to the feds. That's a large difference; how do they get to charge us so much yet have to pay so little to get the money to loan to us?

- According to the Survey of Consumer Finances, 45 percent of Americans don't save anything. Yikes.

Why is this happening? You can blame it on the intersection of a few reasons, some economic, some behavioral, and some biological. The basis is simple economics: the cost of living is outpacing our incomes. Median household income rose 26 percent from 2003 to 2015, while total household expenses rose 29 percent. Some expenses have grown significantly more; medical costs, for instance, are up threefold since 1999, and food and beverage costs are up 37 percent. And don't even get us started on the cost of college.

Another reason is that, as we discussed in the opener to this section, we're programmed to give in to temptation—to satisfy our urges to survive the day. When researchers examine the brain as it makes choices, they find that the brain gets a dopamine rush when we buy things we want. We crave dopamine, because it's one of our feel-good hormones. To continue the brain drip of dopamine, we need to keep the faucet running—that is, the coffee that you buy in the morning is nice for a while, but soon you're craving grander stuff. That's because what becomes typical is no longer novel, so the dopamine flood becomes a trickle. You need to increase the volume or increase the novelty to keep that dopamine coming. In the context of spending, you can see how that snowball works. And that puts us at the wrong end of the financial equation, where the outflow is greater than the inflow.

So our goal in this chapter is to help you balance it all out: increase the inflow and decrease the outflow. When the scale tips in favor of inflow, you can then take the extra and invest it in your future—and watch it multiply and multiply and multiply, creating wealth and opportunities for today and tomorrow.

Inflow: Pumping Up Your Payday

When it comes to health and controlling your calories, the decisions and behaviors are all yours. You decide whether you eat the Lucky Charms or the egg whites, grilled veggies, and fruit for breakfast. You decide whether you'll have a 4,000-calorie dessert or be satisfied with a few bites. Lemonade, or water with lemon. You have full control over what you let into your GI tract.

With money, it's a whole different ball game. It's not as if you just have to decide that you *want* more money. It's partially (at least for most of us) up to a third party, like a boss or a client or a customer or any number of different people who may determine the amount of your paycheck. That, in many ways, makes the economic inflow-outflow equation more frustrating and more difficult than the health one. But make no mistake: the inflow part of the equation is the one that can change your overall financial picture (just as food inflow does to your waistline).

Now, we're all in different job circumstances. Some of you have had stable jobs for a long time. Some have lost jobs. Some of you have changed careers. Some have strung together a professional life that includes working three jobs at once, always looking for the next big thing. Because of this, it's not easy to generalize about what everyone must do to increase his or her income, but we can make a few major strategic points about increasing your inflow.

For one, even if you think you're in a stable situation, you have to focus on your income because your job is your most important investment. That's because it's exponential. As you grow in your career and increase your salary, you have the potential to save and invest even more money. So if it's been years since you evaluated whether you're fairly paid, or asked for a raise, take the time to do it. If you don't ask, the answer is always no. (We discuss workplace income and expenses in depth starting on page 24.)

The other point that's worth making here is this: no matter your job situation, we now live in a world where you can make a lot of money NBN (no boss needed). That's a result of our sharing economy—the growing marketplace of transactions between two parties, usually via a digital platform. You can save a ton of money through these services. For example:

- Rather than buying new clothes at a department store, you can buy used clothes on Tradesy or rent them at Rent The Runway.
- Rather than hiring a moving company, you can get moving help on Taskrabbit.
- Rather than owning a car, you can order an Uber or pick up a Zipcar.
- Rather than staying in a hotel, you can stay in homes or rent rooms through Airbnb.
- Rather than getting a loan from a bank, you can borrow from other people through Prosper Marketplace.

In 2013 the worldwide sharing economy market was $26 billion. It's now over $110 billion (and growing), and there are 80 million sharers in the United States. This sharing economy is booming for a number of reasons. One, technological advances are making these transactions easier (we're all carrying smartphones and getting comfortable with payment systems like PayPal and Venmo). Two, because we live in an era when wages are stagnant, we have had to figure out ways to get scrappy—and to make more out of less. That has created opportunity. Finally, because today's companies are no longer like our grandparents' companies—few standard workweeks, few pension plans, few 50-year careers with the same company—we have all had to rethink what it means to have a career. Employees in prior generations had a single career at an average of three or four companies. Today's workers have three or four careers and an average of 12 jobs. That general instability creates an economic system in which people are searching for independent opportunities to increase income.

Today many people are working in this gig economy—you may have a main job and a side job, you may have four side jobs but no full-time one, you may work your tail off for six months straight on a lucrative contract, then take a month off, or any combination thereof. According to estimates from the Government Accountability Office and Bureau of Labor Statistics, about 30 percent of today's workers operate this way, up from 12 percent in 1999. The bottom line is: this economic structure creates both opportunity and angst.

But here's the opportunity and it's profitable. The sharing economy provides lots of ways to boost your income, depending on your talents and assets. For example, you can rent out part of your home through Airbnb or supplement your income as an Uber driver. But what if you'd rather bake or write or organize or whatever? You can take your talents and extend those services to people worldwide. Sites like Taskrabbit can connect you with people who are looking for your skills in everything from event planning and writing to accounting and computer help (and 35-plus other categories). All of this means that whatever your current salary, you can increase that amount. It may take some work, some time, and some trade-offs, but the opportunities to bump up this side of the equation are greater than in any previous era.

Outflow: How to Make the Cut

You'd think that the goal given by a make-more-money-for-retirement book would be to spend absolutely as little money as you can, so you can put every penny toward savings, investments, retirement accounts—always thinking about having enough money for down the line . Not so here. Our goal here isn't to deny you the subwoofers or the island vacation (or even the island in your kitchen) that you want to have right now. Our goal is to free you from financial handcuffs and debt, so you have enough money for the future *and* to enjoy your life today. So this section on outflow isn't about scolding you and telling you that you really should cut back on your bagel-shop habit, or your love of jewelry, or your antique Pez dispenser hobby. It's about creating a system of spending that works for your own needs and desires, as well as giving you the framework for deciding what's really important to you. It isn't about antispending. It's about spending sensibly. When you can get the outflow to work in

JEAN
SAYS: I have had the experience of being in Starbucks and catching people whispering to each other, "Jean Chatzky is in Starbucks." I get it. I've spent a lot of my career pointing out how much money you could be saving if you didn't spend $4.32 a day on a venti mocha-frappa-whatever. But I am not the money police. You want to spend your money on Starbucks, spend it on Starbucks. The point is to get you to make conscious choices about where you're going to spend this limited resource of yours and where you are not. By the way, my standing order is a grande misto with one and a half inches of 2 percent milk.

DR. MIKE
SAYS: Jean, go with the skim stuff or walnut milk. And make sure they aren't slipping added sugars or syrups in there—that turns coffee that should make you younger into a sugar delivery system that ages you and saps your energy.

JEAN
SAYS: Can't do it, Mike. But I did run six miles this morning.

DR. MIKE
SAYS: Bad food causes inflammation even if you exercise the calories away. By the way, I choose Dunkin' Donuts coffee 'cause I think it tastes better, and I know it is filtered through paper (another factor that is needed to make coffee a LUV-U food that makes you younger).

conjunction with the inflow, that's when you achieve financial security and freedom.

That said, it's also perhaps the hardest part of the financial puzzle. Why? Because of temptation. Because of credit cards that are over-used . Because it's hard to increase income and easy to increase spending. Because we live in a one-click society in which you can order shoes, plane tickets, anything you want 24/7, which makes it easy for us to fall prey to impulse spending.

As with most things we talk about when it comes to health and wealth, the two key points in dealing with these potential obstacles are (1) you have to be aware of where you are and aware of strategies; and (2) the more you can automate your good habits (rather than struggling over decisions every day), the more successful you will be.

As you look at your spending in relation to your income, the following are the strategies that will help you spend less, which will then allow you to save more. And in a way, you'll actually be able to spend more, too—but on the things that you really, really want, as opposed to those things that will just give you a quick fix.

Spending Smarts 1: Embrace the *B* Word

Yeah, yeah, yeah. We know. Budgeting is like a turnip. A lot of people don't like it, even though they know it's good for them. That's because budgeting reminds them of the things they're doing wrong (or the things they're simply not doing). The data are mixed about whether most people keep a budget, but some recent research shows that 60 percent of Americans do not. Whether you call it a budget, a spending plan, or your coffee-addiction-justification formula, it doesn't matter. What matters is that you are staying within the spending lines so that you have enough for emergencies, enough for the future, enough for the things you want that aren't necessarily needs. So creating your MMM (monthly money map, for those who cringe at the word *budget*) is a must-do if you want to make this formula work; there's no debate over whether you're going to create a budget. There are lots of ways to do it (and lots of apps and software that can help). You'll find our recommended work sheet at the end of this chapter, but no matter what system you use, you need to employ basic budgeting principles for your master plan. Here they are:

⤷ Know the end goal. No matter how you shake out the figures, you want the equation to let you pay yourself first by earmarking money for savings.

You'll have some wiggle room in how you get there (that's what a budget is, after all—you choosing what to spend money on), but the goal is to get you to that 15 percent margin in terms of money earned that you will save.

⤷ Log your income. How much do you bring in every month? If you work a regular job, it's easy to know. It is harder, but if you have a fluctuating salary (that is, your income varies from month to month based on the nature of your job, because you work freelance or hourly), here is how to figure it out:

Stabilized Salary	Fluctuating Salary*

Gross income
    – Federal, state and local taxes
    – Social Security and Medicare
    – Health insurance
    – Retirement savings
= Net income/take-home pay
	Last year's gross income
	    – Taxes owed
	= Last year's net income
	    ÷ 12
	= Approximate monthly net income

* If last year wasn't typical—or this is a new job, and you don't know what typical will be—then err on the side of caution and assume you'll earn less than you probably will. Anything extra is a bonus. Managing an irregular income can be tricky for budgeting purposes. The trick to surviving these ebbs and flows is to put a system in place: Deposit your checks into a savings account. Then write yourself a paycheck in the amount of that approximate monthly net (after-tax) income each month. You can set this up automatically, so a certain amount is moved from savings to checking by your bank on a regular schedule, simulating a traditional paycheck. You can pay yourself once a month, twice a month, however you find it easiest to budget.

⤷ Record expenses and track your spending. Use the work sheet on page 195. Go down the page and fill in each line (leaving blank the ones that don't apply and adding in items you have that may not be listed). For variable expenses (groceries, for instance), you need to track your spending for at least a few weeks and then plug in the average. Or use an interactive version of the budget that will do the math for you in real time every time you log any expenses; for it to do this accurately, you need to commit to adding these items every time you spend (and remembering to do so even when no money changes hands, such as when you order the new Adele album off iTunes, or when your automatic payment for cable or car payments goes through). You can find a free interactive version at JeanChatzky.com.

You also have to make sure to add quarterly or semiannual or annual expenses—like insurance premiums or property taxes. Divide the total annual expenses by 12 even if you pay them only four times a year.

➪ Create categories. Once you have all your expenses logged, use our work sheet to see what categories your expenses fall under. This will allow you to make adjustments by looking at our recommended breakdown. This will help you spotlight where you might be overspending, so it's easier to make cuts. The optimum (in our experience) breakdown based on a percent of your total take-home pay:

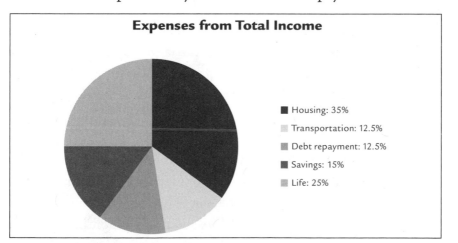

Expenses from Total Income

- Housing: 35%
- Transportation: 12.5%
- Debt repayment: 12.5%
- Savings: 15%
- Life: 25%

Housing: Includes rent/mortgage, taxes, insurance, and maintenance.
Transportation: Car payments, insurance, gas, maintenance.
Debt repayment: Credit cards, student loans.
Savings: Emergency cushion, retirement, college, other 401(k), other.
Life: Groceries, entertainment, clothing, health care, communication.

Here's something important to remember: you can borrow from any category, *except* for savings, to feed any other category. So if you can bring your housing costs in at 30 percent and you want to spend the extra money on transportation, fine. If you pay off your car, you can use the money that you were putting toward the car payment for any other category. If you're not already saving 15 percent, put any extra dollars there.

Spending Smarts 2: Choose Your Cuts

Now that you've created your budget, you have a real picture of where you stand. If you're in line—your income is greater than your expenses and you're saving 15 percent—then you're in great shape. Keep it going. If not, then you need to make some cuts to get to that 15 percent savings per month. To do that you have to ask yourself a series of questions: Where are you out of whack? Is your rent too high? Are you spending too much on transportation because of repairs, or because you're driving a car you really can't afford? Or is your weakness in the living expenses column? Do a little thoughtful (and honest) analysis to see where the numbers are bigger than anticipated. Depending on how far away you are, you will have to make either tweaks or major changes to get those numbers in line. Changes are easiest to deal with when you go from smallest to largest. If you cut small areas first, you may come up with enough money to leave the large ones as is. That said, making one big change—downsizing your abode, for example—can bring you in line with a single bold move. Some ideas for where to look, from small cuts to big ones:

> ↪ Eating out. If you're spending $197 a month for lunches out, that's roughly $9.40 every workday. You could limit yourself to buying lunch three out of five days and bring it the other two. That would save about $75 a month. Or you could limit yourself to $7 a day. That would save $50. Reduce your outflow by eating in cheaper restaurants, eating out fewer times, or finding coupons and deals.

↪ Similar "treats" that you can do without. Look at what you spend in dry cleaning, manicures, gifts, and other expenses that can be trimmed similarly. You'll make the most headway with small things you buy often.

↪ Monthly bills. These include bills for your cell phone, cable, landline (for those of you who still have one), and Internet, as well as payments for things like groceries. (If you spend just 15 minutes a week clipping coupons from the Sunday circular and make an effort to load up on items when they're on sale and avoid buying them when they're not, you can easily lop 10 to 15 percent off your grocery bill and save $1,000 a year.)

Every year, in fact, you should do a bill audit, which involves going through your monthly bills and seeing if you can drive down the costs. That means calling companies and asking them if they can cut you a better deal. Have a flyer from a competitor that was dropped on your doorstep or left in your mailbox? Now's the time to bring it up; often your current company will match it or do even better. If it won't, ask for a onetime credit or special ongoing discount; chances are the company has a promotion running at the time of your call. Finally, consider cutting back to save some dough. You might not be watching HBO this season. Maybe you can make an effort to hop on Wi-Fi wherever it's available and pay for fewer gigs of pricey data (be careful with security, though). Many people are even dropping cable altogether and watching the programs they really want to see online, perhaps with Hulu Plus and a Netflix subscription.

↪ Interest rates. Take a look at what rates you're paying for your mortgage, car loan, credit cards, and other debts. If you can reduce your interest rates and pay off your debts less expensively, it goes a long way. For example, a drop of just 1 percent could save you $120 a month ($1,440 a year) on a $200,000 mortgage. Car loans can be refinanced, too, and you're a good candidate for that if your credit score has drastically improved or you have a high interest rate because you didn't initially shop around for the best rate when you purchased the car. Check out rates at local banks and credit unions; unlike refinancing a mortgage, refinancing a car loan is inexpensive and fast. A drop of 3 percent on a four-year, $15,000 car loan means a savings of over $325 a year. Then there are student loans. Despite what you've heard, you may be able to refinance those as well—even the federal ones and PLUS Loans—and reduce your interest rates.

Finally, those credit cards: If you're a good customer, you pay on time, and you're slowly chiseling your way out of debt, it makes sense to call your card issuer and ask for a better interest rate. You'll be surprised how often they give it to you. That's because it costs them much more to recruit a new customer than to keep an existing one happy. Still, if you're told no, speak to a supervisor. If you're still told no, consider transferring your balance to another credit card with lower rates; just watch out for balance transfer fees, which usually run 3 percent.

▷ The tough choices. If you've gone through the small and medium-size changes and you aren't seeing enough movement to make your budget work, then you have to look at the largest line items on your list: housing, for one. Is your housing simply too expensive? Moving may have to be something you consider, or getting rid of a car, or pulling your kids out of private school and putting them into public school.

It might be worth considering the 80/20 rule, which says 80 percent of effects come from 20 percent of causes.

If you see you're spending a large amount of your money on a small amount of your stuff (usually transportation and housing, but sometimes outsize communication or food expenses pop up), then focus on those outsize areas. If you downsize where you're living, not only do you usually end up paying less on your rent or mortgage, but it doesn't cost as much to heat or cool your place, property taxes are lower, so is your insurance premium, and you're not spending as much on maintenance. Same with your car. If you're driving a car that's more efficient, you're spending less on gas, and often less on insurance and maintenance, too. And if you can go from two cars to one, the savings can be huge.

☞ The Antibudget Budget

Hate budgets as much as you hate getting weighed at the doctor's? You can wing it as long as you pay yourself first: Decide how much you need to save (reminder: 15 percent) and set that amount aside as soon as you get paid (via automation) before you spend anything else. Once that sum is sitting safely in your 401(k) and savings account (as well as your 529 and/or your IRA or any other accounts you're funding), take what's left and use it to cover your fixed expenses (rent, mortgage, utilities, car payment, communications, gas, health care, insurance, and the like). The rest (which should be approximately 15 to 25 percent) is yours to do with as you wish—in other words, you're free to spend the rest of your income on whatever you'd like.

Spending Smarts 3: Employ Spending Savvy

Some research shows that just 5 percent of people never spend more than they originally planned when they go shopping. That goes to show that no matter your best intentions, you (if you are among the 95 percent, and 95 percent of us are, after all) are subject to the impulse buy. From time to time, that's fine. But when it happens more frequently than not, you've essentially deleted your budgetary goals from your mind.

So while creating a budget forms your foundation, it takes a mindset to stick to that budget, to value savings, and from time to time to make the tough choices needed for the inflow-outflow equation.

If you really want to change your financial outlook, you have to make it part of your lifestyle (just the way effective diets work, too, right?). Some of the following tips are gathered from people who save 35 to 50 percent of their total income and thus buy financial freedom much earlier in their lives than most people—in other words, Super-Savers. Here, seven ways to spend and save smarter.

1. *Spend your values.* One thing SuperSavers seem to have tapped into is aligning their spending with the things they really care about. They're not living a monastic sort of life without any frills or any fun. They've just thought about what they do and don't care about. In our research about SuperSavers, one said he realized he had been spending at least $10,000 a year going to fancy restaurants and going out for drinks all the time with his friends. That didn't mean much to him, so he cut back. On the other hand, he did love to travel, so he didn't cut back there at all. One tip to help you: Keep a spending journal. Write down how much you spend and on what. Then go back a week later and again a month later and write down how you feel about having spent that money. You'll start to see a pattern in what's worth it to you and what's not.

2. *Be goal oriented.* The SuperSavers set BIG goals, goals other people might think of as unattainable. But having those goals puts them on the track to success. You can help yourself by committing to your goals on paper. A 2014 study from

Dominican University showed that people were 42 percent more likely to achieve their goals if they wrote them down. It's also important that goals be specific and measurable—involving, for example, an amount you are trying to put away—and that you give yourself a deadline. (Note: A fascinating study of Harvard Business School students showed that only 3 percent of them had written goals. Flash forward 10 years, and that 3 percent with written goals was earning 10 times more than the other 97 percent *combined*.)

3. *Automate as much as possible.* That means employing automatic deductions for 401(k) payments or other savings. Take the time to look at your balances every month or so. When you see how much success you're having, it's like seeing the first five pounds come off. It makes you want to keep going. You can also automate *how* your money is invested; that will keep you from tinkering with everything, especially when the market is down and you're tempted to sell. (Instead, during bear markets do what Warren Buffett does: focus on the total number of shares you have and concentrate on building this number. At lower prices you can accumulate shares faster.)

4. *Give yourself some tough love.* As we said, we're not the money police. But you should be. You should take a look at what you're spending on and ask yourself if it's really worth it. Take coffee. Half of the American workforce buys coffee at work, and two-thirds buys lunch rather than bringing it. That's a huge amount of money—the average American spends more than $3,000 a year on coffee and lunch. These things—along with ATM fees, lottery tickets, soda, cigarettes, credit-card interest, and bottled water—are budget busters. Now, if that daily trip to Dunkin' Donuts is meaningful to you, that's fine. But you should be aware of how much money you're spending on that. Because money is a limited resource, you

have to make choices. And you're going to be happiest if you're making them consciously rather than without thinking about them at all. It can also help to play some games with yourself—for instance, instead of just thinking of that coffee as a four-buck outlay, remind yourself that 10 of them could buy you that shirt you've had your eye on, or that a month's worth could buy you a ticket to the concert you've been dying to see. Reframe the expenditure to represent a goal that's more meaningful to you.

5. *Set up roadblocks.* Sometimes the key to not shopping is simply making it harder for yourself *to* shop, by either putting something in your way or removing a convenience. (When you think about it, this makes sense. One big reason we leave money in our 401(k)s is that there's a barrier—a penalty—to getting it out before retirement.) Some roadblocks you might want to try: don't save credit-card info on websites (so you have to enter it in every time you make a purchase), and unsubscribe from e-mail lists that are especially tempting, or simply make it a personal policy not to shop from the computer at work or after eight at night.

6. *Microanalyze your food choices.* One in three Americans waste $2,600 a year at the grocery store; that's $50 a week. Where food is concerned, a little planning goes a long way. And that's not even taking into account how much is spent eating out. With groceries, shop your cupboards and fridge before you go to the store. Your aim should be to eat it (whatever it is) before the expiration date. And when you go to the store, do it after you eat (a hungry shopper makes for a bad-choice shopper), chew gum to avoid tempting smells, and wear headphones (supermarkets sometimes slow down the music to get you to spend more time there).

7. *Slow down the non–grocery store shopping.* If you find yourself shopping just because, having to have the latest technology or

fashion, or shopping because of a mood—you're bored, tired, angry—it helps to have a set of rules:

- Think "one in/one out." Before you can add another gadget to your already exploding lineup, or another pair of pants to your already exploding closet, you have to get rid of one. Preferably, sell it, and use the money to defray the next purchase.

- Give yourself a discretionary gimme. How much money can you spend—per week or per month, you get to set the rules—without its hurting your budget or affecting your savings? Allow yourself that. If you want to buy something that costs more, save up for a couple of weeks to do it.

- Make a no-cost plan to boost your mood. If you're reacting to sadness or anger, try to do something else that'll boost your mood. Go for a run. Take a walk in nature. Invite a favorite friend over for a glass of wine.

- Keep a 30-day list 🗨. If there's something you want to buy on impulse, put it on your list. If you still really want it when the 30 days have expired, find a way to make it work. Most of the time, the item will be long forgotten.

DR. MIKE SAYS: I love this idea. Maybe I should use it with books, too, as I buy more books than I can read. After 30 days, a subject may no longer interest me. Such a strategy will help declutter my office, too, maybe.

Do research online before you shop, to determine what's actually a good price for the items on your list and what's just a sales tactic. Doing your homework will prevent you from getting ripped off—and help you focus.

Grow Flow: How to Multiply Your Money

Once you've built up some money from savings, you can start to distinguish between the kinds of savings you're keeping. You know that you have to have an emergency savings account, that you have retirement accounts. You may have accounts earmarked for college or for health care. After you have established those accounts, that's when the real fun begins—because that's when you can start to invest the money *in* these accounts, and that's where the real growth can occur.

There are a million approaches to take with investing, so if you're going to try to go at it yourself (or even if you're going to get professional help), you need to have an investment strategy to help guide you. These principles will get you started:

Know the Funds. While there are many nuances and decisions you can make with investments, building a portfolio doesn't have to be complicated. You can do it with just three funds: a total stock market index fund, a total bond market index fund, and a money market fund for cash you're going to need in the next three years. (You may want an international fund as well.) How you divvy up what goes where depends on your age. As you get older, the amount of risk you want to be taking (that is, the amount you will put in the riskiest category, stocks) should go down. One good formula: deduct your age from 110, and that's roughly the percentage you want to have in stocks or stock funds (if you're 40, that's 70 percent in stocks). This changes if you need access to your money sooner (such as if you need it for college). You'll note we singled out index and exchange-traded funds. (There are others we like, too, including target-date funds, which help manage your risk. We'll talk more about them coming up.) We like these funds because they're boring and healthy. All salmon. No cream sauce. They adhere to a particular index—like the S&P 500 or the Russell 2000, or any of thousands of others these days—meaning a computer is at work figuring out what to buy and what to sell in order to stay in line with that index. Where's the excitement there? Yawn. But they're cheap to own, cheap to trade, and cheaper on taxes.

That can make a big difference when it comes to your bottom line. Let's assume you've got $50,000 to invest—and you're choosing between an index fund with an expense ratio of 0.18 percent and a mutual fund with an expense ratio of 1.02 percent. Let's say that no matter how you decide to invest, you're going to earn a 6 percent return. (In other words, we're taking performance out of the equation.) Ten years out you will have spent some $7,000 less on expenses by going with the lower-cost investment, 20 years out more than

$24,000 less, and 30 years out nearly $61,000 less. This is money going into your pocket, not the fund company's. Now let's put performance into the equation. Over time, index funds consistently beat most actively managed funds. Take the S&P 500 for example. Over the last five years, 87 percent of large-cap fund managers have underperformed the S&P 500 index. Over the last 10 years, 82 percent.

What if you don't want to take as much risk as our guidelines suggest? It's important to understand *why* you're taking investment risk. You're doing it because you need your money to work for you. If you put all your money in savings, what happens? It earns maybe 1 percent a year (and a lot less than that in recent history). Thirty years from now, that $10,000 you put away will be worth $13,496. You're thinking, *But at least I didn't lose money.* In fact, you did. It's impossible to predict inflation over the next 30 years—but if it runs at the 2 percent that the Federal Reserve seems to feel comfortable with, that $13,496 will have only the purchasing power of about $7,500 in today's money. (And all of that is assuming you've got this money in a retirement account where it's protected from taxes. If you have to pay taxes along the way, you won't end up with nearly that much.) The only way to shield yourself from having to take investment risk is to save more. Much more. Investing for growth is a lot easier.

Assess Your Own Approach. Ask yourself if you're an ostrich or an anti-ostrich. According to a study from Carnegie Mellon University researchers, ostriches look at their portfolios less when the market is down and are less likely to trade in down markets. That's a good thing. Anti-ostriches do the opposite. They see bad news and act on it. Which are you? Men, older investors, and wealthier investors are more likely to be ostriches. Women, younger investors, and less wealthy investors are anti-ostriches. If you're an anti-ostrich, you need to figure out a way to ignore the bad news in the market, and the volatility. That could mean turning off the TV or not logging on to your accounts. And if you're tempted to take *more* risk than is wise for your age to boost your returns? Don't. Losing too much as you get closer to retirement is harder to recover from—you simply don't have the time.

Rebalance Your Assets. Once a year you should look at your portfolio and make sure that the percentages distributed among the three areas are in line with the kind of risk you want to take. Many people don't rebalance their investments and bring their assets back into alignment even once a year. If you don't do it yourself, you can get some reinforcements. Some options:

⮞ A target-date retirement fund. This type of mutual fund is available almost universally in 401(k)s and via brokerage firms. You buy one with a date in the title that syncs up with your retirement date, and it keeps your asset allocation—which manages the amount of risk you should be taking—on track. The average target-date fund has an expense ratio of 0.84 percent, according to Morningstar.

⮞ A managed account within your 401(k). This is a portfolio customized just for your needs, for which you pay a fee through your plan. About 40 percent of plans offer one, and they cost anywhere from a fraction of 1 percent of the assets you have in your account up to about 1 percent, depending on your plan. The good news is that according to a Morningstar study, people who opt for managed accounts save 28 percent more.

⮞ A roboadviser. This is a computerized financial planning service. (Wealthfront and Betterment were the upstarts in the market, now Schwab and Vanguard have gotten in, Fidelity is in, and there are other services specifically targeting women.) You tell the computer about your goals, age, and risk tolerance. It invests your money for generally one-quarter to one-third of a percentage point in fees. These services are mainly available for IRAs and discretionary funds; robos for 401(k)s and 529s are on the way, too.

⮞ A financial adviser/wealth manager. This is a human who will manage your money, generally for 1 to 2 percent of the amount you have under management per year or more. In general, the more assets you accumulate, the more you can expect a reduction in fees.

Future Flow: Make Your Money Last as Long as You Do

Not to complicate, but the elephant in the room when it comes to figuring out how much money you'll need in retirement is this: What if you live 10, 15, 20 years longer than you might think? That's a topic that scares the pants off a lot of people—in fact, outliving their money is the thing that scares people most about retirement (Allianz found it scares people more than death). A lot of your decision-making comes down to what you have in retirement accounts, Social Security, and other areas. Before you panic, take a moment to figure out where you are:

⮑ Take stock by getting an overall picture of what you're likely to get monthly or yearly in retirement. Add your projected income from Social Security payments to any pension income you're expecting, and then add 4 percent of the current balance in your retirement account. Is it enough? That's dependent on how you plan to live.

There has long been a rule of thumb that you should plan to replace 70 to 80 percent of your preretirement income (that is, your final annual salary before you retire) in retirement—and that that number should be adjusted upward, with inflation, each year. In real life, spending, and therefore the amount you'll need, isn't that linear, because people in their mid-40s to -50s spend the most, and then spending starts to decline before going up again late in life due to health care. Bottom line, the amount people need to replace varies from under 54 percent of preretirement income to over 87 percent. Look at your current cost of living and how you project your expenses will change in retirement. Go back and revisit the results of the retirement diagnostic on page 31—or take it for the first time if you blew it off before. That will give you the level of detail you need.

⮑ Choose the right rate of withdrawal from your retirement accounts. There are a couple of ways to make the money in your retirement accounts last, including annuities, which we'll discuss in a bit. One much-relied upon technique involves pulling out your funds sloooowly and methodically at a rate of about 4 percent. In years where the market is chugging along nicely and your portfolio is up, you can take closer to 4.5 percent; in years where it's dropped, you scale back a bit and take 3.5 percent. (The good news is that retirees are telling us they're doing this already with very little prodding; the difference seems to be one versus two vacations a year.)

⮑ Keep enough in cash—or cashlike vehicles—to get you over rough patches in the market. Once you're not earning an income, you're a little less flexible when it comes to money you need to live. The scenario you want to avoid is having to sell investments—typically stocks—right after the markets have tumbled because you have to pull the money out to pay your bills and otherwise live on. The advantage to long-term investing is that you can wait for the markets to come back and sell in a planned, measured way. That's why once you're in retirement, you need to tweak your asset allocation to increase the amount you're keeping in cash. You need to have at least two years' worth of the money you need to live in cash. How much cash is that again?

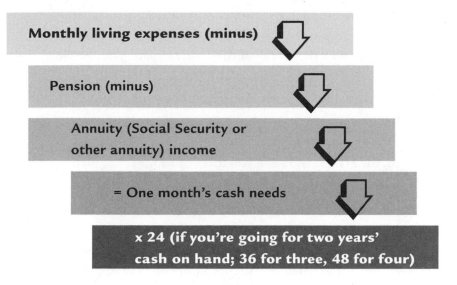

Monthly living expenses (minus)

Pension (minus)

Annuity (Social Security or other annuity) income

= One month's cash needs

x 24 (if you're going for two years' cash on hand; 36 for three, 48 for four)

Then, when it comes to actually withdrawing the money you're going to live on, you look at the markets. If stocks are up, you sell stocks and use that to fund your withdrawal. If they're down, you take from money already in cash or in a short-term bond fund, which shouldn't have seen much damage. And about once a year you rebalance, bringing all these accounts back to the appropriate levels: two years in cash or short-term government bond funds, 110 minus your age in stocks, the rest in a total bond market index fund.

➪ Cover your fixed expenses with insurance. What if you're not comfortable with the feeling that you might be able to withdraw only that 3.5 percent in years when the market is down? There's a way to hedge your bets. You do it by covering your fixed costs—that would be your housing, transportation, food, and health care at the very least—with insurance in the form of an immediate or deferred annuity. Let's just acknowledge the fact that *annuity* is one of those words that make the hair on the back of your neck stand up—and with good reason. Many annuities are lousy deals, laden with fees, incomprehensible even to many experts. A fixed, immediate annuity is not that. It takes a lump sum of money and converts it to a paycheck. You can pick the length of time—five years, your lifetime, even your and your spouse's lifetimes—for which you'll receive your payments. The longer the time frame, the lower your monthly take. You pay taxes only on the part of your annuity payment that is considered earnings, not on the principal. When you die, any money that's left stays with the insurance company that sold you the annuity. But if you outlive the money you gave the company, it keeps paying.

A deferred-income annuity is essentially the same thing, but purchased earlier. Again, you take a sum of money and give it to an insurance company, but then you put off payments, essentially until you need them, which is why such annuities are often sold for long-term retirement planning. The money invested in your account grows tax deferred, and when you're ready (and contractually able) you turn on the spigot and start receiving payments. (Because the money is invested while you're waiting to turn on the payments, you can turn a smaller sum into larger monthly payments than if you'd turned on the tap immediately.)

And now, thanks to some new rules from the Department of the Treasury, you can buy a deferred-income annuity called a QLAC (qualified longevity annuity contract) inside some retirement accounts. Recently the Department of the Treasury OK'd using up to 25 percent or $125,000 (whichever is less) of the money in your IRA or 401(k) to buy a QLAC (say Q-*lack*). You buy it when you're 50 or 60 with the intent of turning on the payments a decade or three down the road. The benefit is that the money you put toward a QLAC doesn't count toward the minimum distributions you're required to start taking from your retirement accounts at the age of 70½, so you're not taxed on it.

⮑ Be strategic about Social Security. Once you've decided that it's time to start taking distributions—or you turn 70½—you want to pull your money out of your retirement and other accounts in a way that minimizes your tax liability. Use money in taxable accounts first. Distributions from 401(k) and IRA accounts are income, and they are taxed as such. That means you need to consider your tax bracket. If you're on the cusp of moving to a higher bracket, and taking a certain amount in distributions will push you there, it's worth cutting your distribution back a bit—and possibly your spending as well—to stay in the less expensive bracket. The other factor to consider here is Social Security. As we noted earlier, for every year that you put off taking Social Security from age 62 to age 70, your monthly benefit grows by about 8 percent. Guaranteed. That's huge. So if you're eligible for Social Security and you need to choose between withdrawing from your retirement accounts and starting your Social Security benefits, you're better off doing the former. If you have a spouse in the picture, that's when things start to get a little more complicated. You may be better off taking one partner's benefits and letting the other's continue to grow. This is a case where it's smart to get personalized advice from MaximizeMySocialSecurity .com or SocialSecuritySolutions.com. For a small fee these companies will run scenarios for you and make a recommendation for how you should tap Social Security. If you're willing to pay a little more, you can spend time on the phone with a counselor. If you're working with a financial adviser, he or she may also have Social Security software that allows them to run these numbers without you having to pay an additional fee.

⮕ If you have a pension, make the lump-sum-or-annuity call wisely. The most important thing a pension can do for you is provide enough money to live—not lavishly but comfortably—for the rest of your life. When you pair it with Social Security, you should know your regular expenses (mortgage, car, food, utilities, Medicare premiums, etc.) are covered. In the rare case that you are not counting on your pension to help with these costs, deciding whether to take your pension as a lump sum or an annuity is easier. Either way you know you'll be OK. In all other circumstances, this is the most important pension decision you have. And many people, driven by human nature and the allure of a large check, make it incorrectly. Every pension plan is required to offer an annuity, or the ability to take your pension in the form of a paycheck that typically lasts the rest of your life. Many plans also offer the option to take your payout as a lump sum, which comes as one big chunk of change to do with as you please. Which is better? Lump sums are calculated based on the amount in your pension and two factors—longevity (or mortality) and the interest rate of high-quality corporate bonds. Our view: A lump sum is OK if you have enough money from other sources that you don't need your pension as a paycheck on which to live, or for your spouse to live on after you pass. It's also a wise choice if you think you can invest the money and get more than what you would earn. But an annuity makes sense if you need the regular income or don't trust your investing ability, especially if you expect to live a long time.

$ Budget Work Sheet

WORKING BUDGET

Use this budget work sheet to track your spending and expenses and figure out how you compare to our pie chart (page 177) recommendations. You may want to make copies before you start filling it out, or use the version at JeanChatzky.com that does the math for you. Work through each of the categories, then put the totals in your spending snapshot to see your overall picture. If the number on the bottom line of the snapshot is positive (and you're saving 15 percent), you're golden.

SPENDING SNAPSHOT

Total income	
Total expenses (includes savings)	
Income less expenses	

MONTHLY INCOME

INCOME	AMOUNT
Take-home pay 1	
Take-home pay 2	
Other	
Other	
Other	
Other	
TOTAL INCOME	

MONTHLY HOUSING EXPENSES

EXPENSE	AMOUNT
Variable home maintenance and decor (from tracking your spending)	

MONTHLY HOUSING EXPENSES (continued)

EXPENSE	AMOUNT
Mortgage/rent	
Second mortgage	
HOA dues	
Taxes	
Insurance	
Heat	
Water and sewer	
Telephone	
Electric	
Gas	
Trash	
Other	
Other	
Other	
Other	
TOTAL HOUSING	
PERCENTAGE OF INCOME	

MONTHLY DEBT EXPENSES

EXPENSE	AMOUNT
Student loan 1	
Student loan 2	
Credit card 1	
Credit card 2	
Credit card 3	
Credit card 4	
Other	

Other	
Other	
TOTAL DEBT	
PERCENTAGE OF INCOME	

MONTHLY TRANSPORTATION EXPENSES

EXPENSE	AMOUNT
Variable transportation costs including gas and parking (from tracking your spending)	
Car loan payments	
Insurance	
Regular public transportation costs	
Other	
Other	
Other	
TOTAL TRANSPORTATION	
PERCENTAGE OF INCOME	

MONTHLY LIVING EXPENSES

EXPENSE	AMOUNT
Dining out (from tracking)	
Groceries (from tracking)	
Clothes and grooming (from tracking)	
Health and fitness (from tracking)	
Child-related (from tracking)	
Entertainment (from tracking)	
Pet (from tracking)	
Miscellaneous (from tracking)	
Education/tuition	
Child support/alimony	

MONTHLY LIVING EXPENSES *(continued)*

EXPENSE	AMOUNT
Cell phone	
Internet	
Cable	
Life insurance	
Health insurance	
Disability insurance	
Long-term care insurance	
Vacations	
Charity	
Other	
Other	
Other	
TOTAL LIVING EXPENSES	
PERCENTAGE OF INCOME	

TOTAL SPENT	AMOUNT

MONTHLY SAVINGS CONTRIBUTIONS

SAVINGS	AMOUNT
Retirement	
Emergency fund	
College	
Other	
Other	
Other	
Other	
TOTAL SAVED	
PERCENTAGE OF INCOME	

AgeProof ESSENTIALS

1. Compound interest applies to both finance and health. When you save more, it grows and grows and grows (as the interest and returns keep building off the principal). The same is true for healthy habits—the better the base you have and the more automated your processes (like breakfast, lunch, snacks, physical activity including resistance exercises, and stress management practices), the more your good habits will grow, and the more energy you'll have.

2. The most important line on your health budget: high-quality foods. The most important line on your financial budget: saving 15 percent of your income.

3. Burn through your calories, not your paycheck.

Part VI
Go Time

The Science of Catching Up

No matter what you've done in the past, it's never too late (till you're six feet under) to get the body or bank account you want

We all know that there's a huge self-help industry in the country. Heck, this book and the work we've done throughout our careers are all part of that industry. The reason we've invested so much of our careers in this world: we believe in the merger of knowledge, awareness, and motivation, and how that union can give you the information and power you need to make positive (and automatic) changes in your life.

But here's a message that we don't like but that the self-help industry perpetuates (sometimes consciously and sometimes maybe not): That you have to be perfect. That, in order to get the body/home/lover of your dreams, you have to follow the prescribed plan *exactly* the way it's supposed to be done. That if you're not a perfect 10, you're an absolute zero.

Let's stop that line of thinking right now.

We're not after perfection. We're after better. We're after small steps that lead to big changes. We're after comfort, security, happiness, joy, energy—all of it.

Frankly, the pursuit of perfection is exactly what derails so many people in their self-help plans: when you go into a venture thinking

DR. MIKE SAYS: Most times when I am a buddy, and my buddy stops e-mailing me, he or she then says something like "Life got in the way on Friday, so I just stopped on Saturday." That's one reason a buddy is so important—for reminding you that one missed day or even three shouldn't stop you. Get back on that proverbial horse again, and ride to become AgeProof.

you have to be mistake-free and then you aren't, that frustration can be what ultimately derails even the best of intentions. Have a doughnut during your 21-day diet, and you convince yourself you might as well eat four jellies and maybe that Boston cream as well. Spend more money on a handbag that you don't need, and you figure why not, throw in the wallet while you're at it. Instead of making a mistake and moving on, so many people use one mistake to justify another 🗨. Life doesn't have to be a slippery slope if you don't let it become one.

Here's the thing. We're not programmed to be perfect, or even close to it. Heck, if people didn't make mistakes, pencils wouldn't have erasers, computers wouldn't have delete buttons, and spouses wouldn't need flower shops.

All of this is a way of saying that it's never too late. Never too late to change bad habits into healthy ones. Never too late to gain optimum health. Never too late to change your spending patterns. Never too late to save the money you need to live comfortably. Until the final buzzer of life sounds, you can call a time-out, change your game plan, and make changes that will count in the win column.

So if you have made mistakes in the past—and even if you have done so for years, decades, or an entire life—you can make up for lost time. Decades-long smokers can repair their lungs. Overweight people can eliminate diabetes. Chronic overspenders can build retirement accounts.

In fact, your body is designed with its own delete button.

That button comes in the form of stem cells.

Here's how they work: your cells turn over every seven years or so, and your stem cells serve as the main driver for repairing your body and regenerating your health. In fact, science tells us that the key to staying young and healthy, no matter what your age, is not avoiding injury but rather *repairing* injury. Take the case of a heart attack: When one happens, you need cells that will come in (you need to restore blood flow to the area so they can come in—get to the hospital to get that done) and repair the damage so your heart will be able to function in the future. Two kinds of cells can handle this repair—inflammatory cells and stem cells. When regular old inflammatory cells are called to duty, they create scabby-type tissue, which is OK for plastering over the problem so dead cells don't cause the heart to have a hole that leaks or spurts blood into your chest cavity and out of its arterial-to-venous plumbing system. But the scab just holds things together and doesn't contract like a muscle, so blood doesn't pump out normally. That's why you need stem cells. They come in to heal the heart by regenerating new pumping heart cells—and making it essentially as good as new.

How does your body decide which kind of cell to send in? Well, you have only a certain number of duplications of your stem cells, so if your body uses them to repair relatively minor damage—say from repeated sunburns—then there won't be enough ready when you really need them.

We want you to take two points away from this: First, that your body has a built-in mechanism to heal you—and essentially erase the mistakes of your past. And second, that you have some control over how long those stem cells last and how they respond—so you should be conscious in your behavior about what you earmark them for. That is, you don't want your stem cells to have to continually perform minor repairs throughout your life—like for sunburn or heartburn from chili dogs or the bad back you have because of inactivity or the other relatively small things that you do have some control over. Better to have those stem cells available to heal your body when it most needs it.

(If you need further evidence, consider longevity studies in Jerusalem that looked at people who started walking regularly at age 75. Those who did so had a 50 percent decrease in disability by the time they turned 88, and 50 percent more were still alive at 88 than those who didn't walk regularly. Never. Never. Too. Late.)

In many ways, what drives that stem cell action—and reverses the course of bad health—is your own actions, right? Your biology is related to your behavior.

One of the most fascinating developments related to reversing the effects of aging revolves around what experts call periodic calorie restriction, which means you eat lean-and-mean and low-calorie meals for five days a month. (It's not fully validated yet, so you want to talk to your doctor before trying it, but it holds promise in being able to repair your body and protect against cancer, diabetes, heart disease, and more.) In a set of new studies from the University of Southern California, Dr. Valter Longo and fellow researchers tested a supershort periodic relative fast diet strategy in which subjects ate low-calorie diets for five days a month for three months. Mice that did a similar program (eating different food from the human subjects) had fewer incidences of cancer, lost belly fat, had stronger immunity, and had sharper minds. They also lived longer.

Though it's still too early to tell, the "CR-or Fasting mimicking diet" (CR standing for calorie restriction) may work by flipping the healthy switches in your body and increasing your cells' resistance to stress. Even better if we humans experience what happened in the mice: when they went back to eating normal portions again (of healthful foods), that prompted some stem cell reproductive action, so they generated the potential to grow more stem cells. All you have to do is reduce calories five days out of every 31 . . . kind of like earning 8 percent on your money every year. Bottom line: when you need 'em, they'll be available to help repair and rebuild tissues throughout your body.

So we know our bodies have the resilience to bounce back from mistakes and problems. But what is the stem cell equivalent in the financial world? What is the five-day per month lean-and-mean plan? Wouldn't it be nice if some sort of cell could increase a credit score or pay off a credit card or get a lower interest rate on a mortgage? It doesn't quite work that way, but there is a similar mechanism.

To regenerate your financial life—that is, to learn from mistakes—takes a mix of motivation and automation. First, you need to understand why you're in a jam. And second, you need to create automated systems to turn the ship in the right direction. If you're looking for the magic action that will repair mistakes, it all lies in one phrase: *Save more, then let it grow.*

Savings can cure a multitude of financial ills—medical emergency, transmission breakdown, adult child on the rocks—just as your body's

DR. MIKE SAYS:

There's a company that provides the food, but basically the plan is 1,000 calories the first day and then 750 calories of a tomato-based soup each of the next four days, then resume your normal Mediterranean diet. The soup I make is 42 ounces of diced tomatoes and 42 ounces of water, plus 14 ounces of corn kernels and unlimited diced onions and spices to taste. I can have 17 portions of that a day without exceeding 750 calories. I continue to take my pills and supplements and vitamins and minerals, too.

processes can stop the blood pouring from wherever it's pouring in the event of an injury or emergency. Compounding—which is your money's version of being fruitful and multiplying, and happens when you invest your money to produce earnings upon earnings while you go about your daily business—is like your stem cells producing more stem cells.

And while it's more behavioral than biological, the key is that if you can get the saving/investing continuum to work without thinking about it, then in essence you have sort of created a financial DNA system—one that works without your having to do much.

Remember our sunburn example? Why would you want your stem cells to waste themselves on sunburn after sunburn after sunburn, when you'd much rather have them at your disposal when you really need them? Think of your money in the same way. Why would you want your savings diverted to the minor things in your life that really don't mean much—hello, impulse purchases—when you can have your reserves available for things that are much more important?

While we know that there's science behind your ability to bounce back from mistakes, that's only the mechanism through which you make those repairs. The real instigator of any repairing process comes down to one word: *values*.

When you ask yourself what you value in your life, it's a lot easier to make choices that will make your body and bank account bounce back—and allow you to live the way you really want to.

CHAPTER 11

Making Up for Lost Coin

«◄──────────────────────────────►»

When you have to play financial catch-up,
some strategies will help you get back in the game

$

Y ou hear this advice over and over: if you start saving for retirement at the age of 20, you'll be set for life. That's because the power of compound interest can take your measly savings as a young adult and turn it into millions by the time you're ready to retire.

Great advice.

IF YOU'RE 20!

JEAN SAYS: Heck, even 30 is great!

But what if you didn't get (or take) that advice when you were younger? What if you're now 40 or 45 without much retirement savings, and you don't want to work at Taco Bell until you're 93? (Not that there's anything wrong with Taco Bell 💬.) What if you're in any kind of less-than-optimum financial situation—like climbing out of debt or digging out from bankruptcy? Is it too late to save more, spend less, or make money?

DR. MIKE SAYS: But don't get the hard tortilla shells, or the soft ones. Or any type of red meat or cheese. Some of the chicken salad options are OK.

It's not. While you can't technically make up for lost time when it comes to the exponential rate of growth of that compound interest, you can strategize about the best ways to erase mistakes and make that murky-as-mud financial outlook look clearer than Caribbean blue.

In this chapter we're going to take you through some very common financial do-over situations—that is, tough spots in which you'd like to turn back the hands of time. And we'll give you the tactics for erasing mistakes and putting those metaphorical stem cells in action—to act as financial healers that will put you in a more secure position. But before we dive into specific scenarios, it's smart to take a look at some of the bigger strategies that will help you climb out of any money-made hole you find yourself in.

➪ Be goal oriented. Those who save a lot of money set big goals—goals that others might think of as unattainable. But those big goals? *They're* what gets you on the right track, especially—as you'll remember from the last chapter—if you write them down. Make sure your goals are specific and measurable and that you have a deadline.

➪ Plan to work longer. Maybe you thought you were going to retire at 62 with a banjo on one knee and a grandkid on the other. Well, enjoy the babies and whatnot, but just think about extending your work life a bit, even if it's part-time.

By keeping income, well, incoming, you do several key things simultaneously that can help you recover from any setback. You give yourself more years to contribute to retirement. You give yourself more time before pulling money out of your retirement plans (which gives that money more time to compound). You reduce the number of years the money in those retirement plans has to last. *And* you delay tapping into Social Security (hopefully until you're at least close to age 70), which is a big advantage. Even if you're determined to stop working at your current job, tapping into the gig economy or consulting part-time can help you accomplish all these things. Or look at alternative ways to add cash flow, like investing in rental properties.

▷ Don't tinker with your investments. Develop an investment plan and focus on funding it—not changing it—unless you discover a fundamental problem with the mix of stocks and bonds in your portfolio. It can be very tempting to try to recover from a setback by increasing the risk in your portfolio to earn more. Bad move. This can set you back even further. Stay the course.

▷ Consider the big cut. Remember those SuperSavers? They work their magic not by cutting out a green tea here and there, but by focusing on the large expenses. Housing is generally the biggest expense in any American's budget (well, it's the biggest after taxes), so it is an obvious place to make a big impact. Choose a home that you can pay off quickly and that is smaller than you can afford, and sock away the rest. And dump the gas guzzler for something smaller and more efficient, keep your car after it's paid off, or go from a two-car to a one-car home. Now, some specific tactics for individual setbacks:

Fix It!

"I have too much debt."

You know how you climb a mountain? One lung-frying step at a time. No matter how insurmountable your debt may seem, you can get back to even ground—and then tip the scales in your favor to begin to save more. It just takes a smart plan (and then you have to stick to it). Remember, if your goal is to climb to the top of the mountain, you don't take three steps down every time you take one step up. Even if you have the occasional stumble—and you might—you keep going until you reach the top. When you get there, you can take in the beautiful view. So no matter if your debt is the size of a small hill or Mount Everest, you just keep plugging away. This is how.

Organize	Write down all the debt you have and the interest rate of each piece of debt. Then put them in order—highest interest rate at the top, lowest at the bottom.
Refinance	Reduce those rates where you can by refinancing mortgages, student loans, car loans, etc. Transfer debt on higher-rate credit cards to lower-rate cards. (Make sure balance transfer fees don't negate the advantage you gain.)
Pick Them Off One by One	Now put all your extra monthly budget toward the highest-interest debt. The return on paying off a 24 percent credit card is substantially greater than the return you get from paying off a 12 percent one or a 4 percent mortgage (the return is *equal* to the interest rate). So wipe out the big interest rates first. With the first one done, move to the next and the next.
Use Debit	Don't use credit cards while paying down debt. If you take out a home equity loan to pay off credit cards, don't use those now-free cards and rack up the debt again. Put 'em in the freezer if you have to.
Close the Cards	If your credit score is above 760, and you have more cards than you need, close the cards as you go through the process. (How many cards do you need? Enough that you're spending only 30 percent of your limit each month, then paying that amount off.) If you need to build your score, you can leave the cards open (as long as you don't use them). Then close one every six months, unless you're applying for a mortgage or car loan (in that case keep them open until that's complete).

Fix It!

"I lost my job."

Whether you get fired, laid off, downsized, or told, "We're moving in a different direction," nobody—absolutely nobody—likes getting the employment ax. While free time might be appealing for a week or two, zero paychecks is appealing for approximately never. That's why losing a job is one of the biggest slam-on-the-brakes moments in the lives of people who experience it. Everything—from mental stability to financial dreams—gets placed on hold as you go from thinking about saving to thinking about surviving. When you lose your job, you have two choices: you can sap your savings and fall apart, or you can keep your financial life in one piece. Here's how to do just that.

DO THIS	DON'T DO THIS
Create an austerity budget—that is, a budget based on reduced spending. Take a look at your expenses over the past six months and prioritize based on wants and needs. Project how long your savings will last based on this new budget.	Spend as you have been by using a home equity line of credit (though it's a good idea to apply for one if you foresee a layoff). In a pinch it can serve as a tax-deductible emergency cushion, but remember you will be borrowing against your home.
Apply for unemployment. You've paid into the system; you are due benefits (just know it may take a few weeks before checks roll in).	Drop your health insurance. It may be tempting to cruise by without benefits, but a large medical bill without insurance will wipe you out. Under COBRA (the Consolidated Omnibus Budget Reconciliation Act of 1985) you can keep your benefits from your previous employer for 18 months, but it's often very expensive. Less expensive options can include going on a spouse's plan or looking for a plan on a health-care exchange.
Find a part-time job or gig while you're looking for a full-time one. Some money coming in is better than no money coming in. Now is also a good time to raise funds by clearing out things you're not using and selling them.	Tap your retirement account. You'll have to pay taxes and a 10 percent withdrawal penalty if you're under 55 (it's usually 59½, but 55 if you get laid off). Better to put a hold on saving than to dip into money earmarked for retirement. The Roth IRA is an exception to this in that you can get at your contributions without penalty, and you've already paid taxes. Still, try to keep your hands off.
Call creditors if you're going to be late. Sometimes they'll let you miss a payment (or work out some other preferential payment terms) without reporting you to credit bureaus. You can also ask creditors to put payments for student loans on hold (though interest will accrue during that time).	Skip the major bills—like mortgage or car loan or utilities. And don't neglect to pay taxes and student loans, because the IRS and federal student lenders have the ability to garnish wages. Credit cards are on the bottom of your list because the only repercussion is a bad credit score if you miss a payment. Not ideal, but the lesser of evils.

Fix It!

"I'm getting a divorce."

It's difficult to generalize divorce scenarios because they come in all shapes, sizes, and varieties. Some are amicable. Some are messy. Some are complicated (especially if they involve children), and some can be quick and clean. But one thing is consistent: there will be some kind of division of assets. And because of that, you must be prepared for all the possibilities. Depending on how the marriage was set up in terms of bill paying and financial responsibilities, you may not know the full picture of your family's fiscal outlook. You can't make a fair and equitable break if you don't. It's especially tough to meet the goals you've previously set (about retirement or paying for college) when you're unexpectedly going it alone.

If you're in this situation, you need to protect yourself. Here's how:

Step 1: *Take precautions if things are messy.* In most states you can remove some of the funds (divorce financial planners recommend no more than 50 percent) from a joint account, provided you have legitimate reason to be concerned that the assets are in jeopardy, and place the money in another account for safekeeping. You can also, if you're a wage earner, deposit some of your money in your own account for safekeeping (although keep in mind these are still considered marital assets). But note: This isn't the time to go on a shopping spree. The court is going to ask you to prove that you moved the money to protect it, not spend it. You'll also need a legitimate reason you felt you had to do so, and spite isn't going to fly. Talk to your attorney before making any major moves.

Step 2: *Create a detailed budget.* Understand what your expenses are, both the necessary ones, such as rent, mortgage, and utilities, and the unnecessary ones, maybe personal training, beauty, and entertainment. If you end up having to fight for your fair share, you'll know where to start your negotiations.

Step 3: *Educate yourself about all the family's finances and assets.* Many people don't know how much money they have as a couple. Some might be surprised to learn that their spouse has retirement plans from past employers or that certain businesses are more (or less) valuable than they thought. Gather all important information, like past tax returns, bank and retirement plan statements, and credit-card or loan balances. The idea is to get a rough estimate of what the marital estate is worth, inclusive of your home if you own it, your 401(k) and IRA balances as well as your spouse's, your mortgage or other debt, your regular bank accounts, and any other assets or liabilities. And don't agree to carry all the fixed expenses of living in the marital home if you're the one residing there, even if it's just while it's on the market to sell. (Selling a home can take substantial time.)

Step 4: *Think carefully about your settlement.* Settlements come in two basic forms—lump sums and sums distributed over time. A lump sum is very good for the person who doesn't want any ties to a former spouse (perhaps you fear the spouse could lose a job and declare bankruptcy or might be difficult to deal with). Plus you get immediate access to the money to pay off debt or buy a house. That access, though, can also be a negative. Are you liable to make mistakes early on—to overspend—particularly if this is the first time you've been in charge of your finances? The one positive of not going with a lump sum settlement is that it does make you budget. As you weigh your options, make sure you understand (your attorney and accountant should help with this) the value of the stream of payments you may be receiving. If you're going to get $10,000 a year for eight years, the lump sum is going to be less than $80,000—the present value of those total payments. Many people also don't realize that maintenance payments can stop if you remarry or cohabitate. So if you see yourself remarrying in the future, that makes a lump sum more interesting to you.

Next you have to consider the assets in your settlement. It seems cleaner to ask for investments to be converted to cash—i.e., for investments to be liquidated before the account is divided. This will reduce fees, make it easier to track transfers, and help eliminate errors, but there are reasons not to do this as well. Taxes will have to be paid, and there need to be agreements about who is going to pay those taxes. Also, there could be investments you don't want to liquidate—say you bought Apple or Google stock years ago—because you don't want to realize a huge capital gain right now. In that case you can split the investment itself (being cognizant of the cost basis on the individual shares) and each decide what to do with your shares independently. Note: to split retirement or pension assets while keeping them in the plan and preserving the tax advantages, ask your attorney about a qualified domestic relations order or QDRO (pronounced *quadro*).

Step 5: *Before or as the divorce comes through, consciously uncouple your finances.* You may have a piece of paper saying you're separated and/or divorced, but many people don't actually go through the process of untangling their finances until it's too late. They might continue to maintain a joint checking account or a joint savings account. Close them all. Then make sure all the assets given to you in the divorce (such as the house) are retitled in your name only. Do the same thing with all the parts of your estate. Make sure your beneficiary (for your IRA or 401(k)) is no longer your ex-spouse. That would be a big no. Review your insurance as well. You may even want to consider adding to your life insurance just in case your former spouse ends up getting married and starting another family, leaving him or her without enough assets (in your opinion) to support your kids.

Step 6: *Get to work at getting back on track.* Take charge of your financial life. Create an emergency fund. Plan for how to start bringing in income, if you don't have an income already. If maintenance is going to be your only support, you should have a life insurance policy on your ex-spouse so that if he or she passes away, you have enough money to continue to live on.

Step 7: *Establish credit in your own name.* This is something to do even if you're not getting divorced. It entails having a major credit card (not a department store card) in your name alone, and a bank account in your name alone. Close out joint bank accounts and lines of credit to protect your credit from future expenditures.

Step 8: *Keep your existing health benefits as long as you can*—and be careful about ending one plan without having coverage elsewhere. Note: Shopping on the exchange at HealthCare .gov (while it still exists) can be less expensive than paying for COBRA coverage through your former spouse's employer.

Fix It!

"I'm getting a late start saving for retirement."

The biggest financial regret that most people have has nothing to do with Louboutins or Lamborghinis. It has to do with the fact that they haven't saved enough money for retirement—that they didn't start saving earlier. If you think you're among them, you probably are. But if you're looking to see how much you're behind, go back to page 31 and retake our retirement assessment. The later you are in the game, the more you're going to have to swing the pendulum from consuming today to saving for tomorrow. And if you haven't started and you're in your late 40s or early 50s, you should understand now that this is not something you can fix by skipping the coffees and bypassing the manicures.

Let's say you're 55, earn $80,000, get 2 percent annual raises and have $80,000 already saved. If you save 15 percent annually for the next 10 years and earn 6 percent on your investments a year, you'll end up with just under $320,000 at age 65. But if you can get yourself to save 20 percent of your income instead, you'll increase what's in your retirement coffers to $380,000. How are you going to come up with that money?

> Use catch-up contribution provisions to enable your extra savings to grow tax-free. Of course, whatever you're stockpiling should go into your retirement accounts. But once you hit the big 5-0, you can contribute more to your retirement accounts each year—and you should. An extra $6,000 in your 401(k) or 403(b), $3,000 in your SIMPLE (Savings Incentive Match Plan for Employees) IRA, and $1,000 in your traditional IRA or Roth annually can go a long way. And if you have a health savings account, you can kick in an extra $1,000 a year once you turn 55. (Note: you and your spouse can make separate catch-up contributions.) These are current catch-up contribution limits; they will likely increase over time.

> Downshift. Pronto. In order to stash away those big numbers, you're going to want to trim your cost of living significantly, sooner rather than later. As we said, the substitutions we're talking about here aren't along the lines of bringing leftovers for lunch rather than buying takeout (although that never hurts). Look at the big items: housing, transportation, education, even health care. You want to sacrifice quantity without quality.

> Make a plan to work longer. Remember the 55-year-old who had $80,000 in retirement funds and was getting 2 percent

raises a year? Boosting his savings rate from 15 percent to 20 percent will bring his total by age 65 to $380,000. But if he enjoys his work enough to continue for three more years, he'll have $515,000. Plus during those years he wouldn't be withdrawing from his 401(k), and Social Security could grow. That Social Security growth is key. Just a reminder: for every year between age 62 and age 70 that you delay starting your benefits, they grow at a rate of about 8 percent guaranteed. You need to live beyond age 80 for waiting to take benefits at 70 to pay off, but these days most Americans—and certainly the vast majority of AgeProof ones—do.

Fix It!

"My credit score looks more like a bowling score."

There are some things in life you want to plummet—your LDL cholesterol numbers, your weight, airfares. Your credit score's not one of them. A low credit score means you're going to have a harder time getting loans on big-ticket purchases (like homes), not to mention that it just clouds your entire financial picture (and, let's be honest, makes you feel lousy). Ideally you want your credit score to be 760 or better. But even 720 or better is considered OK. Anything lower is where trouble begins because you'll pay more if you're looking to borrow money for a car or a home, or even just get a new credit card. Things that will make your credit score drop fast: filing for bankruptcy (up to 250 points), not paying bills on time, letting debt fall into collections, and overusing your available credit lines or applying for excessive credit. Even closing credit cards and reducing the amount of available credit you have can be damaging.

Quickly repairing credit is sort of like a cleanse diet: it sounds as if it can work fast, but the reality is that there's no instant fix. What you can do is work on building back your credit over time (usually a year or two).

DO THIS	DON'T DO THIS
Pull your credit report from AnnualCreditReport.com (you can pull one free report from each of the three major credit bureaus—TransUnion, Experian, and Equifax—via this website each year). Comb over it looking for information that's inaccurate. You can't get negative information removed from your credit reports. Rather, you have to wait for it to fade away like the memory of a bad date. But you can ask to have mistakes removed using the dispute process each of the bureaus has set up on its individual website: TransUnion.com, Experian.com, or Equifax.com. Research from the Federal Trade Commission shows that 20 percent of credit reports have mistakes.	Use more than 30 percent of your available credit lines. Try to stay closer to 10 percent. Credit utilization (the percentage of your available credit that you're using) represents about one-third of your score. It is just as important as on-time payments. And if you're overusing your credit lines (even if you're paying your bills off in full each month), it isn't helping your score. If you know that you're using more than 30 percent of your available credit lines, making a payment in the middle of the billing cycle (or whenever the utilization gets too high) will solve the problem. Or request an increase in your credit lines and then don't use the additional capacity. Utilization is measured both on each card individually and on all your cards combined. So you can't solve the problem by overusing your favorite card (say the one that gives you the most miles or other perks) while not using others in your wallet.
Pay your bills on time every time. This often requires you to set up a system to protect against lateness, such as by putting bills on automatic payments from your checking account or scheduling reminders in your calendar (some billers will even e-mail you a nudge). You  can also e-mail or call your creditors to ask them to adjust due dates so that the bulk are all due at one or two times a month, to help keep you organized.	Apply for new credit while trying to bring up your score. It's better to ask for increases in your current credit lines. An application for credit forces a "hard pull" of your credit report (compared with the "soft pull" that happens when you get a credit-card solicitation in the mail). A hard pull is a sign to the credit bureaus that you need money, which takes your score down a notch.
Maintain a mix of forms of credit. It shows lenders you can successfully pay off a variety of loans.	Close old cards. That reduces your credit lines, which can hurt your all-important utilization.

JEAN SAYS: I pay bills when they come in, which not only protects against lateness but has been shown to boost happiness.

Fix It!

"I filed for bankruptcy."

The dead end of personal finance is bankruptcy. You feel as if you've driven yourself into a corner and there's no way out. Filing for bankruptcy happens when you can't keep up with your debt payments and you have run out of options. If you file, you generally have two choices.

Chapter 7. In the more drastic form of bankruptcy, you have to sell most of your assets (clothes, a car, furniture, and other things that make it possible for you to keep working will be exempt). To be allowed to file Chapter 7, you have to pass a "means test" by which the courts determine you're unable to pay your debts. It's based on your disposable income minus expenses (and varies by location).

Chapter 13. Here you work with a judge to set up a three- to five-year repayment plan, and if you successfully make all your payments, your debts will be discharged. It's the way to go if you have a house or car that you don't want to lose (and have a steady-enough income after your plan is set up to maintain those payments).

Both kinds of bankruptcy stay on your credit report for seven to 10 years and make it tough to borrow money, rent an apartment, sometimes even find a job. That said, in the vast majority of cases filing for bankruptcy is not your fault: NerdWallet conducted a study that showed medical expenses were the biggest cause of bankruptcies, topping credit-card debt and unpaid mortgages. If you are not certain you have to file, a not-for-profit credit counselor can help you run the numbers and figure it out. You can find one at NFCC.org (the website of the National Foundation for Credit Counseling).

Once you emerge from bankruptcy, here are the steps to take:

➪ Build emergency savings to have some available cash to make sure this never happens again. Aim to move $50 every pay period into savings, then increase that number by $10 to $20 a pay period until you're putting away 15 percent of your overall income.

- ⤳ Open a secured credit card. This is a credit card you receive by depositing a small sum of money with the bank that issues the card—the sum you deposit becomes your credit limit. Some of the issuing banks pay interest on your deposit. Then use only 10 to 30 percent of the credit line available to you—and pay it off, in full, every month. You can find a list of secured cards at Bankrate.com.

- ⤳ Check your credit report a few months after your bankruptcy is discharged to make sure the discharge made it onto your credit report.

- ⤳ Don't try to micromanage your credit score. Don't fall for "credit repair" scams that say they can rebuild it overnight. *It takes time.* Just pay your bills as they're due—never late—and keep your borrowing to a minimum, and you'll get there.

- ⤳ Maintain good files, including copies of all your bankruptcy paperwork. Sometimes creditors will try to collect on debt that has been discharged in bankruptcy. If you have copies of your papers, it's much easier to send them packing. Keep these with your permanent records.

- ⤳ Make a plan to pay any debts that weren't discharged in bankruptcy, like student loans or taxes. If you have federal student loans, you are still eligible for one of the federal government's four income-driven repayment plans. This can lower the amount you have to pay out of pocket. Go to studentaid.ed.gov for more information. The IRS, too, will typically help you arrange a repayment plan or an offer in compromise (essentially a settlement for less than you owe). Go to IRS.gov and search for "payment plans."

CHAPTER 12

Never Too Late

《《←——————————————→》》

Steps to take to reverse bad health situations

I n life there are some things you just can't take back, like clearance items. Or telling a spouse that a particular shirt "sure does seem to accentuate your belly." Or the second step out of a plane for a sky-dive. When it comes to your health, however, you do have the ability to rewind—to undo some of the damage caused by whatever health conditions you have or unhealthy behaviors you've engaged in.

That's because actions—through the foods you eat and activities you engage in—can essentially flip a genetic switch. They can tell your genes to act in a certain way. So when you do well, your genes do well.

Everywhere you look are many, many stories of health success— people who have lost a lot of weight, who have quit smoking, who have eliminated the need for blood-pressure or diabetes medicine. They have fixed their problems, reversed the damage, pulled the plaque from their arteries, and recalibrated their bodies to be better than they ever were before.

Now, we don't want to simplify the process so much as to imply that two plus two equals "For the love of God, I'm skinny and toned— I look and feel 26 years younger!" Depending on where you are, the seriousness of your health conditions, and other factors, some rever-sals take longer than others. But the point is that you can erase both mistakes and medical histories. You can get a do-over, a reboot, a reset, a U-turn, whatever you want to call it. What does it take? Smarts, an initial commitment, and working on ways to automate your behaviors so that your body defaults to life's good stuff, not the gunky stuff.

Because all our health conditions are different—someone who's trying to stop smoking may have different prescriptions for reversal from someone who fears breaking a hip—we'll approach this chapter just as we did the wealth chapter by highlighting specific courses of action depending on your main concern or issue. That said, there are some overall approaches you can and should take—no matter what you're trying to reverse, prevent, or improve.

⟳ Eat DMB. No, we don't want you to eat "dumb." (That's what gets many people in trouble in the first place.) We want you to eat with these initials in mind. Why? Not because DMB stands for delicious mouthwatering berries, but because it stands for a substance that may help prevent heart disease—3,3-dimethyl-1-butanol, for those scoring at home.

Here's how it works: Groundbreaking research shows that foods like red meat and egg yolks may be as dangerous for your arteries as smoking. What's surprising is that it may not be because of fat, but because of a heart- and artery-threatening substance (which even threatens your immune system and your brain) called TMAO, produced when bacteria inside your gut chow down on these foods. The bacteria eat the excess carnitine and lecithin and choline in those foods (in an effort to get free carbon and hydrogen that the bacteria use for their energy and life). As a waste product they make TMA, and you convert it to TMAO. And then TMAO does its damage. Why can't you just take something that blocks TMA from becoming TMAO? You can, but then you'd have excess TMA, and smell like dead fish. So scientists are now using DMB to block bacteria from turning their waste from carnitine, lecithin, and choline into TMA.

TMAO is dangerous in your body because it stimulates inflammation in plaque in your arteries, causing clogs. Even worse, it stimulates inflammation that causes your immune system to fail to attack and eradicate some cancerous cells, and, just as bad, it causes chronic inflammation around the neurons in your brain, leading to foggy memories and brain dysfunction. In other words, it is a triple whammy of an inflammation-producing substance. DMB—which is found in some fresh extra-virgin olive oils, balsamic vinegars, and red wines—stops bacteria in your digestive system from turning the substances found in these foods into the compound that becomes TMAO. When this happens, research shows that the plaque buildup in arteries slows down, cancers are killed, and your brain keeps its memories. Whew.

So, what to do? Limit your intake of red and processed meats and egg yolks, for one, but also consider two to four tablespoons a day of extra-virgin olive oil. Grape-seed oil, balsamic vinegar, and red wine may also be good sources. Now, that can be a lot of calories, like 600, or a third to a fourth of all your daily calories, just in olive oil (much more in red wine). Easier to avoid the egg yolks and the red meat, to our minds.

⮑ Move it. You've heard it before and you'll hear it again and again (and again). Exercise isn't just a way to increase your laundry load; it's one of nature's best forms of medicine. Studies from everywhere (Cleveland Clinic, Harvard, Penn, Cooper Clinic, and many others) all point to the same conclusion: physical activity prolongs your life and increases your health. It:

- increases your ability to do daily functions requiring muscular activity, like moving to and from a job

- improves metabolic functions and decreases the risk of obesity, osteoarthritis, bone fractures, and type 2 diabetes
- increases mental alertness and the ability to function in daily activities requiring your brain, increases hippocampal size (the size and connections in the area of the brain thought responsible for encoding and retrieving short-term memories), and improves both long-term and short-term memory
- increases your immune function to ward off cancers and infections and increases disability-free survival if those occur
- changes your microbiome so you have less inflammatory hazard in your body
- keeps you from gaining weight, so you reduce the risk of heart disease and other conditions related to obesity

One of our favorite studies comes from Harvard, which looked at more than 13,000 women who reached or passed age 70 in "super-healthful" condition (they'd had no cancer, diabetes, heart attacks, cognitive impairment, or other limitations). Their commonality: they all did physical activity, and those who were the most active were twice as likely to be healthy 18 years later as the ones who did the least.

As you know, we covered activity in depth just a few pages ago (page 161), so follow the guidelines there for specific instructions on including walking, cardiovascular activity, strength training, jumping (so you'll never break a hip), and flexibility work in your daily routine.

So, yeah, surprise surprise. Your health comes down to inflow and outflow—what you put into your system and what you put out. That's the case no matter what your condition. That said, a whole range of problems can affect you as you age, so if you want to target a particular issue (one you already have, or one you have a family history of and are more at risk of developing), then take a look at the paths that will best help you become—and stay—AgeProof.

Fix It!

"My mom has Alzheimer's and I'm starting to lose my memory. Also, I'm starting to lose my memory."

There's no doubt that one of the scariest prospects of aging is that your brain won't function the way it used to—whether that means putting the car keys in the microwave or forgetting the name of a new grandchild **Q**. It's all understandably scary. Many people have firsthand knowledge of the mental and emotional toll that brain-related problems cause not only the person who's experiencing them, but also the family and other caregivers.

Q JEAN SAYS: Or letting the bills lapse. Finances are one of the first problems to surface when cognitive function starts to slide.

One in five people will experience some form of brain drain, ranging from fuzzy thinking to Alzheimer's disease. While some causes of memory loss are genetic, you can build a bigger brain and postpone memory loss. One study found nine risk factors for Alzheimer's, ranging from obesity to inflammation to plaque in the arteries, and most of them are modifiable. Even if you have the genetics for Alzheimer's disease, a recent UCLA study showed you can avoid the pathology to a great degree just by eating fish with some regularity. Because our brains are plastic (that's a good word **Q** in brain talk) they're flexible enough to grow and strengthen if we empower them to do so.

Q JEAN SAYS: But a bad word in wealth talk!

So to combat brain-related problems, do the things we recommend throughout the book—like getting that physical activity, ditching foods that cause problems (remember those SSSSnake oil foods), de-stressing, and building healthy relationships—and make one especially important addition. Play a specific brain game that has been shown in a multicenter randomized trial to decrease dementia by 48 percent over a 10-year period (the ACTIVE trial). Remember, food and exercise are key, too. For example, exercise for 30 minutes three times a week for six months consistently enlarges the hippocampus 2 to 22 percent. Your hippocampus is the brain region responsible for memory. No exercise, and the hippocampus decreases in size by 0.25 percent in that same six months. Some other specific tactics for creating a brain built for a centenarian:

↪ Learn something new. Trying a new skill, hobby, or game, or even trying to find new directions (ahem, without GPS) to a place you visit regularly, will create more connections that also help enlarge your hippocampus, which shrinks your risk of memory loss. Pickleball, anyone? The best of the new things that has been demonstrated in the ACTIVE trial is "speed of processing training" available from BrainHQ. In that trial of over 2,800 people followed for 10 years, 18 hours of reasoning or memory training had little or no statistical effect on the number of 73-year-olds who developed dementia over the next 10 years. But 18 hours of "speed of processing training" (two hours a week for five weeks with booster two hours a week for two weeks in months 11 and again in month 35) decreased this risk by 48 percent over 10 years. WOW 💬.

↪ Manage stress. Stress is the greatest cause of memory loss and is linked to a shrinking hippocampus (pruned connections). You can use meditation and behavioral modification to control your reaction to stressful events. See more about stress starting on page 71.

↪ Lower your blood sugar. Slightly raised sugar levels—even if you don't have diabetes or prediabetes—will affect your memory. Excess blood glucose causes inflammation, which damages brain cells. In one study, people had their long-term sugar levels tested and were asked to memorize

DR. MIKE SAYS: Yes, I have done the 10 hours and am doing 20 minutes more each week! And a second trial showed increase acetylcholine release in the brain with a second "speed of processing game." DOUBLE WOW!

15 words, then repeat them a half hour later. Those with chronically higher levels of blood sugar remembered, on average, two fewer words. Lower blood sugar is linked to a bigger hippocampus, which means more connections for long-term memory storage.

↪ Take in enough magnesium, folate, B12, B6, and D2. Magnesium ensures strong links among your brain cells, so you have a big network ready to solve problems. You need 420 milligrams daily, but most of us fall short. Turn to brown rice, almonds, hazelnuts, spinach, shredded wheat, lima beans, and bananas to top off your tank. The B vitamins are key for brain functioning, too. Vitamin D2 can protect your DNA to prevent damage from free radicals (rogue oxygen molecules that attack DNA). Aim for 1,000 international units (IU) daily from a D2 supplement. Get yours measured; you want to aim for a level over 35 💬.

DR. MIKE SAYS: How much over 35 no one knows, but toxicity doesn't set in till your D2 level is over 80 and maybe over 110. So I aim to keep my D2 level in the 50-to-80 range.

↪ Don't shortchange sleep. When you're busy, it's easy to say that the thing you want to sacrifice is sleep. But you need sleep for lots of reasons, and one of the biggies is that it acts as a scrub to clean up your brain and get it in condition for optimal learning, problem-solving, and memory.

↪ Keep inflammation low. Inflammation damages your brain's neurons, causing long-term dysfunction. While other things you are doing—like avoiding the SSSSnake oil foods, exercising, managing stress, getting appropriate sleep, and avoiding periodontal disease—reduce it, you can monitor it with blood tests for hs-CRP and TMAO. If these are high, add some DMB foods and a dental visit, and talk to your doc about adding 162 milligrams of aspirin daily as well as DHA omega-3s and a newer statin. (We think atorvastatin or rosuvastatin should be considered for all over age 50—the older statins do not have as much or any anti-inflammatory effect; see below.)

↪ Consider supplementation. Your brain is more than 60 percent fat, and half of that fat is DHA omega-3; randomized controlled studies show an improvement in cognitive function in those worried about memory loss who take 900 milligrams of DHA omega-3 daily. You can use supplements from plant sources like algae or eat 18 ounces of wild salmon or ocean trout (the only fish species in the USA with predictable omega-3) weekly. Remember that study saying that just a little fish weekly decreases the risk of Alzheimer's? You get more than DHA omega-3 by eating fish, like other healthy proteins (potentially) and other fatty acids, like omega-7 palmitoleic acid.

Fix It!

"I'm deathly afraid of falling and breaking a hip."

Just because a certain popular commercial ("I've fallen and I can't get up") was once a source of public mockery doesn't mean that this isn't a serious problem. As we age we do fear falling, not necessarily because we fear the pain we'll feel right then and there (though admittedly that's no picnic), but more because of everything we've heard about what happens after the fall. *Oh, Aunt Edna fell and broke her hip, came down with pneumonia, and died a few weeks later.* It's such a prevalent—and distressing—narrative that we put it in the title of this book, and it's prevalent for good reason: when you age you lose some of your ability to navigate the world around you (making you more susceptible to falls), and you also have bones that resemble not so much a steel beam as a wooden one enjoyed from the inside by an army of termites. The chance of dying in the six months after a hip fracture is 15 to 25 percent. (Surprisingly, it's two times greater in men than in women. While men fall less frequently, accounting for 15 percent of total falls, 40 percent of those men who do fall and break a hip die within a year.) Why? Being prone to falling and fracturing (or fracturing and then falling, which happens much less commonly) can be a sign of some other underlying pathology such as inflammation in your body, which makes you more susceptible to other acute types of problems, like pneumonia.

Bones are not the perfectly solid structure that most of us imagine them to be. The outer layer provides rigidity and structural integrity, while the spongy bone on the inside imparts flexibility and compressive strength to the skeleton—making the design of bones similar to that of the Eiffel Tower. But here's the great thing: bone is dynamic; it's able to remodel itself according to what you need, such as by fusing back together after it's been fractured. Bone is so dynamic that you often can't even see in an X-ray where a bone was broken after it's healed. So what does that mean for you as you age? As you lose some of the density, you actually have the ability to build it back up. (Remember our discussion of this process on page 165.)

You reach your peak bone mass at age 30, and up until then can increase your banked calcium. After that, both men and women lose a half percent of bone per year. For the first five years of menopause (without hormone replacement therapy), women's bone loss increases to 2 to 4 percent of the spongy bone on the inside and 1 to 2 percent of the hard surface bone per year. After that the decline levels out to a half percent a year again. (For men it remains constant at that half percent.) What you can do to protect your bones:

⇨ Engage in jumping games. The reason any kind of resistance training, or preferably jumping, is so important: both stimulate that charge we talked about and put more force on the bone, to cause bone remodeling (and, importantly, to build muscle and increase your sense of balance, so you're less likely to fall). Weight lifting turns on a gene that makes a protein that eventually turns on osteoblasts to do the work of building bone. Sports that require some jumping or quick movement, like tennis or badminton , are also good.

DR. MIKE SAYS: I'm a big squash fan, myself (and not just the vegetable).

JEAN SAYS: Don't be modest! He once captained the US squash team at the Pan American Games.

In a randomized controlled study—the gold standard—women aged 20 to 50 were randomly assigned to jump 10 or 20 times twice a day or not at all (control group). After eight weeks the jumpers who did it 40 times a day had an increase in bone density (0.5 percent), compared to a loss of 1.3 percent in the control group. So jump in place 20 times twice a day, or do 10 jumping jacks every time you use your car.

⟳ Choose calcium and leafy greens. You need calcium to mineralize (provide more rigid structure to) the collagen proteins that help build your bone. Aim for 1,500 milligrams a day in foods and supplements (though that's on the high side if you're at risk for developing kidney stones). And no more than 600 milligrams a day should come from supplements. Get 300-milligram chewable calcium citrate tablets, put them in the car, and take one when you put the key in the ignition to go to work, then another when you're on your way home. (If you don't drive, use another habitual reminder to take them.) Since you can absorb only about 600 milligrams in a two-hour period, this helps make sure the doses are spread out throughout the day. Your other option is calcium carbonate, but that should be taken only after a meal. (If you have GI issues when taking calcium carbonate, switch to calcium citrate.) For vitamin D, take 1,000 IU daily (or 1,200 for women older than 65). Get your level measured after three months, and aim for a value above 35 (we actually aim for 50 to 80, but there's strong data only for a level greater than 35 🗨).

DR. MIKE SAYS:
I know I said this before, but vitamin D is that important.

Plus, it's smart to add 400 milligrams of magnesium a day to prevent the constipation that calcium causes. (This is roughly the same amount of magnesium we spoke about above—you only need 400 or 420 milligrams a day, so don't double it.) Getting magnesium is important—magnesium deficiency may be more common than calcium deficiency in women with osteoporosis. Eat whole grains, leafy green vegetables (which also give you vitamin K, important for bone health), and nuts (almonds are rich in both magnesium and calcium).

 ⇨ Stretch regularly. Stretching won't do anything to the physiology of your bones per se, but it will give you the ability to maneuver yourself during a fall or get yourself up after one. See the discussion of our recommendations on page 166.

 ⇨ Take some tests. While you can't always predict tripping over a stray toy/curb/Chihuahua, you can get some sense of whether you're a prime candidate for a fall. This balance test, for example, will be one indication and can let you know if you really need to work on strength training and balance. Stand on one foot, extend your arms to any place you balance best, and keep yourself balanced. Now close your eyes. Stand as long as you can before you have to grab something to get your balance. (Best to do this with a spotter or next to a wall.) The threshold for success is 15 seconds at age 40 and 30 seconds at age 30. If you can't make those times, it means that you shake more than a salsa dancer—meaning that your lack of balance makes you more susceptible to falling, putting you at a higher risk of breaking your bones. Fix this by practicing, playing sports like Ping-Pong or badminton that make you change direction fast, and making the choices above that protect your brain.

Fix It!

"I'm addicted to [fill in your vice]."

When it comes to addictions and health, the three most chronically dangerous ones are tobacco, alcohol, and food. While you can be addicted to anything (if *addiction* is defined as a habit you can't control that has destructive consequences), these three are the ones with the most potential to do long-term damage to your body. All are a tad different. Why? Smoking is something you don't have to do to live. Eating is something you have to do to live, so you can't just cut out eating entirely. And alcohol isn't something you need, but it's not entirely bad, because a moderate amount of alcohol does have some health benefits. But while these addictions aren't created equally, it is fair to say that the way we approach each is fairly similar.

We also know you can repair the damage done by your addiction over time. For example, if you haven't yet done structural damage or developed a tumor, your lungs, your brain, your arteries, and the rest of your body can get back to pretty darn close to normal after five years of not using tobacco (smoking, vaping, and/or chewing). Easier said than done, you say. And while we don't think we can quote-unquote cure an addiction in a few pages (after all, there are whole books, programs, and treatment centers dedicated to the cause), it is worth exploring this issue—and assuring you that even if you've been addicted to your vice for decades, you can reverse the damage if you can stop the cycle.

The reason breaking addictions poses such a biological challenge is that repeated and addictive behavior actually changes your brain circuitry. When you adopt a behavior, neurons communicate with one another to learn the task. While those neurons are strengthening to learn the task, the neurons that aren't being used lose their power. So when you're addicted to drinking or cigarettes, the repeated behavior rewires your brain to perform that action over and over. Your brain circuitry reinforces those unhealthy habits because your brain wants the temporary high that comes from them, no matter the damage that follows. The key to breaking any addiction is to take advantage of that very same circuitry. How?

⤷ Discover new habits. These new habits allow you to build new connections so you can prune the destructive ones from your memory. You have to find new circuitry boards to build so your brain stops investing its energy in the connections that make you want to do the destructive behavior. A habit can be a repeated behavior that gives you a high (the hormonal and chemical high you experience when you engage in a behavior is the driver of why you want to do it again and again). As long as no adverse effects are associated with that repeated habit, you are going to rewire your brain away from the addiction and into a healthy habit. So the new habit could be exercise. Or the new habit could be some kind of healthy drink in place of an alcoholic one.

○ Forget about cold turkey. Cold turkey is a fine decision as it relates to Black Friday shopping, but other than that, it just doesn't work 💬. There are some outlier cases where quitting cold turkey succeeds because the addicted person makes it his or her mission to stop, and does have the willpower to overcome his or her brain circuitry. However, the fact is that most people who successfully break the chains of addiction over the long term (*long term* being the key phrase) don't just stop abruptly—they can't, because of the wiring system we described above. The data shows that people who try to quit smoking cold turkey have only a 2 percent success rate. If you try to kick the habit using just an anticraving pill, there's a 3 to 5 percent success rate. If you use an anticraving medication and a nicotine patch, the success rate rises to about 10 percent. But if you use medication and a patch, and substitute another habit for the addictive behavior (like taking 10,000 steps a day), and enlist the support of a buddy (in person or electronically), the success rate soars to over 30 percent. The success rate in Dr. Mike's work with more than 3,600 tobacco users was an astounding 62.8 percent after seven months.

○ Consider reinforcements. Many antiaddiction programs involve some kind of anticraving prescription drug, such

DR. MIKE SAYS: Confession time: I did give up my extreme diet soda habit cold turkey. But I used the principles of substitution to do so, subbing in coffee and water.

as bupropion or a benzodiazepine. These drugs help mitigate the withdrawal symptoms you feel when trying to break an addiction, giving your brain time to cut through those entrenched wires so you can rewire your brain with healthy habits. It should be noted that different drugs are used for different addictions, because each is designed to work on the mechanism that causes a specific addiction. For example, bupropion (we recommend it in a lower dose than the brand-name preparation, Zyban) is used in smoking-cessation programs because it quiets the addictive properties of nicotine.

Fix It!

"I feel like, well, blah. All the time."

Without sounding too flip about it, depression comes in a variety pack—there's postpartum depression, seasonal affective disorder, major depression, bipolar disorder, situational depression, depression associated with a heart attack, depression associated with medication, and many other types. But while the causes may be different, the effects are pretty similar. Being depressed can change sleep patterns, decrease energy, change the way you eat, and much more—all of which threaten your long-term health. Depression is reported to be more prevalent among women, but that may be because women are more often classified as depressed, while men are more often classified as alcoholics (because men are more likely to self-medicate their blues with bourbon).

Some believe that depression may be related to an abnormality in the functioning of hormones in the brain. That's because people with severe depression tend to have abnormal levels of the stress hormone cortisol or other hormones, and the size of their brain's memory relay station, the hippocampus, actually decreases. Depression is actually one of the signals your body uses to tell you that something isn't working quite right—and that you should be thinking of coping strategies to get your mind and body on the right track.

- ➪ Get professional help. Remember, depression is a tricky proposition because so many of the symptoms can be either on the subtle side or similar to symptoms of other problems. Your doctor can put together a good treatment plan, but only if she knows the whole picture. In an exam, she'll ask you about medical problems that could be related to depression. But you also want to be up front about your recent history—the changes in your life that might not be medical but can certainly influence your mood. While it may sound as though you're going to confession, you should talk to your doc about major life events (such as deaths in the family or financial stresses, and, yes, changes in sexual pleasure or frequency), as well as changes in job and family situations (retirement, for example).

- ➪ Consider meds. If you have a chemical imbalance in your brain that's altering your mood, you should get it treated. Your doc will prescribe drugs that best match your symptoms. She may prescribe medication based on symptoms alone, or she may do further testing, such as blood tests to ensure you are not short of thyroid hormone or vitamin D2, B6, B9 (B9 is folate, but its substitute is methylfolate, as a high percent—maybe as high as 36 percent—of depressed people actually have a genetic change that means they cannot metabolize folate appropriately and need methylfolate to restore biochemical pathways), and B12, all of which are linked to depression. Antidepressant drugs should rarely be given without psychotherapy, because they dull us to the realities of life. In some cases they're essential to turn back the tide. Typically they take three to six weeks to have substantial effects. This delay occurs because the brain appears to accommodate to the accumulation of the drug in the brain. Thus the drugs are usually used for six to nine months for the first episode of depression. Recurrent episodes require longer-term treatment. Selective serotonin reuptake inhibitors (SSRIs), such as Prozac and Zoloft, are especially effective if you're experiencing anxiety. SSRIs work by boosting serotonin in the brain, with one common side effect—decreased libido. That can be addressed a few ways, including by decreasing the dose, switching to another SSRI, switching to a different class of antidepressant drug, or using a second drug to offset the sexual side effects. Good non-SSRI choices are bupropion (Wellbutrin) or Remeron, which appear not to have much of an effect on sexual function or desire. Different drugs affect different parts of your brain, which is why you should discuss changing drugs or drug classes with your doc if you feel you're sacrificing quality of life at the same time that you're trying to restore it.

AgeProof ESSENTIALS

1. You can't take back time. But you can make up for lost time.

2. Don't think of problems as dead-end streets. You always have the option to find side streets, alleys, and other routes to get you out of trouble—and on the highway to healthy and happy living.

3. The thing that scares many people about the problems they're having is that they know they might have issues that need to be dealt with, but they don't confront them. Only when you get a full assessment of where you are can you make the changes and employ the tactics that will help you catch up. If that applies to you, reread our opening section on the science of diagnostics and make a commitment to assess yourself as the first step to making up ground. Become aware, and then automate the solutions.

Part VII
Making a Living

The Science of Working

Why what you do influences how healthy you are

Picture this: Two people stand on opposite sides of a room. There's a band in the background. The music starts, and the two people meet in the middle. No matter whether it's a salsa or a waltz, no matter whether one is wearing a glittery dress or a tux, no matter whether the couple is alone or amid a frenzy of fellow dancers—they meet, they clasp hands, and they follow the direction of the music. And each other.

They dance, they glide, they shake, they feel the music, and the two people move together as one. You don't have to be a *Dancing with the Stars* fan to see the scene—two different people joining forces to create an artistic, elegant, and beautiful moment together.

In a way, everything we talk about in this whole book is like that ballroom interaction—two distinct areas (health and wealth) that appear to be quite separate, mingling and coexisting to create a strong and AgeProof life.

Perhaps this is nowhere more evident than in the work environment. We tend to think of health and wealth as separate areas (though we hope that by now you no longer do), and many of you probably think that addressing the work environment is really about making money. But the reality is that the dance—the blending—of health and wealth is so intertwined that you should really think of the work environment as a dance floor on which your most important decisions about long-term health and financial status play out. Just consider the ways they're tied together, and you can see the blurring of the lines:

- Work is the way in which you make your money.
- Work is also typically the primary vehicle through which you gain health benefits and choose a plan that you can use to motivate yourself to stay healthy, and that keeps you from financial Armageddon if a health problem does occur.
- Work often dictates what kind of retirement benefits you'll receive, which influences how long you plan to work.
- Work can be a primary source of stressful events (as can not having enough money to live comfortably).
- Stress can be a primary infliction that manifests itself in health problems, which can keep you out of work.
- Your ability to work—perhaps affected by various health issues—determines your earning power, and therefore your chances of living comfortably today and your outlook on retirement in the future.
- What you do at work has a direct impact on other areas of your health (as with excessive sitting leading to back pain, other on-the-job injuries or disabilities, or exposure to toxins or toxic work conditions).
- Your overall health can determine how much you work, which can determine how well you can perform, which can influence your income and the size of your nest egg.

See what we mean? All these reasons go a long way toward explaining why many major companies and organizations are spending so much time and so many resources on developing workplace wellness programs—that are, more than ever, dipping into both physical wellness and financial wellness. They know that *your* health affects your productivity, your absences, and your medical expenses, all of which affect *their* bottom line. They also know that if you don't get your financial act together, you likely won't retire until further down the road. That they could end up with a workforce comprised of older, more expensive, potentially less healthy employees explains why more and more companies are starting to see your financial wellness (or lack thereof) as a potential future drain on their balance sheets. It's also why you—if you don't work in a place where wellness is a priority— need to recognize the blending of the two areas, so you can take steps to improve your own medical and financial bottom lines.

It's also important to acknowledge that we are—more than ever before—a society of workhorses. Our work has become our lives. Consider: Americans work more than people in any other country— England, France, Germany, even Japan. We work more days, retire later, and take less vacation (we're given 15 days on average, but we take only 14; Europeans get and take 28 days, Asians get 19 but take fewer). According to Gallup, Americans work nearly 48 hours a week (the equivalent of a six-day workweek), which is up one and a half hours from a decade ago. And some research indicates that Americans worry they're not making enough money and feel they should be working *more*.

Now, it should be said that this may be changing, thanks in part to millennials, who as a whole work to live rather than live to work, at least compared with other generations. Big companies like Deloitte, Goldman Sachs, and some top law firms have had to change the way they expect young people to work in order to attract the best talent (and compete with the Googles of the world, where you can show up in jeans, eat multiple meals for free, etc.). These companies have issued policies about *not* being required to check e-mail on weekends and into the night, and Deloitte goes through an onboarding process with new clients where everyone from both sides of the team—the Deloitte side and the client side—is given a chance to say, for instance, "I'll be out of here on Tuesdays by 6 p.m. to catch my kids' games." The United Services Automobile Association, a large financial services company, offers the option to work a 40-hour four-day week and take Fridays off. And PricewaterhouseCoopers and JPMorgan Chase have just made every day casual Friday.

We'll be addressing a number of work-related issues in the following two chapters, but perhaps the big message to take home about work isn't about the volume of work; it's about the satisfaction you get from it. A 2015 study shows that only 48 percent of us are happy at work; in 1987 the number was 61 percent. There's no question that having a passion for what you do will have major health benefits. So the underlying message is to find work that you're passionate about and satisfied with.

Now, we know that you can't just snap your fingers and change your boss, your job, your commute, your coworker who crunches chips in the next cubicle all day long, or any of the millions of things that can cause you stress and dissatisfaction. It can be a long process to change jobs or careers, rekindle (or find) your passion, or find new inspiration in an old job. But there are some ways to jump-start your happiness:

- **Find some autonomy:** Even if you're just rearranging the furniture in your office or setting your hours so they're slightly different from those of people around you, feeling that you are the one in charge makes you happier.

- **Challenge yourself:** If you're trying to get better at something, you're going to feel more energized. This may mean taking on a new project or volunteering to learn a needed skill (which makes you more valuable to your employer as well).

- **Find the flow:** Everyone has a zone—maybe you've found it playing video games or gardening: It's that state of being in which the clock ticks away and you don't notice, you don't stop to eat, you may not even stop to pee. All of a sudden you look up and hours have gone by. That's flow, and you want to find it at work. So look at your strengths. When you're doing something that makes you feel like master of your domain, you're more likely to find the flow.

- **Search for a calling/importance:** If you're doing something that makes you feel you're serving someone other than yourself—that you're fulfilling a purpose or doing something important—you are likely to be happier.

- **Make a friend:** You don't need to have a work spouse, just a buddy—someone you enjoy spending your lunch hour or chatting with—to help you handle stresses or simply to increase the satisfaction of being around others during the day.

- **Fake it till you make it:** Sounds silly, we know. But if you walk around pretending to enjoy yourself—with a smile, when appropriate—you will eventually begin to actually enjoy yourself. There's science behind this.

Why is all of this important? Because you spend so much time at work that if you're happier there, you're going to be happier with your life. And if you're happy with your life, you're going to be healthier and wealthier. Happy people have younger hearts, younger arteries, fewer infections and cancers, better brain function, the ability to recover more quickly from surgery and cope better with pain, lower blood pressure, and longer life expectancies than unhappy people. They also get job interviews, land those jobs, and receive better performance evaluations that culminate in raises and promotions—in other words, more money. While we know that happiness is about half-genetic, the other half is determined by you—your choices, your decisions, and your ability to have a positive outlook about what you're doing—to enjoy it and know it is meaningful.

CHAPTER 13

Being Worked to ~~Death~~ Life

How to make your day job a healthy one

I f you discount the 9 percent of the population that works in the
health-care industry in some capacity, the rest of the country has
other things to think about when they're at work. Right? Your
main job is your main job. You build things with your hands or your
brain. You write reports or e-mails. You serve customers and clients.
You answer to bosses or manage employees or both. You play office
politics. You try to get ahead. You meet. You think. You do.

Whatever it is you have decided to pursue as a career (or careers),
you have value to your employer or the greater world for the role you
serve; you wouldn't get that paycheck if you didn't. So it's no wonder
that thinking about your health while you work sometimes takes a
backseat to the 423 million other things you're responsible for from
day to day, minute to minute. Add in the fact that we now work *all*
the time—because we're technologically tethered to clients and
bosses and customers with occasional respite periods to watch kitty
videos—and it's that much harder to keep healthy living at the top of
your to-do list.

And when you pit the two things against each other—work versus
health—it's admittedly hard to make health a priority. There's always
another e-mail to send. There's always a client lunch that you could or

should do. There's always more work, more stress, and more volume. There's always pressure. And for so many people, that means there's less time for two-minute walks around the hall, a lower chance you're going to choose a handful of nuts over a monster-truck plate of nachos with the after-work crew, less opportunity to manage stress or think about *your* well-being. Life just gets in the way.

Traditionally, that's the way the world works. Health and work go together about as well as red wine and toothpaste.

That's changing, thankfully, because corporations are realizing that people work better and are more innovative and more productive when they're healthier. And if people work better when they're healthier, that means the company is more profitable and efficient, and able to serve customers better. When the two are intertwined—health *and* work, not health *versus* work—it's a win for everyone: the employer, the employee, the customer, and the family.

JEAN SAYS: I'm looking into getting one of those.

DR. MIKE SAYS: Go for the treadmill desk (I use one)... many more benefits.

Now, we're not suggesting that you have to turn your cubicle into a minigym by doing bicep curls with your laptop (though standing desks and treadmill desks sure are nice), but we do believe that you can rethink how you view the relationship between health and work. Health isn't just something you do after hours; it's something you should make part of your entire life. When you consider how much of your waking life is spent working, it only makes mathematical sense that being healthy while you're working provides the foundation for being healthy all the time. And in the end that means a better life—and more financial success—for you.

The interesting part about this work-and-health relationship is seeing what employers are doing to help inspire, educate, and incentivize their employees to live more healthfully. While you can't always control what the corporate suits (or HR folks) decide when it comes to wellness opportunities, there are lessons you can take from these places and apply to your own working life. So let's start by looking at some of the trends in the corporate world—and then talk about some ways you can develop strategies for making your work environment as productive and positive as possible.

Lessons from Workplace Wellness

There are some jobs where you're simply expected to be healthy (doctor, personal trainer). And there are some jobs where it's sort of expected that you're, well, *not* (a restaurant critic is gonna try the fondue). But for all the places between the two—where there's zero expectation of either optimum health or unhealthiness—health has been an ancillary topic; it hasn't been tied to the qualifications or responsibilities of the job. Until recently. Companies now understand that health affects work and work affects health. And the better they dance together hand in hand, step by step, the better off they will be.

It took some time for companies to realize this, and it took hard numbers to influence the decision to bolster workplace wellness programs around the country.

Want to scare a company? (We mean besides by making it endure a major social-media faux pas.) Give it evidence that it's losing money. Here's one set of numbers that does just that: In the 1960s about 50 percent of all medical costs were accumulated in the last year of life. Today that number is about 15 percent—meaning that most medical costs are associated with having to treat chronic diseases, with a good percentage of those costs coming during typical working years. Who absorbs that cost? Well, you do, for one. But the companies do, too, in the form of insurance costs. (Make no mistake: employers spend a lot of money on health care. The annual amount spent by employers for individual health care increased $9,822—from $4,247 to $14,069—from 2000 to 2018, while the amount spent by the individual increased $4,003—from just $1,543 to $5,547 a year—during the same time.)

So in response, companies did what companies do: they put on their thinking caps to figure out ways to reduce those costs and cost increases (and in the meantime get their workforces healthy). They figured out that if they put more costs on the employee, they might motivate many to stay or to get healthy. They started programs to help their people eat healthfully, move more, and stop smoking, so they and their people would have a shot at reducing the risk factors associated with chronic disease. (Four factors cause 75 percent of chronic diseases: tobacco and other toxins, food choices and portion size, physical inactivity, and unmanaged stress. You can see how work can strongly influence these. While declines in smoking can be attributed to a number of factors, it's no coincidence that once workplaces banned smoking, rates also dropped. People had to make an effort to smoke, by going outside to designated areas. Employers changed the environment to make it difficult to maintain the behavior that causes ill health and easier to choose the behavior that fosters good health.) By the same token, if companies could get you, the employee, to choose the grilled chicken over the fried chicken, or the piece of fruit or some nuts over the piece of trans fat–laden candy, then, well, costs could go down and productivity could go up. Thus the daily LUV-U foods like the BWell meal at places like the Hearst Corporation's employee café.

Literal belt tightening for you (and health for you) equals profitability (and financial health) for them. See, the two work together.

Corporations and health-care providers like M&T Bank, IBM, LafargeHolcim, and the Cleveland Clinic are saving huge amounts of money over what they were projected to spend (and even have stable costs compared to prior years despite older workforces) in insurance and medical care for employees and dependents when their employees and their dependents get and stay healthier. Plus their employees are happier, more engaged in life, more productive, and productive longer, which is a plus for the company financially. (It's also a plus for the individual financially—not only in money earned, but also in money not lost to major medical costs associated with treating problems and missing work, as well as in additional years of retirement plan contributions.)

And you know how they're doing all this? With the same strategy we've been suggesting throughout this book—changing your environment to make your decisions automatic. If a company doesn't have a machine selling or in some way dispensing sodas—making it difficult for you to impulsively buy a bottle of hip-thickener —then you likely won't have that soda.

JEAN SAYS: Mike, just the fact that you call it "hip-thickener" is enough to make me steer clear. A personal trainer once told me, "Eat a bagel, be a bagel." I don't think I ate a bagel for a solid year.

Eventually, as the environment changes, your decisions become automatic (sound familiar?). Companies put well-thought-of managers or other leaders at the forefront as "team leaders" urging colleagues to join them in a walk or run for a charity or simply modeling good behavior by holding business meetings, literally, on a run. (Nike employees, not surprisingly, do this all the time.) Something else companies do—which we can all learn from—is offer incentives to people who are able to prove their good health. For example, in some programs, if people show they're at a normal level for the 6+2® major risk factors for chronic disease (blood pressure, blood glucose or hemoglobin AIC, body mass index or waist size, LDL cholesterol, presence of cotinine, stress management program completed and practiced, and [the 2] see a primary care physician and immunizations up-to-date), they can earn financial rewards—like lower insurance deductibles. Now, that doesn't guarantee that everyone will jump on the bandwagon—incentives seem to provide a 20 percent increase, according to some research, although larger incentives at some work sites like the Cleveland Clinic have motivated over 69 percent to try to improve their health, and 95 percent of the healthy to stay healthy over nine years—but large incentives certainly do help push people into initiating and sustaining the behaviors that might seem difficult at first, but eventually become good habits. (Note: the Affordable Care Act or ACA allows business to offer up to 30 percent of insurance costs as incentives and penalties for people who do or don't participate in corporate wellness programs, respectively.)

These programs do work. Since 2009 the 37,000 employees in the Cleveland Clinic weight management program have lost a combined 455,000 pounds. That's the equivalent of five and a half fully loaded 18-wheel tractor trailers. In addition, rates of chronic disease and now per-member-per-month all-in medical costs have decreased, in contrast to the upward trend we see in other populations. And while you may not be able to control the umbrella programs your company offers, you can steal their strategies and apply them to your own life.

Be Your Own Chief Wellness Officer

It's one thing if your company offers wellness programs. Our message is simple in that case. Take advantage of them. Use the company gym, choose the healthy food, learn a stress management technique that works for you, take advantage of the financial incentives, maximize your health while bulking up your wallet. And be thankful that your company has made your wellness and productivity a priority, because even if there aren't financial incentives for the company—and some employers do this even though they haven't quite figured out the ROI, simply because they think it's the right thing to do—taking advantage of such a program still benefits you, big-time.

It's quite another thing, however, if you don't have systems in place that make it easier for you to get and stay healthy. Worse, what if you work in an office where the culture is outright unhealthy—doughnuts every morning, toxic levels of stressful events, toxins in the air (HQ is just off a busy freeway), and a guy whose major mantra is "Let's hit the unlimited buffet for lunch"? What if you are the owner of your own small company and don't have the financial infrastructure to create some of these systems? Or what if you work in the gig economy and your home is your office and your spouse likes to collect tins of Pringles? Our message is not quite the same, but it's very similar: become your own Chief Wellness Officer. Develop your own plan, mission, goals, and opportunities to make your work environment the healthiest (and thus most lucrative) one possible.

Essentially, that means you're creating an environment in which your butt is out of your seat, the junk is out of your mouth, and your stress levels can taper off as much as possible. We're not saying that every day should be an oasis with spa music and cucumber water, but we are saying that being your own CWO means you develop a plan with good habits you can stick with long term.

Let's start with this quick test: on a scale of one to 10, rate how healthy your work environment is, as a whole and for you individually.

Be honest with your assessment, and rate in the following five categories (two points each):

1. Promotes tobacco-free campus, and uses only materials that are toxin-free

2. Promotes sustained (not one-off) physical activity

3. Makes healthful food choices available (not necessarily free) in places that offer food (whether vending machines or your own fridge) as well as during meetings

4. Helps you manage stress, and facilitates life-work balance

5. Provides an environment and financial programs that facilitate health (yoga lessons, plants—there are many options here) and financial well-being (such as 401(k) programs, health savings accounts, and insurance incentives)

If your rating is anything but a nine or 10, you likely can make some small changes to create a better environment. If it's below a three or four, you may need to shake things up in order to foster improvement. Our suggestion: Pick three of the following strategies and make a plan for integrating them into your work environment. As they become automatic (and you feel healthier and stronger), choose another one or two. Within a few months, you will have installed your very own metaphorical door—from a work environment that's built to damage you to one that's built to strengthen you.

Walk and Talk. Why does every meeting have to occur at a table or a desk? If you have a one-on-one or even a three-way meeting, why not schedule it so that you're walking? Q The obvious benefits are that it will help you get steps in (you're aiming for 10,000 a day) and keep you from sitting (which isn't great for your back or your entire musculoskeletal system). But another is that when you're walking, meetings that can be contentious are actually less confrontational because you're side by side rather than eye to eye. (This is a good tactic for couples who need to have difficult conversations, because

JEAN SAYS: Or running! Over the years I've become running buddies with several clients. It's not just healthier for you, but good for business. Getting out of work clothes and into shorts and a T-shirt somehow enables the ideas to flow a little more freely.

it's a little less threatening.) How to get started? Pick one coworker you suspect would be amenable to a walking meeting and initiate it for the next time you need to confab. Aim for once a week. Soon that once-a-week will turn into people asking *you* for on-the-go work sessions.

Park in Papua. This habit isn't hard to pick up, and it's not hard to figure out the benefits. Choose the parking spot farthest from your building and park there. More steps and activity at the start and end of your day. Always running late? Tighten up your morning routine to save you that five minutes.

Change the Candy Bowl. Yes, the people who keep a bowl of mini-Snickers may be popular around 3:30 every afternoon, but they're also contributing—albeit through a slow drip—to individual and collective obesity issues. Besides the fact that simple sugars lead to fat storage, they also won't help your productivity, because the initial surge you get from the sugar only results in a bigger drag when that sugar high wears off. You're better off with whole, good, unprocessed foods as snacks. Bring apples to meetings. Keep nuts in your office for when you need some energy. After a few weeks you'll see that sustained energy is much better than extreme energy in a chocolate-covered sugar burst.

Don't Rely on the Keyboard. Here's a novel idea for the tech crowd. GET UP AND TALK TO SOMEONE WITH YOUR MOUTH, NOT YOUR THUMBS. There's no denying that e-mail, social media, texting, and all forms of digital communication have made work life easier. But every message doesn't have to be sent through one of these media. Make it a point to talk to people in your office. Not only will you likely save time because a conversation can be taken care of in three minutes as opposed to 44 replies, but you'll also get the added benefit of getting up and moving, as well as strengthening relationships with face-to-face interaction (which has been shown to improve health outcomes). Make it your starter goal to choose a face-to-face interaction over a digital interaction once a day.

☞ Make Your Work Space a Healthy One

The Issue	The Plan
Noise	*Acoustic comfort* refers to a space free of potentially distracting and dangerous noises. The easiest fix is to use music or a white-noise app to drown out distractions, or noise-cancellation earphones if it's really bad.
Air quality	Use dehumidifiers to reduce mold and allergens. Add plants to help with the circulation of oxygen. Ask your company supply chain guru to buy only stuff that doesn't off-gas formaldehyde and is safe enough to chop up and eat. Lead that guru to the WELL Building Standard (wellcertified.com).
Light	Rather than relying on bright office lights around the clock, it's worth having an adjustable light for your desk so you can supplement natural light (if your office has it) with artificial light. Dim lights help foster creativity, while brighter lights will be better for grind-it-out productivity. Use blue lights near sunup, and red-light wavelengths after seven p.m. 💬
Screen time	Keep your computer monitor at a distance from your eyes that's equal to or greater than the screen size—nine-inch screen, at least nine inches; 20-inch screen, at least 20 inches. Every hour, focus on a distant spot, like the hulk 200 feet from you. Then start walking.
Water	Keep a jug of water at your desk at all times. This will help curb your hunger, plus water is much better for you than other tempting at-the-desk options (save black coffee or tea if you are a fast caffeine metabolizer). It's also smart to keep healthy snacks in a desk drawer to prevent vending-machine impulse buys.

DR. MIKE SAYS: All the night-lights in our bathroom are red-wavelength only, so going to use the throne in the middle of the night does not mean we are up for the rest of the night. These red-wavelength-only bulbs are available at the big-box hardware stores or online.

Get Vertical. See your HR contact or your direct supervisor and make a request for a standing desk or an accessory for your desk that allows you to raise your computer (a cheaper option). Setting aside some time every day to work from a standing position helps prevent back problems and encourages more movement throughout the day. (Standing desks add only two calories per hour to your outflow, so the real benefits are in back-problem prevention and getting you moving.) No matter what kind of desk you have, make a habit of getting up to walk at least two minutes every half hour. You can even set calendar, phone, or watch reminders just to tell you to move about.

Create a Tribe. A hallmark of many wellness programs is that they offer support groups or social groups that let people unite around common goals, whether through weight loss classes or yoga classes or other activities that encourage healthy behavior. The best of these do this not in a top-down way (someone tells you what to do) but a we're-in-it-together way (where people feed off each other's support and energy—and often those of top managers who act as cheerleaders—to make smarter choices). Nothing says you can't create your own informal groups to the same end. We'd like you to do that. Some ideas: a walk-at-lunch group, a group that does a healthy potluck every Friday for lunch, a recipe-exchange club, a few people who would like to take the spinning class every Thursday, a team getting together to run the local 5K. The key is that someone (cough cough...you) needs to take the lead and recruit a small number of people who share similar goals and are willing to buddy up to sustain wellness.

BYOI. This stands for build your own incentives. In corporate programs, incentives help people initiate change and adhere to long-term wellness goals. We know from commonsense parenting and general life experience that the proverbial carrot or stick gets people moving in the right direction. The trick for many, though, is making sure that carrot or stick isn't something unhealthy. You don't want to reward yourself for having six walking meetings a month with a hunk of lasagna. Defeats the purpose. But you can create some personal incentives and goals to help move you along.

So, for example, set a goal to have one walking meeting a day for a month. If you hit that goal, you schedule a massage (though it costs money, there's a health and bodily benefit to massage). Or maybe you say that if you hit your daily goal of 10,000 steps every day for three months, you will take a personal day to do whatever *you* want with no obligations to work or family. Are incentives a guarantee that you'll adopt healthy behaviors at work? Of course not. The guarantee comes in the form of automatic behavior, which happens when you make the environment support your doing the right thing. But the incentive works in a very important way. It kick-starts the action and turns motivation into automation.

CHAPTER 14

Paid in Full

«‹•————————————————————•›»

How to make the most of your health and retirement benefits
(even when you're paying for them yourself)

$

These days there are as many work scenarios as there are ice cream flavors. Some people work so-called traditional jobs for traditional hours. But there are loads more who do it differently. Some start their own businesses. Some cobble together their own gigs that change from month to month. Some work days for a major corporation and nights for themselves. Some work for a few months, then save money to travel for a month. Each one of these scenarios can be great if you're doing what you love, having enough time to keep healthy, making enough money to take care of yourself, and saving. Then, well, you've got quite a bit figured out.

But you still need the safety net we call benefits. Whether you work for a traditional employer, for yourself, or for some combination of the two, there are two really important benefit streams that you have to have (besides the most obvious one that goes by the code name *paycheck*): health and retirement benefits.

More and more, the money for both of these benefit streams is coming out of that paycheck. As you know, health care isn't subsidized the way it used to be, and pensions have made way for you-funded 401(k)s and other retirement accounts. And if you aren't traditionally employed, then the ball is 100 percent in your court; *you* have to make use of tax incentives and health-care subsidies to make sure your benefit streams are as robust as possible.

So when we think about the work environment, it's not just about your salary per se; it's also about the two benefit streams that can really work against each other. You have to pay for health care now—and use it wisely now—so that poor health doesn't bankrupt you in retirement. And you have to save for retirement (or your older self—see page 54) now, so that a lack of funds doesn't prevent you from maintaining your health—and, of course, a comfortable lifestyle—in the future.

☞ What to Do When You Start a New Job

New job? Congrats—it means new friends, new business cards, new challenges (and new office politics to learn!). While you want to jump in and immerse yourself, don't ignore the financial pieces that come with this transition. In other words, pay attention to the benefits. Get to know your main contact in HR, or at least read the materials that can help you make smart decisions. Here's a quick to-do list for making the transition from one job to another.

Get Transition Health Insurance. If you have any time between jobs in which you're not covered, extend your former employer's benefits under COBRA for up to 18 months. It may be expensive, but you can't go without. The alternative is to get a short-term policy on the public health-care exchange at HealthCare.gov (while it still exists). Not doing this can be the short road to bankruptcy if a medical emergency hits.

Decide What to Do with Your Old Retirement Plan and Sign Up for the New One. If you have at least $5,000 in retirement, you can leave it in your prior employer's plan, roll it into your new employer's plan, or roll it into an IRA. (The check should be made out to the new plan's administrator, not you, so you don't get taxed or penalized.) Administratively, rolling over may be easiest because you'll have more assets in a single place. Then enroll ASAP in the new employer's plan and set up automatic contributions from your paycheck. If your new employer doesn't have a plan, open an IRA (or other retirement account) and start making automatic contributions on your own.

Meet with Your Benefits Rep. Get all the info you can on health insurance and retirement benefits. Consider life and disability insurance as well.

More and more traditional employers are getting this: there's a financial incentive for them to make sure that you save well for retirement. Consider this: What happens if you haven't saved enough for retirement? Maybe that's OK because, what the heck, you see nothing wrong with pushing paper for a few more years, so you'll just work more years than you thought you would. That's not quite the lens employers use. They've come to understand that if their workforce isn't saving enough money for retirement, their workforce *will not retire*, thus saddling them (the employers) with an older cadre of employees who are more expensive to insure and to employ in general. Eventually these workers are going to slow down when it comes to doing their jobs—some, although certainly not all, may become set in their ways or less innovative—and that doesn't make for efficiency. So while we can't generalize for everyone, it is safe to say that your employer *wants* you to take advantage of retirement benefits so you can save enough to set yourself up for your postwork years (see ya!).

DR. MIKE SAYS: I did notice the *s* on *accounts*—that is, Jean says, to segregate the emergency, retirement, investment, splurge, and other accounts (like your Health Savings Account) from each other, as well as to make sure you diversify who is holding your money. It's important because keeping different accounts for separate purposes actually helps you make more headway toward your goals.

Not only that, but employers care about the interaction between money and health, and how yours affect them. What happens when money stresses you out? Maybe you take a day off, as more than one in five employees said they had in the prior year, according to a study from MetLife. Or maybe you're just plain distracted or inefficient.

So this chapter is really about creating space for financial wellness when it comes to saving for retirement and paying for health coverage. Work, after all, should fill not only your soul, but your bank accounts 🗨 as well.

Health Benefits

Things that can cost $30,000: a car, having a baby, a year of college tuition (or half a year at some places). You know what else? Three—*three!*—days in the hospital. That, in a nutshell, is why health insurance is a must. It's not just because you have to have it for legal reasons; it's also for your financial and mental health—so you have the financial wherewithal to handle acute treatments, preventive care, and everything in between, without sucking dry your retirement as well as your emergency accounts.

Simply put, insurance lets you see a doc and have a trusted medical team; even if you have a high deductible, you'll have peace of mind knowing that you'll be covered for routine exams, and (once you hit that deductible) an X-ray if you roll your ankle or get run over by an uninsured motorist, visits if you need to see specialists, and many other benefits that can become necessary.

So the hard part isn't deciding *whether* to have insurance; it's navigating all the choices, knowing the differences between options, and figuring out what's best for you and your family. This decision involves both health and finances—you want the best care that your money will buy, but you also want to be smart about spending those dollars. Now, we do hope that following the health steps throughout the book reduces the number of times you'll need to call on that insurance, but that doesn't mean you shouldn't be prepared (remember, medical costs are the number one reason for bankruptcy). Below we detail how to figure out the various choices that you will have to make.

⤷ Through your or your spouse's employer. Make sure that your favorite doc and hospital are covered by whatever plan you choose.* You may have to divide and conquer (maybe a favorite pediatrician is on your plan, but not your spouse's). You're also free to shop on your own through private or public health-care exchanges or marketplaces, but you won't qualify for premium subsidies from the government if your employer offers insurance.

---

*If doctors you prefer are not in your plan, you may have to pay the whole cost out of pocket to see them, or a greater share of the cost. Before you sign on to any plan, check this; most have online directories of doctors and hospitals listed. If you don't have a regular doc or you live in an area where health care is sparse, choose a plan with a larger network, because you'll have more choices.

⟿ On your own. Go to HealthCare.gov (while it exists) and enter your zip code. You'll be directed to your state marketplace if your state indeed has a marketplace. Otherwise you'll shop through HealthCare.gov itself. You can shop on private marketplaces, but you won't get any subsidies you're entitled to (essentially tax credits that defray your premiums) on sites run by anyone but the federal or state governments.

⟿ What it should entail. Every plan sold through the ACA exchanges (while it exists) has to cover these 10 things. Most plans your employer offers will cover them as well (but note that the coverage may not be complete— that is, some lab tests must be covered, but not all lab tests; and there are exceptions, especially if you work for a small company). Ask for the summary of benefits and coverage to be sure.

- emergency services

- hospitalization

- laboratory tests

- maternity and newborn care

- mental health and substance-abuse treatment

- outpatient care (services you receive outside a hospital; make sure your doc is included)

- pediatric services, including dental and vision care

- prescription drugs (but not all drugs will be covered; if you have an expensive one, make sure the plan you choose has it in its formulary, and for the indication appropriate to you)

- preventive services (such as immunizations and mammograms) and management of chronic diseases such as diabetes

- rehabilitation services

Types of Plans	
PPO or preferred provider organization (most common offering from employers)	Typically doesn't limit you to in-network health-care providers (or make you get referrals for specialists), but you will pay higher out-of-pocket costs for out-of-network health-care providers (often much, much higher, so go with the plan that covers your doc and hospital "in network"—you can ask your HR department to use its leverage to get them in network, too).*
HMO or health maintenance organization (old standby)	Typically limits coverage of medical services to in-network health-care providers with whom it contracts. You need a referral to see a doctor other than your primary provider. Out-of-network care is not covered or is limited to medical emergencies, and sometimes you even have to call from the emergency room to make sure they will cover you—be careful if you travel where the HMO isn't.
Consumer Directed Option (fastest-growing option)	This is a high-deductible health plan with a Health Savings Account. You pay for most of your care (doctors and prescriptions) until you meet your deductible, so less comes out of your paycheck. To help defray the costs, you'll have a health savings account into which you and your employer can deposit pretax money. It can be invested and grow tax-free as well. If you use the money to pay for qualified health-care expenditures, you generally won't have to pay any taxes on it when you use it (see above—and check with the plan administrator 💬).

DR. MIKE SAYS: High-deductible plans are becoming so popular that docs are really busy in October, November, and December—so book early if you go through your deductible and are thinking about elective surgery or some other needed but postponable health procedure or treatment near year's end.

*The reason out-of-network care is so pricey: the insurance company, and consequently you, don't get the benefit of the negotiated rates of in-network care. A 2015 study by AHIP's Center for Policy and Research found that the average out-of-network charges for the majority of 97 medical procedures examined "were 300 percent or higher compared to the corresponding Medicare fees" for the same services. Yes. Yikes. Some docs at "in-network facilities"–hospitals or surgicenters or emergency rooms, etc.–are "out of network." Super BIG bills. Surprise BIG bills. Yes. YIKES!

Your Cost: Premium Plus Out-of-Pocket Expenses	
Premium	If you buy through the public health-care exchanges, this cost may be subsidized. If you buy through your employer, your employer may also chip in for some of your share.
Out-of-pocket expenses	Includes co-pays, coinsurance, and deductibles. A co-pay is a fixed amount you pay per prescription or per visit. Coinsurance is a percentage of the cost that you're expected to cover. Ask your HR rep or employer if there is a premium reduction for healthy behaviors or biometrics. (At the Cleveland Clinic, for example, employees pay 2009 rates—a saving of over 90 percent of the premium and co-pays they would pay in 2016 and 30 percent of the total cost—if they are adopting behaviors and hit biometric goals,

Your Cost: Premium Plus Out-of-Pocket Expenses	
Out-of-pocket expenses *(continued)*	like achieving a normal blood-pressure or blood cholesterol level, with or without medications.) One other tip: don't focus solely on the cost of deductibles. That's easy to do because it's often the biggest number, but a low deductible may mean a more expensive plan overall. You need to look at the whole picture (co-pays, premiums, and deductibles in parallel comparisons—monthly, annually).
Factors to consider	⇨ If you're generally healthy (be honest here) and not planning on having a child, and do not have to worry about pediatric visits, then buying a plan with a higher deductible/ higher out-of-pocket costs and a lower premium generally makes sense. ⇨ If you know you have an expensive (chronic) medical condition or you know one is coming up (baby, hip replacement), you're usually better off buying a more expensive policy that covers more of your cost. Make sure as you do your calculations that you consider any incentives your employer is offering.* Another case in which a plan with a lower premium and higher out-of-pocket costs makes sense: when you can't afford the pricier one. A cheaper plan is better than no plan at all.

*Some employers are now paying their employees extra *not* to participate in the health plan and to essentially buy their own. Keep in mind that if you pay for coverage through your employer, you're doing it with pretax dollars; if you buy one through the exchange, you're doing it with after-tax dollars.

☞ Other Work Benefits

You have probably seen headlines about companies offering some outrageously cool benefits to their employees—Google provides the surviving spouse of a deceased employee 50 percent of that employee's salary for 10 years, Netflix gives a year of paid paternity and maternity leave, PricewaterhouseCoopers offers $1,200 per year in student loan repayment (up to $10,000). Even if your company doesn't capitalize the *b* in *benefits*, it might have other options you should look into. Some of the main ones:

Flexible spending account (FSA)	You can contribute up to $2,550 in pretax dollars that you then use to pay for medical expenses that aren't reimbursed. This essentially allows you to shave up to one-third off the cost of say, braces, because you're paying for them with pretax dollars. You can also have an FSA for dependent care expenses for kids and older parents (and can contribute up to $5,000 if you're married filing jointly or a single parent, $2,500 if you're married filing separately). Contributions usually come right out of your paychecks, so these are easy to make. However, if you don't use the money, you lose the money, so be very careful to put into the account only an amount you know you'll use. Schedule a calendar reminder to load up on contact lenses or chiropractor visits before the expiration date.

Group life and disability insurance	If your employer offers these insurance policies, chances are that buying them is more cost effective than buying them on your own. The Social Security Administration estimates one in four 20-year-olds entering the workforce will become disabled over their working career.
Disability insurance outside work	If you're single and relying on your own ability to earn a living, a disability policy should be high on your financial priority list. Think about it: Two-income couples could fall back on each other's earning power for support. But singles—or individuals who are the only wage earners in the family (and likely to remain so)—don't have that luxury. Shop around for a disability insurance policy that covers at least 60 percent of your income to age 65 (see if you can get one with an inflation rider, too). You can bring down the cost by electing to wait three to six months until your benefits kick in.
The gym	If your company has a gym on site, joining it (and using it) can be a way to get your fitness in during lunch hour, as well as to save yourself a pricey gym membership elsewhere.
Training classes	Many companies offer reimbursement for education, sometimes even outside your current field. If you're one of the many Americans not especially satisfied with their jobs, this can be a free way to move yourself in another direction.
Transportation savings accounts	As with FSAs, some companies allow you to use pretax dollars to pay for public transportation. This shaves up to a third off the price, depending on your tax bracket. This set of accounts seems to be disappearing after the 2017 tax law changes went into effect.
Employee discounts	Your employer may have deals with other companies to give you discounts to purchase their items or services. Check with HR.

Retirement Benefits

We all know the goal here: save enough money to take care of yourself for the length of your life, without having to work beyond the age that you want to. The trickiest part of this goal is that the equation for saving for retirement includes two variables that are, well, just plain squishy. That is, you don't exactly know how much you need, because you can't totally predict expenses that will come, partly because you don't know how long you'll live or how well you'll live. And you'll likely live longer than you now think you will.

So what we're after is the ultimate financial security blanket—assurance that you will be able to provide for yourself if you live to 80, 90, 100, or beyond 💬.

DR. MIKE SAYS: Some people refer to these years as the break points for how they feel about travel: Go-Go, Slow-Go, or No-Go. Do the AgeProof method and they may all become Go-Go years. That means more savings are needed, but that's why we tied 'em together for you.

DR. MIKE SAYS: I love helping people choose healthier behaviors.

JEAN SAYS: I'm with you. I don't really want to ever stop working completely. (Don't tell my husband.)

Of course, the biggest factor in the question of how much you need to save each year stems from another question: How long do you want to work? The answer influences income, savings, and more. We don't necessarily believe that it's all about trying to retire as soon as you can so you can live life with piña coladas and hammocks and a few tennis matches a week (not that there's anything wrong with that). Some people love what they do for a living, and continuing to pursue that passion 💬Qhas substantial health and financial benefits. But because of all the variables, approaches to retirement are very individualized. (That's why a financial pro can sometimes help. See page 113.)

That said, there is a common goal for all of us: save as much as you possibly can for that day, whenever it may come (and for 60 percent of people, according to a recent survey by financial firm Voya, the timing comes as a surprise), preferably without sacrificing too much of what you want and need *today*. Ultimately you want to be able to choose— to retire when you want to, when you're ready, when you're able.

You already know the ideal way to budget retirement and other savings (see page 31; for minimum amounts you should have saved by certain ages, see page 32). Remember to start by creating that emergency cushion to protect you and your family in times of unexpected crisis.

After you have that established, dedicate yourself (and a portion of your income) to a long-term savings plan. Here's where to put the money:

▷ If you have a retirement account at work. You know that 15 percent of your take-home pay we've been talking about incessantly—you're going to first put that money in a 401(k) or 403(b) or other vehicle where you get matching dollars, meaning your employer is pumping money into your accounts as well. If you don't get matching dollars, you still want to put the money first in a work-based plan, because it's the easiest thanks to the fact that your employer will pull money out of your pay (automatic!). The money in these accounts can grow, tax deferred, until you hit age 59½. At that point you can pull it out without facing a 10 percent penalty (though you will have to pay income tax at your current tax rate); but you don't have to start pulling it out until you hit age 70½ (or later if you're still working; check with your benefits department). Trust us: later is better. This goes hand in hand with working longer. (And note: If your company has added a Roth 401(k) to the menu, you may want to put some money into it. Unlike the Roth IRA, there's no income cap on participating—that's a big benefit—and it'll give you a pool of money on which you've already paid taxes to withdraw from in retirement, allowing your tax-advantaged funds more time to grow.) See page 191 about withdrawing your funds so they last as long as you do.

▷ If a work-based retirement plan isn't available. If you work for yourself, work a string of part-time jobs, or work for a very small company, you may not have a 401(k) or similar plan. No problem. Contribute automatically to an IRA or Roth IRA or to a retirement plan like a SEP that was designed specifically for the self-employed. But like ice cream and fathers-in-law, retirement plans come in all kinds of flavors. Your choices:

- **Traditional deductible IRA:** A traditional IRA is available for anyone under age 70½ who has earned income. Currently you can put in $5,500 a year, plus another $1,000 if you're 50 or older. Your spouse can do the same as long as one of you is in the workforce. Your contributions are tax deductible up to the income limits (these change every year), and the money grows tax deferred until you withdraw it at retirement. At that time it will be taxed at your current income tax rate. You *may* begin withdrawing from your IRA without penalty at age 59½, and you *must* begin making withdrawals the calendar year you turn 70½.

- **Traditional nondeductible IRA:** If you have another retirement plan at work (or your spouse does), you may not be able to deduct your IRA contribution. But you can still make one at the same rate: $5,500 a year, plus $1,000 for people 50 and over. You should contribute if you max out your work-based plan (and your HSA, 529, and other tax-advantaged accounts; see below) and still have money to invest for retirement. The money will grow tax deferred until you withdraw it (the rules are the same as for traditional deductible IRAs) and pay the taxes at retirement.

- **Roth IRA:** There aren't any age requirements when it comes to a Roth IRA, but for you to be eligible to contribute the maximum to a Roth (again, $5,500 plus $1,000), your modified adjusted gross income can't currently exceed $117,000 if you're single or $184,000 if you're married filing jointly. Other differences? Your contributions to the account won't be tax deductible, but your money grows tax-free. When you pull it out in retirement, you won't have to pay taxes on it. You aren't forced, as you are with a traditional IRA, to ever make withdrawals, which means you can pass this money on to the next generation tax-free. And you can make preretirement withdrawals for education and your first home, as long as the money has been in the account for five years, without penalty. You can also pull out your contributions, but not your earnings, at any time, penalty-free.

- **SIMPLE (Savings Incentive Match Plan for Employees):** This is for people who work for themselves or who have side gigs (they're easy to set up and administer). As employer, you have to make matching contributions of 1 to 3 percent of each employee's compensation (including yours). The current max is $12,500 for people up to 50; people 50 and older can kick in another $3,000.

- **SEP (or Simplified Employee Pension):** This is really good if you are a solo practitioner or work with your spouse, but it gets expensive if you have employees, because whatever you do for yourself, you have to do for them. You can contribute up to 25 percent of employee compensation (20 percent of net self-employment income if you're the owner) up to $56,000 in 2019. There are no catch-up contributions for SEPs.

- **Taxable accounts:** In some years, you may max out your ability to save in tax-advantaged retirement accounts and still be able to save more. Do it. Not only does that give you some wiggle room in leaner years, it gives you money on which you've already paid taxes to draw down in your earliest retirement years—before you must begin taking withdrawals from IRAs and other tax-advantaged accounts at age 70½. That way the money that's not being taxed on growth can continue to pile up.

⇨ If you're maxing out the above options and still have money to put away. First, congratulate yourself! Then get right to the options that give you tax advantages and will let your money grow.

- **529 college savings account:** For new parents, college tuition is like a colonoscopy—it's something you think is way off in the future, but before you know it, it's something you have to take care of. If you're in good shape saving for retirement, it's best to start deferring money for college as soon as you can. Each state offers at least one version of this savings plan, which allows your investments to grow tax-free, as in a Roth IRA. Contributions aren't deductible on your federal return, but your state may offer tax breaks for contributions. The best part? Distributions used to pay for the account beneficiary's college education are tax-free. If you don't use the funds for college, however, you'll pay a

10 percent penalty and income tax on earnings. To avoid penalties—or for any other reason—you can change the beneficiary to another qualifying family member at any time.

- **Health savings account (HSA):** If you're covered by a high-deductible insurance plan, you're likely eligible to establish an HSA, which allows you to either deduct your contributions or make them on a pretax basis, depending on your employer. There are no income restrictions, but in order for you to have an HSA, your deductible must be at least $1,350 for individual coverage or $2,700 for family coverage. You can then contribute $3,500 if you have self-only coverage, or $7,000 if you have a family plan (plus an extra $1,000 if you're 55 or older, in the form of a catch-up contribution if you like). Once the money is set aside, you can use it for qualified medical expenses—everything from doctor visits to over-the-counter medicines. If the money is used for anything else, you'll be taxed—and, if you're not over 65, penalized 10 percent. Once you turn 65, you can use your account for other expenses without penalty. But here's the thing. You can also *not* use it, which can turn your HSA into a supplementary retirement account.

☞ What Is a HSA?

Over the last few years, the use of HSAs—health savings accounts—has grown like a toddler's vocabulary. They can make a lot of sense financially, because the tax benefits can both save you on current medical costs and allow you to amass a supplementary retirement stash. Here's a primer:

What It Is. An HSA is a tax-advantaged savings account you open and fund for the purpose of paying for health care. In 2019 the deductible has to be at least $1,350 (for singles) or $2,700 (families). You can contribute up to $3,500 (singles) or $7,000 (families) and use the money to cover your deductible, co-pays, coinsurance, and other IRS-qualified health care expenses. You won't pay taxes on what you contribute or what you use for medical expenses. This makes an HSA different from an FSA (flexible spending account); with these accounts you lose any unused funds every year. Your HSA will grow and is yours forever.

How to Set It Up. You can open one with any bank or brokerage firm (there will be fees involved, and you can compare them at HSASearch .com). Then you can invest the money and it can grow tax-free.

What It Covers. A lot. So much that the IRS has a 40-page document detailing what you can spend the money on. (Over-the-counter painkillers are not included, but things like acupuncture and health-related travel are.)

How to Turn It into a Supplemental Retirement Account. Open it and contribute as much as you can each year. Invest the money (you may need a minimum of a few thousand before your HSA provider allows you to flip this switch) in a long-term portfolio similar to the one your retirement savings are in. When you have medical expenses you can cover out of current cash flow—without pulling money from your HSA—do it. Let this money grow instead. When you hit retirement and age 65, you can of course withdraw money for medical expenses without paying taxes. But you can also withdraw and use the money for anything else—like money out of a retirement account. You won't be penalized; you'll pay ordinary income taxes at your current rate, just as you do with a 401(k) or IRA.

AgeProof ESSENTIALS

1. Work isn't just a place to think about what you do for a living, but also a place to think about how you can keep on living. You can use your workplace to become healthier, and you should examine your retirement and health benefits to maximize your financial future.

2. Find a way to move around at work. Stand up. Have walking meetings. Park farther from your office. The more you sit, the unhealthier you are.

3. During every open enrollment period, it's worth taking time to examine your health and retirement benefits to make sure you're using the smartest strategies for protecting yourself now and in the future.

Part VIII
Domestic Engineering

The Science of Home

Finding peace—and financial security—amid the chaos of your castle (and using that castle as a supplementary retirement safety net)

In baseball, home base is the place where you score. In the game of tag, home base is where you stay safe. In military operations, home base is the central command center. In nature, home base—in the form of nests, caves, or holes—is sacred. All for good reason: Our homes are more than just a place to eat, sleep, and store 1983 yearbooks in the attic. Our homes are symbols of security, love, family, financial success, and—really—our entire lives.

If we extend the metaphor of home, it's not difficult to see the comparison of a physical home to an anatomical one: the human body serves that function. The structure in which we live comes with a plumbing system (your GI), a fuse box through which all power runs (your brain), a foundation (your skeleton), and even that pile of junk in the corner (your fat).

With both homes—your physical one and your bodily one—you invest a lot of time, energy, and money into making them functional and happy places.

But here's the reality of the home scenario for many people. Greeting-card writers can go on all day about how home is where the heart is, about how there's no place more special than your home, about how you are king or queen of your castle. That's all well and good, yes, but we know that the reality of life is that our homes lie somewhere between the fairy tale and the horror movie. Sometimes our homes cause conflict. Sometimes our homes cause stress. And sometimes our homes can drain us—emotionally and financially.

Because home base is so important, you should consider how it contributes to your health and how it can influence your wealth. Perhaps the biggest takeaway when it comes to your home is the notion that it should be the place where you strive for peace, where you try to smooth rough waters, to create for yourself an oasis in a world of conflict and noise—your sanctuary. But that's difficult to do when your home—as many are—is cluttered with stuff. Stuff to do, stuff to put away, stuff to look at, stuff to listen to, stuff to stress over, stuff to remind you that you don't have your life totally in order.

So while we don't want to turn this section into an episode of *Hoarders*, it is worth exploring the role of managing clutter and distraction as a proxy for managing your overall stress levels (and thus your health and wealth levels at the same time). With very few exceptions, we all have too much stuff—not just in the amount we have, but in the way we keep it. Clutter, things, junk, paper, reminders of chores unfulfilled—just overall noise.

JEAN SAYS:
Very similar to spenders, interestingly. Some people find spending money to be pleasurable; others find it painful. The latter group hoards cash.

OK, we promised this wouldn't turn into reality TV, but it's important to also note that there has been a lot of research in recent years into why we allow our environments—and our lives—to be overtaken by stuff. Hoarding has become a hot topic, and the medical establishment is taking it seriously as well. It officially became a disorder in 2013. At the Yale School of Medicine, researchers compared the brain activity of hoarders against that of nonhoarders when throwing something out. Hoarders found letting go of something painful, whereas keeping things made them feel calm and safe **Q**.

In addition, research into the brains of hoarders has shown that a part of the brain called the ventromedial prefrontal cortex is highly involved when they think about whether to keep things or throw them out. That part of the brain is tied to your feeling of identity—the idea that you do things, or keep things, because they make you *you*. For other people, throwing things out actually produces the opposite brain reaction: It's freeing. It's *fun*. Until it's not. Compulsive *de*cluttering is actually a form of OCD.

Where you are on this continuum is really up to you to discover. But what Elaine Aron, a psychologist in California, has documented is that some people are much more likely to be bothered by clutter (and noise and other stimuli) than others. She calls them highly sensitive people—and says that about 15 to 20 percent of the population falls into this category. If you're among them, getting a grip on your environment using the solutions in this section will be particularly helpful to you.

All of this really points to a key word—*excess*. And in the pursuit of an AgeProof life, part of the journey is about stripping your life of excess so you can make the most of what's most important to you. In other words, this isn't just about shredding some old papers or giving away your 1994 shoe collection or coming to grips with the fact that your garage doesn't have to look like a junkyard. This is about a mind-set—a mind-set that excess is unnecessary, it causes an unnecessary stress response, clutters your space and your mind, diverts your attempts to become financially AgeProof, and isn't any way to live.

If you look at the financial scenario you call home over your lifetime, you see that excess shaped like a bell curve. When you're young, fresh out of school and in your first couple of jobs, you likely rent a small, hopefully not too shabby but certainly not too nice studio or one-bedroom. You buy your furniture at IKEA, scream at the wall as you're trying to Allen wrench it together, and pray that your salary increases keep up with your landlord's hikes. Fast-forward a decade: you're married or otherwise paired up and buying a starter home. The carpeting has seen better days, so you invite your friends over for some beers, rip it out, and—hey—discover that some numbskull covered up actual wood with that pile of wool. Party time! Another 10 years down the road, you've made the move into your forever house. Now your salary supports the latest technology, the kitchen and bath renovations, the furniture you know you're going to live with for a long time, and the walk-in closet that can hold as much as you can put into it.

And that's the point. For the next 20 years, you add and add and add. Clothes and gadgets and art and stuff. You pay down that mortgage (or at least you should—we'll talk more about excessive refinancing in a few pages) and accumulate equity. Property values increase over time. Then the kids leave, you retire a car, and all of a sudden you're feeling that it all may be too much. You're tired of the excess. You're ready to simplify.

There's a financial payoff to the real estate cycle as many people go through it. When you're ready to retreat to a slightly smaller life, you can cash out, downsize, move to a place where the school taxes don't read like a second mortgage. There's value in your property. But in your quest to make your money last as long as you do, you've got to know how to tap it.

In the following two chapters, we're going to get more granular about your home—specifically, how you can design your home to maximize your health, and how you can deal with the specific home-oriented financial issues that limit or foster your financial security (from insurances that protect you to ways to organize your finances to how and where to store your data and documents to limit the risk of identity theft). As we launch into those more specific strategies and issues, the bigger picture is really about making your home your sanctuary and making sure the value it provides brings peace of mind.

If we're being realistic, we know that decluttering your life takes some time. You don't just rent a front-end loader to remove the junk from every room of your house. You don't just decide you're going to downsize, then move next week. First it takes a mind-set and a commitment to create a space and place to live that just *feels* better. Then you can get your home in order. Get your space in order. Get your life in order. When you do that, that's when you will have mentally prepared yourself to think, to dream, to strategize, to do, to live.

Your new start is going to come more easily when it's a clean one.

CHAPTER 15
Home Bases

*Your favorite comfort zone should also be your
first-line health zone*

When it comes right down to it, your home is most likely your favorite place on earth. It's where you unwind and relax. It's your sanctuary and safe haven. It's where you gather with kids, with pets, with friends, with all the people close to you to share meals and laughs. It's where moments are made. It's *you*.

With all the good that your home provides, however, it's smart to realize that it also has land mines, at least when it comes to your health. The couch can suck you up into evenings of inactivity .

Your computer can force your eyes and your mind into too much zombie-esque screen time (which can be as much of a financial hole as a boat). Your pantry—if you stock it just so—can tempt you with crackers and cookies and all kinds of junk. Now, don't get us wrong. We're not saying that your home should look like an oasis of health perfection, but we are saying that you shouldn't think of being in your home as retreating into sloth city. There's nothing wrong with relaxing and watching Netflix and enjoying a glass of wine while you decompress and enjoy your family. (Those things, particularly with the family, can be healthful.) But there is something wrong if your

> **JEAN SAYS:** My mother always says that good couches have ether.

derrieres are glued to the chair and chocolate chips are consumed by the bowlful.

Your home should be a place for health and happiness. So at the risk of your thinking that we're going to sterilize your whole abode (we're not), we're going to take you on a tour of the best ways to improve your overall health via your home environment.

Your Bedroom

You already know four of the sides of the pentagon of health—LUV-U back nutrition, stress management, avoiding toxins, and activity. The fifth? It's sleep, and it's just a little less important to your rate of aging than the other four. Most obviously, that's because getting optimal amounts of sleep allows you to get rid of waste that would ordinarily accumulate in your brain and cause inflammation that leads to memory loss. Good sleep also helps you have the energy to do what you need to do, make smart decisions, and avoid falling into health traps—because fatigue tempts you to choose shortcuts that may feel good at the time (sugar fix!) but that aren't good over time (right to your hips!). Perhaps less obviously, sleep is important because of the systemic influence it has over your body. For example, sleep is when you get to strengthen your brain connections (to help solidify your memory, improve concentration, and more). Decreased quality of sleep is associated with many health problems, including obesity and depression. Lack of good sleep also means you're compromising your immune system. So if there's one area of the home where you can really make exponential gains in your overall health picture, it's the bedroom.

From a health standpoint, there are only two things you should do in your bed—sleep and have sex. A quick word on sex: high-quality sex (whether it's the dueling banjos variety or a game of solitaire) is linked to greater longevity and better overall health (and makes you as many as 16 years younger). We're not going to spend time discussing relationship issues that can help you improve your sex life, but we do want to point out that quality sex (meaning not only frequent and enjoyable, but that it helps to be in a caring relationship) does have many health benefits. OK, so that means the bed shouldn't be used for work or watching TV or checking your phone or eating ice cream or anything else except sex and sleep. Your goal is to create an environment in which your body can wind down, shut down, and fall asleep to gain the health benefits we just mentioned.

The unfortunate part is that most Americans simply don't get enough snooze time. And it's not because you're not tired enough. It's because you're so frazzled, overworked, and time crunched that you are always tempted to do other things than call it a night. It's because you don't set yourself—or your environment—up for sleeping success. It's not always easy, but if you can make a commitment to attempt to get the appropriate amount of sleep (usually more than you're getting now), you will see compound interest on the investment—more energy, less weight gain, lower amounts of pain, and so much more. Some strategies for making room for more downtime:

⤷ Prep your sleep. For good health you have to do some prep work—whether it's shopping for ingredients and making a meal or changing from your work clothes into your gym clothes. Same goes for sleeping. You can't expect to be wired from a Facebook frenzy and then plop down into bed and fall right to sleep. So your prep work includes creating a sleep environment that's conducive to shut-eye. To do that, dim the lights in the bedroom an hour before you go to sleep and turn the thermostat down (a good sleep temp is cooler than whatever temp you're used to living in; research shows that the optimal choice is about 67 degrees 🗨). It also will help if you can do some light meditation or stretching (for maybe 10 minutes) to get your mind into a quiet place 🗨. Build into your schedule time to prepare all the things for tomorrow you might have forgotten (your child's or your lunch), and another 10 minutes for hygiene.

JEAN SAYS: A programmable thermostat can be set to reduce the temp automatically for an hour before you go to bed. You'll save about 3 percent off your heating bill for every degree you turn it down.

JEAN SAYS: I like the four-seven-eight trick. If you can't fall asleep: Inhale on a count of four. Hold your breath for seven seconds. Then exhale for eight seconds. Repeat three more times. You should be asleep.

Stop eating or drinking three hours before bed, and make sure all screens (phone or tablets) are away from the room.

⤷ Shoot for eight hours. To get there you obviously have to work backward from the time you need to get up, and plan to be in bed about 15 to 20 minutes before the eight-hour mark. (This is one of the reasons you shouldn't do other things in bed; if you work or play Words with Friends on your phone to wind down, you're teaching your body to be alert while you're in bed, rather than ratcheting down.)

⤷ Make sure you don't have sleep apnea. That's when you stop breathing during your sleep. You won't know it because you'll likely stay asleep (or at least not be conscious you awakened for a short time), but someone who sleeps with you can have an indication because you briefly stop breathing. Sleep apnea is often the sudden stopping of snoring (that's the apnea part) punctuated by progressively noisier snoring. If you or your partner suspects you have sleep apnea, talk to your doc about tests (these can often be done at home) and medical options to help open up your airways to reduce the risk of high blood pressure, mental fatigue, food cravings, brain dysfunction, and heart-related problems (and also normalize your sleep).

⤷ Supplement your sleep. With a power nap. At less than 30 minutes, a nap can be invigorating. Naps enable your body and brain to reboot and are commonly practiced in societies that boast great energy and longevity. (Any longer than 40 minutes risks making you feel drowsy when you wake, because you could slip into a deeper sleep cycle.) In terms of sleep supplements, there's no strong research to show that they should be first-line choices, but some people like valerian root (though it has an energizing effect in 10 percent of people), passionflower, theanine, or melatonin, 0.5 to 3 milligrams (especially if you're jet-lagged or working weird shift hours ). Aromatherapy seems to work for more than 30 percent of people, with lavender a large component of several blends that are successful. Use only 100 percent essential oils—no phthalates, etc.

ᗢ If you have serious sleep troubles, it is worth trying an online program like GO! to Sleep (which uses a restrictive sleep program that forces you to sleep less, so you grow so tired that you will get to sleep at a normal time; see ClevelandClinicWellness.com). And if that doesn't help, see a sleep specialist, who can prescribe some more aggressive monitoring and treatments.

Your Kitchen/Pantry

For many people the kitchen is the Grand Central Terminal of home. It's the hub of activity. It's the center of family discussion. It's where the action happens. It's also where pounds are gained or lost. It's where health is improved or threatened. It's where you make in-the-moment decisions that can affect your future. So it's no surprise that the nerve center of your house has so much influence over so many things you do throughout the day. On page 155 we discussed the foods and nutrients that serve as the foundation for healthy eating, so we won't review them again here. Instead we'll detail some other tactics you can use when making your eating decisions.

ᗢ Make food a two-way relationship. Too often the food battle is all about your love for it, as in, *Oh, I just can't live without creamed corn and cheesy potatoes.* Fine. Maybe you can't, and maybe there's a way for you to—occasionally—have small portions of the foods that you associate with comfort or sin, but that give you joy. But we'd like you to change your mind-set a bit. After all, you wouldn't accept one-way relationships when it comes to, well, relationships.

DR. MIKE SAYS: Stopping eating 3 hours before start of planned sleep time and finishing 75 percent of your calories 7 hours before start of planned sleep time seems to improve sleep initiation, duration, and quality substantially (see my book *What to Eat When*).

JEAN SAYS: I actually have a two-sided clock in my kitchen labeled "Grand Central Station."

So why should you accept them with food? That is, so what if you love trans fat–laced puff snacks? What have they ever done for you? Nothing, nada, not a damn thing. All they've given you is a momentary fling of the taste buds and then a lifetime of misery in the form of overstretched waistbands, arthritis, diabetes, heart disease, and less brainpower. So instead of thinking that you have to succumb to every one of your taste-based temptations, maybe you need to think about your relationship with food the way you think about other relationships in your life. Is your food loving you back—in terms of promoting good health, clearing your arteries, preventing cancer and brain rot, and keeping you satisfied for the long haul? If that's what you want—and it *is* what you want if living an AgeProof life is your goal—then you will be more likely to choose fruits, veggies, lean proteins, 100 percent whole grains, and healthy fats.

▷ Use a chef's secret weapon. There's an easy knock on "healthy eating." Tastes like cardboard, right? How much grilled chicken and steamed broccoli can one have before wanting to gnaw through an actual cardboard box to get to the Pop-Tarts? (More than 150 million boxes are purchased annually.) But that—like any form of stereotyping—is just plain wrong. There are literally thousands of ways you can change tastes, flavors, and approaches to your basic staples simply by experimenting with herbs and spices. And every culture has traditional spices and herbs that make food that loves you back easy to love and to create. The best part is that herbs and spices have no negative effect on your weight (and many have health benefits). You can experiment with all kinds of spices, ranging from sweet to spicy-hot to exotic, and you can change the makeup of any dish just like that. As you try new combinations, you'll come up with formulas that feel right for you and your family.

⤳ Create an emergency food kit. If you live in a hurricane or tornado zone, you know the drill when it comes to emergency preparedness. You want batteries, flashlights, water, canned goods (and a can opener), a propane stove and flint lighter, a solar-powered radio, even a solar-powered cell phone recharger, and other essentials to keep you going in case of a natural disaster. While we don't mean to directly compare such an event to an 11 p.m. craving for a mocha-something-ccino, the principle is similar. You create emergency plans to get you out of trouble, and you can do the same when temptation is the internal storm that's brewing. Every kitchen or pantry should be stocked with foods that you can go to when you just have one of those days and all you want to do is obliterate some salt-and-vinegar chips. Your go-to can be nuts, olives, and an apple, or maybe it's some carrot sticks with some all-natural almond or walnut butter (try to get crunchy, sweet, and salty all at once). But the point is that if you create your emergency kit, you know that's the protocol to reach for when your urge is to stray somewhere else.

⤳ Some areas you should also think about cleaning up in an effort to stay healthy: the garbage disposal area (bacteria spray up after each use) and the dishwasher (put a cup of white vinegar in a container on the top shelf and run the dishwasher through a cycle while it's otherwise empty). Also, you can cut down on germs and get rid of bacteria by cleaning up your rags and sponges. These are fertile bacteria breeding grounds, containing more than 100,000 germs per square inch. Microwave wet sponges (dry ones can catch fire) for two minutes on high when they're particularly dirty (preferably each day) to kill bacteria, or get rid of them (best choice, as we believe sponges are just about impossible to get clean) and just use dishrags cleaned in a diluted bleach solution. And if you have the choice, use wooden cutting boards, which are safer than plastic ones in terms of reducing the growth of bacteria. Clean all your counters with water after preparing food. If your food is contaminated with bacteria, as all chicken and hamburger are, kill them by wiping your counters down with Lysol, bleach, or a green alternative such as vinegar. Ditto for your fridge and freezer.

☞ Your Home Emergency Kit

It should include:

- fire extinguishers in key areas (kitchen, garage, at least one on every floor)

- fire plan (so family knows what to do and where to go)

- batteries in smoke alarms changed every six months

- list of emergency contacts (family, doctors, authorities) in a location that your family knows

- backup generator if you have medical devices that require electricity (in case power goes out for extended periods)

Your Main Living Areas

Besides the kitchen, there are probably one or two spots where you spend most of your downtime. It could be a family room or maybe even a home office, but it's the spot where you plop down your butt, get a cold beverage, and settle in for a night of *Real Housewives of Whatever City Is Next on the List.* And you know what? We're not going to sit here and come up with a laundry list of things you need to do (you already have enough laundry) to make your living areas a beacon of health. After all, you *should* have rooms that are yours and that are where you de-stress and veg out. That said, there are a few simple things you should think about when it comes to your main spaces.

- ⇨ Spring-clean even if it's not spring. As we talked about a few pages ago, decluttering your life is one of the most crucial steps to finding peace and getting a solid grounding in healthy living. If all your main areas are filled with piles of papers, with junk on every shelf, it creates a low-grade (or maybe even high-grade) disturbance that has a trickle-down effect on other areas of your life. The more you can simplify your space, the better the frame of mind you'll be in to tackle other issues, whether they're health related or money related. Your spruce-up project may take only a few hours—or it can take a few days or weeks to clean up, clean out, and live simpler. But we encourage you to make it a family project, and to take one small piece at a time (maybe a new room or corner every weekend for a few hours at a time), and eventually you'll dig yourself out Q.

  JEAN SAYS: Alternately, if you're a Marie Kondo disciple, you pick one thing—clothing, books, kitchen utensils—to tackle at a time. Going room by room (or drawer by drawer) also works; this is just another way to do it.

  While there is some research to show that a cluttered life can make you more creative, don't use that as an excuse. There is also a bounty of research that shows making your bed makes you happier, which, by the way, we find to be true; it's easier to think in a room where even the bed is clutter-free. The benefits of decluttering will extend into other areas of your life.

- ⇨ If you have trouble working exercise into your daily schedule, make a commitment to weave it into your screen time Q by finding a place for it at home. Maybe it's worth the investment for a Schwinn low-cost dual-action stationary bike that you can put in front of the TV. Maybe you can commit to doing lunges, squats, and push-

  JEAN SAYS: I schedule exercise in my calendar. I also try to exercise with friends—knowing that I'm meeting someone makes me more likely to show up.

DR. MIKE SAYS: I have all the key papers in a box in our safe—the box is labeled "In case I die." Hope Nancy (and I) remembers the safe combo when the need arises. AgeProofing should help us with that, though.

ups during the first commercial break of the hour-long show you're watching, or take a three-minute walk every commercial break (not to the fridge), or do some jumps outside every hour between dinner and bed. Maybe you can invest in some resistance bands that don't take up any space but that you can use while catching up on the news. Maybe instead of sitting, you roll out a mat that you can stretch on. The point: it's about making your environment conducive to the behaviors you want to adopt.

⇨ Create a paper space. Even though much of our lives are digitized, you should keep all your financial and related records in one space, in organized and easy-to-find files (preferably locked up). This spot should include not only all your account info, but also your paperwork as it relates to your estate, your taxes, your directives, and any other "home base" paperwork. An organized financial picture is half the battle when it comes to making financial gains and creating financial freedom 🗨. To do it right might take a day or two of some pretty heavy organizational work, but you will be thankful in the end that you did it—and that you can call upon any paperwork very quickly when you need it.

🖙 Taming the Paper Tiger

Let's just acknowledge that when it comes to the piles of paper on your desktops and kitchen counters and wherever else you choose to plop them, many of them are financial. You need some ground rules for how to handle all that. Here are ours.

⇨ Keep, Toss, Shred:

Anything tax-related: Three years

Anything tax-related where you lost money: Seven years

Paperwork relating to assets (homes, investments, cars): As long as you have the asset

Receipts (ATM and otherwise): Until the monthly bill or statement comes in

Monthly bills and statements: Until the annual reconciliation statement arrives

Legal documents: Birth certificates, divorce papers, military discharge papers, adoption records, citizenship papers, powers of attorney, wills, living wills, health-care proxies: Forever

Shred anything you no longer need that contains identifying details, like addresses, account numbers, Social Security numbers, etc.

▷ Create a road map someone else can follow. Write a list of accounts, passwords, contact information for important people in your financial and legal life (lawyer, accountant, financial adviser, doctors, etc.), contact information for important institutions in your financial and legal life (banks, brokerage firms, insurance agencies, etc.), and the locations of other important info. Update this once a year. Keep it locked up if possible. Make sure your nearest and dearest know where it is and how to access it.

▷ Keep parallel filing systems online and off. Today most people pay bills online and receive bills in the mail. You know what this creates? Chaos. The solution is to create the same system of folders and files on your two desktops (real and computer). For example, you'll want a folder for investments. In that folder you'll want files for your 401(k), IRA, 529, and discretionary brokerage accounts, and the documentation you got when you gave your nephew a $10,000 friends-and-family investment to start his small business. Set up the same files—some other categories would be credit cards, house (mortgage, taxes, common charges, maintenance), insurance (auto, home, life)—on your computer that you have in your filing cabinet. Once a year, go through both sets of files and move the things you no longer need from day to day to the filing cabinet in your basement or storage in the cloud.

Your Bathroom

Forgive us for going behind locked doors here, but since your day often starts and ends right here, it's a good spot for reminding you of ways you can influence and monitor your overall health. Some quick reminders:

▷ Brush and floss religiously. Poor periodontal health is linked to poor heart health. Change your toothbrush every three months, and avoid alcohol- or antibiotic-based mouthwashes (so your mouth bacteria can metabolize nitrates to nitrites and then load your arterial walls with nitric oxide to make blood flow better).

▷ Keep your medicine cabinet stocked with the essentials:

Dental floss

Soft-bristle toothbrush (don't brush as you brush a toilet, and change every three months); a sonic brush is even better

Healthy toothpaste (if you have frequent mouth ulcers, avoid the foaming agent sodium lauryl sulfate and whitening agents)

Home blood-pressure-testing device

Alcohol-based hand sanitizer

Skin exfoliant (removes dead cells and reduces adult acne)

Pain relievers and medicines: Topical muscle reliever, such as Bengay, Tiger Balm, capsaicin cream, or arnica; aspirin (162.5 and 325 milligram doses)

General first aid kit: Butterfly tape strips (to close little cuts); Band-Aid Liquid Bandage (cyanoacrylate Dermabond for blisters and small cracks—this liquid bandage is like the stuff doctors use, it's like superglue, but tested for safety in humans); petroleum-based Vaseline, Neosporin, or bacitracin cream (to keep wounds moist)

Tea tree oil (for pilonidal cysts and feet)

Burt's Bees beeswax lip balm

Gly-Oxide (soothes canker sores)

Pepto-Bismol (for traveler's diarrhea)

Antacids (such as over-the-counter Prilosec)

Epsom salts (use in bath for soreness)

Elastic bandages for tight wrapping (as part of the RICE protocol for injuries—rest, ice, compression, elevation)

Benadryl tablets for minor allergic reactions

➪ Check your waste (both kinds). Any changes in color or frequency warrant further investigation.

➪ Wash your face. Skin is a proxy for overall health, so keep it clean with a wash, and use a moisturizer and sunscreen.

☞ Safeguard Yourself from Falls at Home

As you age, your chance of falling rises. And that means you're at a higher risk of not only breaking bones, but also suffering adverse effects associated with falling (such as developing pneumonia). You can greatly reduce the risks by doing things like getting rid of throw rugs and cleaning up stray wires (easy to trip on) and making sure you have grippy mats and rugs in bathroom areas (and handles on showers and tubs—we all need them, even 24-year-olds).

CHAPTER 16

Home Runs

‹‹‹———————————————————›››

*You put a lot of money into that place you lay your head; if you
plan right, it can give you something substantial back*

$

It doesn't matter whether you live in a mansion or a condo, in a
city or the country, by yourself or with a small army, your home is
more than just a place that holds your stuff, keeps you warm, and
protects you from rain, snow, and bird droppings.

Your home is an investment. And although we're sticking with
what we said earlier about your job's—i.e., your earning power's—
ranking highest on the list of all the investments you have, this one
comes very close to the top. And unlike, say, stocks (unless you have
a sheaf of shares left to you by your favorite grandfather, or a position
in a company where you've worked your whole life), your home has
emotional value. Your home is where you raise your
family. Your home is where you make decisions. Your
home is where you snuggle up with your favorite
pet or glass of Chardonnay (or maybe a pet named
Chardonnay 💬?). Your home is where you host holiday dinners. Your home is about making—and
storing—memories 💬.

If you've read this far through the book you've
learned that pairing emotions and money is the equivalent of pairing a Scorpio with a Leo. You may think

**💬 JEAN
SAYS:** Not
as crazy as it
sounds. The dog
next door while
I was growing
up was named
Michelob.

**💬 MIKE
SAYS:** Some of those are
about clutter, but many are about
the times spent playing with kids—
like pitching and catching with
Jeffrey and being his soccer goalie,
and the shaving cream fight for
Jenny's seventh birthday. We still
had many cans left for another
one on her 16th; I wish I had more
pictures. Wonder if the cloud will
keep memories made now forever.

you've got a love match in the beginning but it rarely ends well. Emotions lead you to make financial decisions that are better for today-you than future-you, and when we're talking about a very long-term investment like a house, those heart-not-head type decisions are often pricey mistakes.

Before we dive into it and show you how to manage the money you plow into your home, we think it's important to acknowledge that there is a bit of conflict over whether your home is actually an investment (and, beyond that, over whether it's a good one). Research by Yale economist Robert Shiller shows that from 1890 to 1990, housing prices appreciated at just about the rate of inflation. In the last two decades we had a boom—in which prices outpaced inflation—followed by a notorious bust. Some people are still suffering from that.

Our view: Unless you're a real estate investor purchasing properties to fix up and flip (and believe us, that's a lot more complicated than it looks on HGTV), or buying rental properties to manage as a means of generating income, you're best off not counting on your home as the place where you're going to make a killing. Rather, you should think of it as what Shiller found it to be in that 100-year period: a supplemental savings account.

By purchasing intelligently—we'll talk about how momentarily—and making an effort to pay off, or come fairly close to paying off, your mortgage before you retire, you end up with... well... a paid-off house. And you can do a lot of things with that. You can continue to live there, of course, paying only real estate taxes and insurance. That's a nice low-pressure way to enter retirement, the time of life when your income will likely begin to tail off. You can sell it and use the proceeds to buy something cheaper, smaller, more convenient to your kids, easier to maneuver (i.e., horizontal rather than vertical living), with facilities to provide you with a social structure or continuing care (or whatever your needs happen to be). Or you could—by taking advantage of a reverse mortgage—pull some of the equity out to fund your other living expenses while you continue to age in place.

So that's what we're going to talk through in this chapter. Strategies for buying right based on your stage in life. Strategies for paying down your mortgage (and, when it actually does make sense, for refinancing or using a home equity loan/line of credit to tap some of the savings you've amassed). And strategies for your eventual exit (even if you have no desire to go anywhere at all).

Your Home: The Place

We all remember the famous line from *Forrest Gump* comparing life to a box of chocolates. But when it comes to all the financial issues involved in home buying, home owning, and home maintaining—which for most individuals (no matter their age) is the largest item in the monthly budget—it may feel like that other Tom Hanks movie, *The Money Pit*, and the line should go something like this: "Life is like a slot machine. You just keep putting more money in, more money in, and more money in, and the damn thing doesn't spit out a single nickel." There's no doubt that there's a ton of dough tied into just plain old living expenses, which is exactly why you need to be smart about how you approach home-related items in your budget (see page 195). There's a lot to consider—so much that, depending on your goals and situation, you may decide that owning a home isn't even for you. This section will help you answer some of the most important home-related questions.

☞ Protect the Rents

Nearly 95 percent of homeowners have homeowner's insurance (their mortgage company makes them buy it). But only 37 percent of renters have renter's insurance. That's a pretty dumb move, particularly when you consider that with home ownership rates at a 50-year low, more people are renting. And that it's not all that expensive—just $15 a month on average, according to the National Association of Insurance Commissioners—and it can bail you out if you're robbed or have a fire. You can save by bundling your auto and renter's insurance with the same company, by increasing your deductible, or by doing other things like improving your credit score.

Should You Buy?

The fact that home ownership is still considered part of the American Dream—even after the Great Recession—makes it seem like a no-brainer that at some point you will choose to buy a home instead of renting. But the added costs of home ownership (moving, insurance, maintenance, property taxes paid directly by you) mean that each time you make the choice between buying and renting, at various stages of your life (including when the kids are grown and you're thinking about that next phase) you should take a good, hard look at both financial and other quality-of-life issues.

Home Ownership: The Right Choice for Right Now?	
PROS	CONS
When you want to sell, years' worth of mortgage payments (as well as any growth in your property's value, if you get that) help provide a supplemental pot of money for buying a larger home or, eventually, for retirement.	If you plan to move within five years, it may not make sense. That's because of potential ups and downs in the market as well as the other costs associated with ownership—like the costs of moving and maintenance. If you sell for a price lower than you paid, you lose. (From 1968 to 2004, home prices increased more than 6 percent a year every year. But then prices flattened and crashed, so buying and selling is all about timing. You don't make money until you sell.)
Ownership gives you freedom. It's yours and you can do with it what you want. You can paint the walls purple (though if you want to sell the place in a reasonable time, any good home stager will tell you you're going to have to paint them white or off-white).	Investing in a home and all the related expenses means you're tying up a lot of income that you could otherwise invest. Even if the money you spend on your mortgage is the same as what you'd spend renting, the down payment on a house is money you might want to spend on other investments. It may be more lucrative to invest a lump sum and watch it grow than to put it into a house.

Home Ownership: The Right Choice for Right Now?

PROS	CONS
You're not "throwing money away." The argument is that when you're paying rent, you're not putting anything toward a property you own. When you own you're saving, at a modest interest rate, which historically has been roughly the rate of inflation. This is not a bad thing, as you build equity in the home over time. It can be wise to pay a little bit more toward the equity of the home, rather than just the interest. But what many people don't understand is that during the first half of your mortgage, most of the money you are paying goes the way of stray hairs—down the drain. It doesn't build much equity. (Don't believe us? Run any mortgage calculator, then look at the amortization schedule. Ooof!)	You pay interest on your mortgage. Again, you have to ask yourself if you would make more money if you invested it elsewhere. The fact that mortgage interest is cheap has led some people to argue that you should always have a mortgage; borrow money on the cheap, invest it, reap the rewards. This doesn't always work. Consider the stock market in 2008 and human behavior overall. You say you're going to buy term life (because it's cheaper than whole) and invest the difference, but do you ever really do it? Not so much.
You win if the value of homes happens to outpace inflation—which has happened a few times nationwide, notably after World War II and again at the beginning of this century, as well as locally in booming places (Austin, Seattle, San Francisco/Palo Alto, Boston, Brooklyn).	Property taxes go up continually (seemingly without end ●), and homeowner's insurance is more expensive than renter's insurance. That's why it usually costs more to own than to rent.
Various studies show that owning a home has many benefits, not just financial ones. One study showed that homeowners were happier than renters, and that children of homeowners got better grades. And homeowners were also shown to have lower stress and other health advantages. We should note that there is conflicting research. One study of female owners showed no increase in happiness; in fact, these owners felt more pain than renters, resulting from having less time to spend with friends and pursue leisure activities.	Not only do you have to pay to maintain your home (which costs 1 to 2 percent of the average value of the property a year, according to Harvard), but money you put into improvements like new baths and kitchens are, in reality, just sunk costs. You'll get a portion of them back, but only if you sell within about 15 years. Wait any longer than that and your "new" kitchen is no longer new, but shockingly out of date. That brass hardware, or convenient desk you put in the kitchen? Passé. As are faux finishes and whirlpool tubs.

JEAN SAYS: You should grieve— in other words challenge—your property taxes if you haven't. I did this the easy way, by hiring a lawyer who took one-third of the savings for the first three years. Mike did, too. Money well spent.

Home Ownership: The Right Choice for Right Now?	
PROS	CONS
Research has shown that people are happier when spending their money on experiences rather than things. Are homes things or experiences? They're somewhere in between. So if you can use your money to find ways to change and improve the way you experience your home, you'll more likely derive the happiness benefit 🔾 from it.	Home ownership is stressful 🔾. Something goes? You have to fix it or get it fixed. The grass needs mowing? The snow needs shoveling? The weeds need pulling? You have to do it or get it done (and use your time to do so, or pay the homeowners' association an onerous amount of money to take care of it).

🔾 **JEAN SAYS:** I'm writing this at the desk in my bedroom, a room I modeled as closely as I could on Diane Keaton's bedroom in *Something's Gotta Give* (a movie on which many real estate fantasies rely; director Nancy Meyers has been lovingly accused of churning out real estate porn). This room is done in light blue and taupe. My writing desk (as hers was) sits looking out a window. We've decorated minimally with black-and-white photography. It's as close to a sanctuary as I'm ever going to get—and it gives me great pleasure to work in here, watch TV in here, or simply lie on the chaise in here and talk on the phone. Yes, like Cleopatra, I have a chaise (albeit no one to peel me grapes).

🔾 **JEAN SAYS:** In 2009, shortly after we got married, my husband and I bought a place in Long Beach Island, New Jersey. The following summer we drove out on a Friday night; we were expecting guests the following day. When we walked into the house, the whole place looked weird. The dryer was working, but not the washer. The instrument panel on the oven was blinking as if we'd had a power failure. Upstairs in the kitchen, there were little pieces of plaster all over the floor. We thought maybe we'd been invaded by raccoons. (That had recently happened to my aunt and uncle in Florida. Raccoons are evil and clever; they trashed the place.) But no, we'd been hit by lightning. It had traveled from a TV satellite dish left on the roof by the prior owners, down the chimney, and along some metal piping used to hold the walls together (inside the walls; we never saw it), and blown out a decent-size hole above the fireplace. Anyway, we called in the insurance company. The damage was covered. A few years later, Hurricane Sandy swept through, and although we had minimal damage compared to some, we did have water in the basement, and that water brought on mold. Another claim. There have been tornadoes. Other major storms. Leaks in the roof for no reason in particular. Just. House. Stuff. You deal with it because you have to—and if your house brings you enough emotional benefit, which this one does, it's worth it. But it's not especially easy or fun.

☞ Add Emotional Value to Your Home

You can't always measure the value of a home in Zillow stats. There's plenty you can do to make your home feel good—which has quality-of-life and stress-reducing benefits. Some ideas:

- Buy things that enable you to have quality home-based experiences. A new patio set for outdoor entertaining, or a new outdoor grill. Or a new tub if a good soak is one of your favorite pleasures. New experiences bring us happiness because they're exciting and challenging. If you can include friends, even better.

- Swap out your lightbulbs. Not for cheaper ones—but sometimes these new energy-efficient ones are harsh (and ugly). Some brands give you the old-fashioned/softer feeling of good old incandescents.

- Put up blackout shades. If you can't sleep, you're going to be cranky. And while you're at it, flip and rotate your mattress a couple of times a year.

- Invest in security. If you feel secure in your home, you're more likely to be able to relax there.

- Get a pet. For full-on happiness, make it a puppy. Pets make us happier and healthier.

Smart Buying

Some tenets of smart home buying hold true no matter what phase of life you're in. These factors always matter: school quality; proximity to health care, emergency services, shopping, culture, and the place where you work; and curb appeal. But it's also true that many people get so caught up in, yes, the emotion of beautiful countertops or other small details that they fail to make a smart overall choice. A few suggestions for getting it right:

⮕ Think about what you can't live without. On HGTV they call this your "must-haves." You shouldn't have too many (or you'll never find a place to live), but you should have some and not deviate from them. The length of your commute, for example. If you don't want to go over 20 minutes each way, a place that's 30 miles out will eventually make you miserable (and no, buying a new car won't help 💬). Or a bedroom on the ground floor. This can be particularly key as you age; even if you're fully able to handle stairs (and all Mike's suggestions for staying fit) today, think about what happens 10 years from now.

⮕ Try it before you buy it. If you're moving to a new city or state (or country!) because you think it's where you want to be, do yourself a favor and rent something for at least a full season before committing. We all know too many people who sold their place, moved halfway across the country, and were back home again before the calendar turned.

⮕ If you're downsizing, don't wait. You may have many reasons for wanting to stay in your forever home a little longer—the kids have memories, your friends are still in the neighborhood, it's familiar. But here's one big reason to make the move as soon as your life will accommodate it: perhaps there's no other one move that will make such a big difference in your retirement fortunes. (If you're looking for proof of this, use the helpful calculator developed by the folks at the Financial Security Project at Boston College— it's at SquaredAway.bc.edu/move-or-stay-put.) Any money you manage to pocket from swapping a bigger/more expensive home for a smaller/less expensive one gets added to your retirement coffers. That immediately increases

MIKE SAYS:
Maybe autonomous cars will change that?

the amount of money you have to live on each year you're retired. For example, if you come out $150,000 ahead, you're looking at an extra $6,000 every year for retirement (assuming you're withdrawing at a 4 percent rate). And that doesn't count the thousands you're not spending on care for the bigger lawn and higher property taxes. The differences, though they seem small, add up. Finally, the older you get, the tougher it is to move at all. Go while you have the energy to do it.

↪ Factor furniture (and the cost of living where you are) into the equation. The cost of housing isn't just the house; it's filling up the rooms, keeping the flower beds full (and watered), paying for gas and electric, and the list goes on. If you know people in the area, ask them to share with you their monthly upkeep costs so you know what you can bank on. Otherwise, local utility companies often have estimates.

Smart Borrowing

Finding the house you want to buy is only half the challenge; you also have to borrow smart. Although there are several steps, the key here is to try to time the period for which you borrow against the next antici-pated major change in your life. So, for example, if you're buying your first home and you know you'll outgrow it in a decade, you may want to look into a 10/1 adjustable rate mortgage (ARM) with an interest rate fixed for the first 10 years before it starts adjusting, rather than a plain-vanilla 30-year fixed. Why? The 10-year fixed rate will likely be slightly lower than the 30-year, so you can bank the money you're saving for other goals (like retirement). And you'll be out of there before the adjustment hits. On the other hand, maybe you're 50 and moving—finally—into your dream home. Retiring the mortgage before you retire from work is a smart idea, so you want to look at a 15- or 20-year fixed-rate loan (depending on your retirement timetable) rather than a 30-year one. Yes, the payments will be higher. But by paying up front you'll give yourself a great deal of breathing room down the road.

Preparing for a Mortgage

Credit reports	Before you apply for a mortgage, make sure you're in great standing (740 or better credit score for most loans, 760 or better for jumbo loans). Pull all three credit reports to get a complete picture. While you're at it, don't apply for any new credit for a year before applying for a mortgage.
Down payment	You'll typically need to put down 10 to 20 percent of the cost of the home (though some loans will require less). The more you can put down, the more you'll save—you won't need mortgage insurance if you put down more than 20 percent, and you may even qualify for a bigger loan. Lenders—who learned their lesson when the housing bubble burst—will make sure your housing payments don't exceed 28 percent of your gross adjusted income.
Budget in costs	Your related home costs can be about 1 or 2 percent of the value of your home, according to Harvard's Joint Center for Housing Studies. This doesn't include taxes and insurance, just maintenance.
Decide your loan length/type	A 15-year mortgage will have higher payments, but you'll save tens of thousands of dollars on payments and interest over the life of the loan. Adjustable mortgage rates (actually hybrid adjustables, which are fixed for the first five, seven, or 10 years of the loan, then begin adjusting yearly) make sense when you plan on being in a home for 10 years or less. The goal is to pick an initial term that jibes with the amount of time you plan on staying in the house. It's typical to save about half a percentage point on a 5/1 ARM versus a 30-year fixed-rate loan. Fixed-rate loans make the most sense if you plan on being in the house forever—or you're uncertain of your plans.
Don't take the first offer	You should shop around among different lenders to get a good deal—lowest rates, reasonable down payment, etc. Preapproval (a piece of paper from a lender that says yes, we'll give you a loan) can make you more attractive to a seller as well.
Check out the CLUE report	The seller can provide a copy of the Comprehensive Loss Underwriting Exchange report—a detailed history of claims against it (if there are many, you may be charged more for insurance, and it may be a red flag about home quality, integrity, potential mold, etc., as well as location). Request one online from LexisNexis.com.

☞ Should You Pay Off the Mortgage?

This is an emotional decision, rather than strictly a financial one. Having a mortgage weighs heavily on some people's minds; they lump it in with debt, a word that has negative connotations all the way around. But mortgage debt is generally good debt. You're paying toward a home that you will eventually own outright. In many cases that home will appreciate at slightly over the rate of inflation. You're also getting a tax advantage, because the interest you pay on first and second mortgages of up to $750,000 ($375,000 if you're married, filing separately) is tax deductible (the old limits of deducting interest on loans of "$1 million" and "$375,000" still pertain if you secured your loan before 12/15/17).

On the flip side, you're taking money that is liquid, that you can use if you have an emergency, and you're locking it up with a lender. If you suffer a job loss or an illness, or you just need a bit of quick cash, you won't have it available to you. Sure, you may be able to get a home equity line of credit, but in this market that's not a given. So as a general rule, don't pay off the mortgage unless you're in retirement or getting close to it and you don't want the extra payment weighing you down.

Otherwise you'll be better off investing that money in a mix of stocks and bonds that is appropriate for your age and risk tolerance. What we're looking at here is the opportunity cost of leaving that money in savings (where it's likely earning 1 percent) over putting it into your mortgage (where, if you have a good rate, your return after the tax deduction will be 2 to 3 percent). The question to ask yourself is this: If I invested the money in another way instead (by putting it into my portfolio) could I do better? If you put it into a 401(k) for which you get matching dollars, the answer is an absolute yes. If you put it into another account where it could grow tax deferred, the answer is probably yes. And if you put it into a taxable account, the answer is also going to be, historically, yes. History has shown that the return on your money will be greater than the interest you're paying on your mortgage.

Unlocking the Value in Your Home

So we've talked about how it's a good idea to try to retire your mortgage before you retire yourself. It takes the pressure off. But is it ever a good idea to pull equity out of your home? Yes, in several cases. But they're not without their risks.

During the housing boom—when the value of real estate was growing faster than your grandma's sourdough starter—a number of homeowners realized their houses had become the equivalent of an ATM. As interest rates dropped and home prices soared, they could execute one "cash-out refi" after another, reducing their monthly mortgage payments and padding their bank accounts with money they used for vacations, college, cars, what have you. The hitch was that because they pulled money out, they owned less of that home than they did before. And when the housing market went pop—and their values tumbled—many found that they owed more on these houses than they were worth. They were upside down, underwater, up a creek without a paddle. Some lost their homes. Others took years to get their financial lives back on track. There are still some with debt hangovers nearly a decade later.

We are not recommending you go down this road. But there are three instances in which you can look at unlocking some of the value in your home . . . as long as you do it carefully. Here are the three scenarios and the corresponding solutions:

⤷ Scenario: You need cash to renovate, maintain, or do something else that will (in all likelihood) improve the value of your home.

Solution: The home equity loan (and its cousin, the home equity line of credit or HELOC) was developed specifically for this purpose. These are both basically second mortgages; you borrow money against the equity built up in your house to do something else with the cash—in this case, improve the place. These secured loans have their advantages: they have fairly low interest rates and allow you to deduct interest on loans as part of your regular mortgage interest deduction. But you have to have good to great credit and equity in your house to borrow against it, and some lenders won't deal with sums of less than $10,000 or $20,000.

Now, these cousins do have some genetic differences. A home equity loan is a fixed-rate loan that you receive as a lump sum, then pay off monthly (usually over five to 15 years). These are good for when you need a big chunk of money all at once to, say, put on a new roof or renovate the kitchen. A HELOC, on the other hand, is a line of credit that you tap only as you need it; then you pay off only the part you've tapped. It's better if you are looking at a series of improvements you may want to undertake over several years. The interest rate is generally variable (and tied to the prime rate), which means your monthly payment amount will vary, too.

⤷ Scenario: You need cash for college, credit-card consolidation, or fill-in-the-blank, and borrowing from your home is the cheapest way to get it.

Solution: Because there is a big, valuable asset—your home—that can be used as collateral in the case of both home equity loans and HELOCs, these second mortgages are a lot less risky for the lenders that make them than, say, unsecured personal loans with nothing backing them up. For that reason the interest rates on home equity loans and HELOCs are lower than the rates you'll get if you borrow specifically to buy a car, pay for college, or do pretty much anything on a credit card. (And the fact that the interest may be [see above] tax deductible makes them cheaper still.) This is why using home equity to pay for college and credit-card consolidations as well as other things has become so popular.

The big caveat: *you are putting your home on the line.* Here's what we know about people who took out home equity loans/lines for credit-card consolidation (i.e., to pay off expensive credit-card debt with debt at a much lower interest rate and wipe the slate clean). A few years after they made this move, 40 percent of them had gone out and charged those credit cards right back up again. At that point they had to repay both the home equity loan/line debt *and* the new credit-card debt. In other words: double trouble. You cannot allow yourself to do this if you want to be AgeProof. The goal of the mortgage has to be retiring it before you retire. And so, if you do borrow from your home because you can't borrow elsewhere cheaper, you must put yourself on a payment plan to satisfy that second mortgage before retirement, too. Which means, those credit cards? They have to go.

Note: There is one other scenario in which a HELOC makes some sense. If you are entering a period of economic uncertainty—perhaps your company looks as if it's going to be sold and you think your position could be eliminated, or maybe your industry is going through a consolidation— apply for and secure a HELOC before you lose your job. Consider it a back-pocket emergency cushion. Then don't use it unless you have no other choice. If it comes down to a choice between pulling money out of your retirement funds (and paying taxes and penalties) and using the HELOC, the HELOC may be the better way to go. But scale back your spending as far as you can so you don't put yourself in a significant hole.

➭ Scenario: You want to stay in your home forever, but you're running short of funds. Do you have cable TV? Then you've heard about reverse mortgages. They're the financial instruments peddled by Arthur Fonzarelli (without the jacket). Reverse mortgages (like annuities) have a pretty bad reputation, which, by the way, they've earned. Default rates on these products are high (about 10 percent) and they are fairly expensive. That said, in the past few years, changes in the marketplace have both improved the products overall and made them a good deal for some people—if you use them right.

Solution: A little background: Reverse mortgages, or Home Equity Conversion Mortgages (HECM), offer a way for people to borrow the equity in their homes while continuing to live in them. The loan doesn't have to be paid back until the homeowner dies or has been moved out of the house for a year or longer. To qualify you have to be 62 or older, have a substantial amount of equity in your home, and be able to pay taxes and insurance.

How much you are able to pull out of your home is based on three things: the amount of equity in your home (the more you have the more you can take), your age (the older you are, the more you can take, because the lender has to assume it won't get its money back until you die), and interest rates (which are fixed). And you can take the money in three ways: as an annuity (or paycheck), in a lump sum, or as a line of credit you can draw on if need be.

This last option is the most intriguing. If you're heading into retirement with your money invested in a diversified portfolio, one of the realities of life is that the market will have good years and not-so-good ones. It can be damaging to your long-term investment prospects if you're forced to sell investments when they're down to fund your day-to-day expenses. An untapped reverse mortgage, taken as a line of credit, can come in handy at times like these (much as a HELOC can function as a back-pocket emergency cushion). You pull the money out of the reverse mortgage when you need it, then repay it from your investments once the markets have recovered.

That said, the closing costs on a reverse mortgage are still not inexpensive. And a 2015 report from the Consumer Financial Protection Bureau says that consumers don't fully understand the risks (which include defaulting on the loan if you're unable to pay your property taxes or insurance). Nearly all the reverse mortgages available today are HECM loans, which are insured by the federal government and available through lenders approved by the Federal Housing Administration (FHA). If you go this route, you'll have to go through a financial assessment to make sure you are able to afford the liability long term, and counseling with an FHA-approved housing agency to make sure you understand what you're doing. Both, in our minds, are good things.

Aging in Place versus Moving to a Place to Age

Surveys of Baby Boomers make it clear that the vast majority of us would prefer to grow old (or at least older) exactly where we are rather than moving to a place specifically designed to help us move through the stages of aging. According to a 2010 survey by AARP, nearly three-quarters of people age 45 and over said they'd like to stay in their homes as long as possible; two-thirds expressed a wish to stay in their communities. A 2016 report from American College puts the numbers even higher. It says 83 percent of seniors want to stay in their own homes.

The term we use for this is *aging in place*. But what exactly does that mean? Typically it involves staying either in your current home or in your current location. You generally start out independent but bring in help in the form of caregivers (family or paid) if you need it. And you may have to modify your current home to make it possible.

What it takes to make a home into one you can age in is, well, money. A 2014 report from Harvard's Joint Center for Housing Studies says that there are five features a home must have to make it suitable for aging:

- "A no-step entry,
- single floor living,
- extra-wide doorways and halls,
- accessible electrical switches and controls and
- lever-style doors and faucet-handles."

Just 1 percent of the housing stock in the US has all five. (Though there are, as the report points out, huge geographical variations. Houses in the South are much more likely than those in the Northeast to be built, ranch-style, on a single floor.) AARP's 26-page HomeFit Guide is substantially longer than Harvard's and includes everything from nonslip rugs to shower and bath grab bars to temperature controls that prevent sink and shower water from scalding. We recommend taking a look if aging in place is something you want to do.

Once you get a sense of the extent of the changes you'd have to make to your home, you can start to weigh the options. For example, perhaps your current home doesn't have a bedroom on its first floor. What it does have—along with a kitchen and powder room—is a formal living room no one has used in years. Reconfiguring that as a master bedroom and adding a full bath could be substantially cheaper than moving somewhere else entirely. Or maybe your current home just won't do it. The hallways aren't wide enough, too much of the living is done up a flight of stairs (or two), even getting into the place is a bit of an ordeal. In that case you can start the hunt for another home more conducive to aging but within your community. Or consider the third option—a continuing care retirement community or CCRC.

Another buzzword, yes, and one you're probably hearing more often, *continuing care retirement community* refers to something a little like a summer camp for older folks —in that different groups of people are given different amounts of supervision. (At camp the youngsters—tadpoles, freshmen, or whatever they're called—receive the most care. In CCRCs they tend to receive the least.) Typically adults move in (actually they buy in—we'll get to the finances in a moment), while they're still able to live independently. They occupy apartments, houses, or condos, where they can go about their business on their own, if they choose. But they can also take advantage of on-premises meals, social events, medical care. Depending on the price of the CCRC, it can seem more like a country club (or, again, adult sleepaway camp) than anything else.

As you get older or need additional care, you generally move into a part of the facility set up for assisted living. Here you may no longer have a full kitchen, but instead a kitchenette. You may take all your meals in the dining room—or have them delivered. And eventually, if need be, you may move to a part of the facility where skilled nursing care is available around the clock.

DR. MIKE SAYS:

My 99-year-old mother-in-law still drives, and lives in a senior living community called Judson Manor— which is exactly that, a manor. She goes to the botanical garden, to the orchestra, to Cavaliers and Indians games, to yoga classes, to knitting groups, to dances. WOW!

This amount of care—and the guarantee of it down the road—doesn't come cheap. Typically it requires a deposit (or buy-in) of between $100,000 and $1 million to enter a CCRC. The number varies widely with housing prices in the area, but the average is about $250,000. This is essentially collateral against your future care requirements. Then there will be monthly fees of $3,000 to $5,000 and up. But note: You're not, typically, buying a home. Instead you're buying the right to live in the community.

You'll buy in by signing one of three types of contracts:

- ➲ A fee-for-service contract is the least expensive option. You'll pay a lower fee (or sometimes no deposit at all) to enter the CCRC, but you'll pay more for assisted living and skilled nursing down the road.

- ➲ A modified contract is the middle option. It provides you with services for a certain number of years at an agreed-upon rate. When your contract expires, rates will generally go up.

- ➲ A life-care contract is the most expensive way to buy in. You're paying up front to lock in the cost of your care down the road, and you know that cost won't rise in the future, no matter how much care you need. Additionally, some of your deposit may be refunded to your heirs.

Which is best? That depends on how long you're going to be there. If you fall ill and pass away within the first few years of moving in, you likely will not have used up all the care you paid for with a life-care contract. But if you live for decades (which you will, of course, because you're AgeProof), the pricier option can be the better bet.

If a CCRC is an option you're considering, make sure you spend enough time touring different communities to get a sense of what's available and what suits your needs. Take a good look at the facilities (are they nicely kept?) and the staff and residents (are they happy and engaged?). Then there are a number of questions to ask before you make the move:

▷ What happens to couples if one spouse needs more care than the other? What are the financial implications of this?

▷ If I decide living there is not for me, is all or part of my deposit refundable, and for how long?

▷ Can I spend a week there as a visitor before making the decision?

▷ What are the rules about visitors? How about pets?

▷ What sort of credentials do staff members have, and what is the staff-to-resident ratio?

▷ Could you provide me with a copy of your financial statements and inspection reports?

▷ How have your prices increased in the last five to 10 years? (Compare this with others in the area.)

▷ What sort of memory-care services do you have available?

▷ What happens if I can no longer pay?

Finally, take time to read the contract and have your attorney, accountant, and financial adviser take a look. If this sounds like overkill, it's not. Unfortunately, CCRCs aren't regulated in many states (unlike nursing homes). For that reason your grown children may want to give the contract a read as well.

AgeProof ESSENTIALS

1. Home should be about comfort, yes, but it's also a place you can use to get healthy and stay wealthy.

2. The most important dynamic in your home environment is free and honest communication with your family. Every good strategy about finances (and many of them about health) starts there.

3. You will sleep better when your finances are in order. Better sleep means better health overall. That's why your bed may just be the single most important thing in your home. Invest in a good one, and treat it kindly.

Automate good habits.

Get a handle on your financial and health behaviors
by tracking them.

Eat LUV-U foods (lean protein, unsaturated fat,
vegetables and fruits, unprocessed grains); you should love
food, but it must love you back.

Pay yourself 15 percent toward your future
as part of your monthly budget, to prepare for your future
and reduce stress.

Rally a team of pros and friends to help
you reach your goals.

Offer to be on others' teams.

Organize your health and financial worlds
to help you think clearly.

Find your passion and live it.

acknowledgments

From Jean Chatzky and Mike Roizen:

We pulled together another great team of experts, all wanting to live longer without running out of money or breaking a hip, while remembering where they put it (the money).

Ted Spiker crafted an uplifting, enjoyable text that thrills readers with insights spiced with humor. Professor Spiker (he is one in real life at the University of Florida) keeps his classroom lively as we (Jean and Mike) were pumped with weekly homework assignments.

Erik Feingold is the genius behind the Sharecare App; his knowledge of stress kept us from fighting, running away, or freezing as we learned much we didn't know. His ability to help us communicate this is demonstrated in this text. His ability to make that knowledge accessible to you is demonstrated in the clarity and use of the Sharecare App, and his desire to help us all "Live in the Green."

This book contains so broad a range of topics that compelled us to ask advice from many world experts who selflessly share their insights in the true academic tradition. We cannot possibly list them all here if we are to have space for the actual book, but we deeply appreciate your dedication to your specialties and willingness to sacrifice your time in helping craft the most scientifically accurate book on how to live well longer possible.

We want to especially thank our many "volunteer" readers: more than two dozen contributed comments that made the style and content of this work much better. And we appreciate the efforts of the *Dr. Oz* and *Today* show teams, especially Mehmet Oz and his executive and senior producers Amy Chiaro, Stacy Rader, Laurie Rich; producers Nicole Romanella, James Avenell Sr., and all the great production team members who make our day-to-day lives so much fun; *Today* producers Noah Oppenheim, Don Nash, Tom Mazzarelli, Jackie Levin, and Melea McCreary and all the *Today* anchors who made waking up early to discuss finance and health a pleasure.

We also want to thank the group at Grand Central Life & Style (Hachette Book Group) who so enthusiastically supported this material and have dedicated themselves to bringing our ideas to the world. Karen Murgolo always sought solutions to our many needs and the suggestions of our "volunteer" readers to make this book the best possible experience for you dedicated readers. And thanks to the team at Grand Central—Amanda Pritzker, Nick Small, Morgan Hedden, Mari Okuda, Giraud Lorber, and Lisa Honerkamp—for bringing it to life.

And a special thanks to our agent, Candice Fuhrman, who kept us focused on the goal of writing a compelling book that helps many embrace the challenges of the new and exciting age of longevity.

From Michael Roizen:

Dr. Mike wants to thank his administrative associates, especially Beth Grubb and Jackie Frey, who made this work possible. And thank you to many of the staff at the Cleveland Clinic and physicians elsewhere who answered numerous questions. Many of the Clinic's Wellness Institute staff and associates made scientific contributions and constructive criticism, and allowed the time to complete this work.

Cleveland Clinic CEO Toby Cosgrove has said that while the clinic will continue to be one of if not the best in illness care, wellness is what the clinic will do for every employee and person we touch. I am fortunate to work with such a talented and creative group who helped our thought processes, such as Regina Chandler, Drs. Rich Lang, Mladen Golubic, Anthony Miniaci, Raul Seballos, Roxanne Sukol, Steve Feinleib, Dan Neides, Scarlet Soriano, Anthony Bang, nutritionist Kristin Kirkpatrick, super chef Jim Perko, Jane Ehrman, Dr. Kellie Kirksey, Drs. Martin Harris, Joe Hahn, and Brian Donley, as well as Cindy Hundorfean, Paul Matsen, Bill Peacock, and many nutritionists and exercise physiologists, as well as clinicians and leaders who run the gamut from inner-city schoolteachers to executive coaches.

But most of all, I am indebted to our close partners at RealAge .com, including Keith Roach, Carl Peck, and Axel Goetz, and the really incredible team Jeff Arnold has assembled at Sharecare, including the above superstar Erik Feingold, Donna Hill Howes, Dawn Whaley, and Monda Roquemore.

Our family was fully engaged—with Drs. Jeff and Jennifer as critical readers, and joined full-time by the woman responsible for our kids' developmental successes, Nancy, as well as by the "enlarged family" of the Katzes, Unobskeys, and Campodonicos. I also want to thank Diane Reverend, Eileen Sheil, Susan Petre, Zack Wasserman, and others for encouraging and critiquing the concepts.

Having a great partner to ablate stress daily is clearly a magnificent way to help life be better—thank you, Nancy.

From Jean Chatzky:

I'll always be grateful to the folks at Endemol for introducing me to Dr. Mike Roizen. They brought us (and a handful of other fun folks) together for a television pilot that sadly went nowhere, but I emerged with a new friend. Thanks to Mike for being willing to undertake this collaboration—and for teaching me so much about how to live my longest along the way. And to Ted Spiker for helping us channel our thoughts and energies so seamlessly. I will miss our Wednesday night calls. Thanks, too, to Dr. Mehmet Oz for scripting the foreword. I so appreciate your support!

I'm so lucky to have people in my life who helpfully (sometimes painfully) weigh in on my projects. Thank you, in particular, to Diane Adler, Mark Eskin, Dr. Nancy Snyderman, Elaine Sherman, and Alexandra Taussig for your feedback on this one. Thank you to Heather Jackson for brainstorming the title; I'm so glad you're back in my life. Thanks to Ash Sandberg and Beth O'Connell, who always have my back. And to Kelly Hultgren and Hayden Field, who get me through the day.

Finally, to my mother, Elaine Sherman, and stepdad, Bob Cohan, my children Jake and Julia Chatzky, Sam and Emily Kaplan, and my husband, Eliot Kaplan: I love you all, more than you know.

From Ted Spiker:

My deepest thanks to Mike Roizen and Jean Chatzky, two of the country's best thinkers and doers in the areas of health and wealth, for letting me tag along in this book. I appreciate not only your wisdom and your passion to help the world but also that you appreciate and embrace the fact that how-to can be served with a sprinkling of spice.

I'm appreciative of my colleagues and students at the University of Florida, as well as many influential editors, writers, and others I have worked with throughout my career. Most thanks goes to my wife, Liz, and my boys, Alex and Thad, as well as the rest of my family and friends, for their continued support of my work.

index

about the authors

Jean Chatzky, the financial editor for NBC's *Today* show, is an award-winning personal finance journalist, AARP's personal finance ambassador, and host of the podcast *HerMoney with Jean Chatzky* on iTunes. Jean is a bestselling author; her most recent books are *Women with Money: The Judgment-Free Guide to Creating the Joyful, Less Stressed, Purposeful (and, Yes, Rich) Life You Deserve, Operation Money*, a free financial guide for military service members and families, and *Money Rules: The Simple Path to Lifelong Security*. She believes knowing how to manage our money is one of the most important life skills for people at every age and has made it her mission to help simplify money matters, increasing financial literacy both now and for the future. In 2015, Jean teamed up with *Time for Kids* and the PwC Charitable Foundation to launch *Your $*, a financial literacy magazine reaching two million schoolchildren each month. She lives with her family in Westchester County, New York. www.jeanchatzky.com

Michael F. Roizen, MD, first chief wellness officer, Cleveland Clinic (@DrMikeRoizen), initiated and developed the RealAge concept to motivate behavior change. He has served as Cleveland Clinic's first chief wellness officer from 2007 to 2019 and founding chair of its Wellness Institute. The Clinic's Wellness Programs helped the Clinic not spend over $665 million for its 101,000 employees and dependents over ten years compared with national averages, and help 43.6 percent of participants achieve 6+2 normals® for health. He is certified in internal medicine and anesthesiology. He is a Phi Beta Kappa graduate of Williams, AOA from UCSF School of Medicine. He has authored over 190 peer-reviewed scientific publications (he really is a science nerd), four *New York Times* #1 bestsellers, nine overall bestsellers including his initial #1 bestseller in five countries, *RealAge: Are You as Young as You Can Be?*, *AgeProof—Living Longer Without Running Out of Money or Breaking a Hip*, and his latest book, *What to Eat When: A Strategic Plan to Improve Your Health and Life through Food*, and served sixteen years on FDA advisory committees. He helped start thirteen companies, co-invented a drug approved by the FDA, and has a weekly podcast now in its 930+ week; he and Dr Oz co-author a daily column syndicated to over 100 newspapers that translates current scientific reports into actionable steps for lay audiences. He is a recipient of an Emmy, an Elle, and the Paul Rogers best medical communicator award from the National Library of Medicine. Dr. Roizen is devoted to helping people live younger. He consults with patients in Cleveland Clinic's Executive Health Program and is an avid believer in smartphone technology tied with human coaching and large incentives to motivate health through behavior change to reduce need for illness care and thereby to substantially reduce health-care costs.

Ted Spiker (@ProfSpiker) is a professor and chair of the department of journalism at the University of Florida. He is the co-author of about 20 books, including the bestselling YOU: The Owner's Manual series. He is the author of *DOWN SIZE*, a book about the biology and psychology of weight loss and dieting struggles, as well as the writer of the *Big Guy Blog* for *Runner's World*. He was once named one of the 100 most influential people in health and fitness by Greatist.com. www.tedspiker.com